GOD

ED

A PASTORAL READING OF THE CUMBERLAND PRESBYTERIAN CONFESSION OF FAITH

Roy Hall

The Historical Foundation
of the Cumberland Presbyterian Church
& the Cumberland Presbyterian Church in America

Memphis, Tennessee
2016

God So Loved. Digital preparation by Matthew H. Gore for the Historical Foundation of the Cumberland Presbyterian Church and the Cumberland Presbyterian Church in America.

First Printing: May 2016

ISBN 10: 0692707042
ISBN 13: 978-0692707043

About the Cover: The photograph is of a trail marker on a tree. It was taken by Matthew Gore at Montgomery Bell State Park near Dickson, Tennessee, within sight of the McAdow log house and near where the footbridge to McAdow Spring crosses Acorn Creek. That marker is a device to keep hikers on the trail in much the same way that this book can guide the reader's exploration of Cumberland Presbyterian doctrine, keeping them on the right trail, so to speak.

Historical Foundation of the Cumberland Presbyterian Church and the Cumberland Presbyterian Church in America
8207 Traditional Place
Cordova [Memphis], Tennessee 38016-7414

God So Loved

For Eston, Addison, and Rose

Children of the Covenant

Contents

God Acts Through the Holy Spirit

God Creates the Church for Mission

Christians Live and Witness in the World

God Consummates All Life and History

God So Loved: A Pastoral Reading of the Cumberland Presbyterian Confession of Faith

INTRODUCTION

At the beginning of all theological perception, research, and thought —and also of every theological statement—stands a quite specific amazement. Its lack in even the best theologian will threaten the heart of the entire enterprise, while even bad theologians are not a lost cause in their service and their duty, as long as they are still capable of amazement. Amazement occurs when we happen upon a spiritual or natural phenomenon that we have not yet encountered, that we are not used to, that is initially unfamiliar, strange, and new. It is a phenomenon that we do not know how to begin to integrate into the realm of what we believe to be possible, and about it's origin and essence we can only ask, until further information is available. The amazement that overcomes us when we get involved with theology, however, is of a different kind. To be sure, it also brings astonishment and forces us to learn, but in this case there can be no talk of one day learning all there is to know, of the unusual ever seeming usual and the new becoming old hat, of the foreign ever becoming domesticated. Here, progress in study can only mean that the stopping short and the questioning in regard to the object of study will only increase, and far from ever in some sense letting us go, this amazement will more and more gain the upper hand. If we ever really experience this amazement, we will become, once and for all time, totally amazed human beings.

Karl Barth, Insights (Louisville:
Westminster John Knox Press, 2009), p. 3.

During forty plus years as a Cumberland Presbyterian pastor, I probably have heard it at least a score of times. People have said, when somehow becoming acquainted with the Cumberland Presbyterian *Confession of Faith*, something like this, "Wow! Cumberland Presbyterians have a really good theology." Or, "This is what I always have believed, but I didn't know it." Or, "This is a theology with which I can be comfortable." These kinds of comments have been made by new members of a congregation, some who have come from other church backgrounds, from candidates for the ordained ministry, from ministers transferring from other denominations, and from friendly readers of our theology. We Cumberland Presbyterians do *have* a really good theology. I have written this book because I hope that this theology will, more and more, come to *have us*?"

Perhaps what I mean by "*have us*" can be clarified by a personal illustration. Some years back I stood in a Kroger grocery store talking to a dear friend whose wife recently had passed away. He was the pastor of the Lutheran congregation in our town and was left alone to raise three young children. It was late in Lent, only a couple of weeks before Easter. A mutual friend approached and the three of us talked for a few minutes. When leaving, the friend said, "Ed, I'm sorry about Connie's death. I hope you can have a happy Easter." Ever the wise theologian, Ed replied, in a gentle and respectful way, "Thank you. But Easter is not something you have. It is something that has you." This is precisely what I mean with regard to the theology in the *Confession of Faith* (hereafter designated as *COF*). What if the really important thing is not that as Cumberland Presbyterians we have a good theology, but that this theology truly has us?

Karl Barth (1887 - 1968), the great Swiss theologian, once spoke of "The strangely wonderful world within the Bible." The *COF* provides one way, our shared way, of being guided into and around in this "strangely wonderful world." It can lead us, if we let it, on the adventure of a lifetime.

Speaking of adventure, I am reminded of my mother-in-law who was born and raised in pre-World War II France. At the end of the war, she married an American soldier. This marriage meant coming to America. It meant leaving behind one world and entering into what was, for her, a whole new world. She had to learn a new language. She had to learn a bewildering variety of new customs and behaviors. She had to learn a new national story, as well as many new local stories. It was an incredible and demanding adventure for her. After living in Alabama for many years, she began making trips back home to visit her relatives. They delighted in telling her that she now spoke French with a Southern accent!

Theological work (here meant reading and reflecting on the *COF*) is entering into the biblical world and learning our way around, or rather being led around by the best of all tour guides, the Holy Spirit. It is learning to speak the language of the Bible, the language of our faith. It is learning, and relearning, the old but ever new story of God and God's people. And, when returning to the everyday world, it is discovering that we may find ourselves speaking with something of an accent. It is the accent of prophets and apostles and original witnesses to the mighty acts of God.

A few years back Dr. Jay Earhart Brown, President of Memphis Theological Seminary, presented a seminar to Robert Donnell Presbytery on the theology of the Cumberland Presbyterian Church. He reminded us that every Cumberland Presbyterian is a theologian. Anyone, he said, who thinks about and seeks to serve God is a theologian. He then spoke about the difference between "inherited theology" and "reflective theology." Inherited theology is the theology we have picked up along the way simply from being members of the church, having Christian parents, or living in a dominant Christian environment. Some of this theology, probably most of it, is good theology, sound and solid. But sometimes inherited theology might not be so good. It can be simply what everyone thinks and everyone may be quite wrong. Reflective theology, on the other hand, is theology that has been hammered out on the anvil of sustained prayer, study, reflection and dialogue with others. Reflective theology is important because what we truly believe, and in whom we truly believe, significantly impacts what we truly are and what we truly do.

The Cumberland Presbyterian (and Cumberland Presbyterian Church in America) *COF* is a reflective theology. It also is an ecclesial, or churchly, theology. It doesn't express the faith of only two or three theologians, or even a considerable group of theologians, but the faith of our churches as a whole. The introduction to the *COF* of 1984 includes these words, "The committee submitted to the General Assemblies of 1981 its draft of the Confession, the Constitution, and the Rules of Discipline for study and response by the churches at large. Responses were received from study groups, sessions, presbyteries, and individuals. Subsequently, the committee again revised its work in light of these responses as a mark of its intention that the Confession be the work of the entire church rather than that of a committee." The *COF* of 1984 reflects what our churches were thinking at the time, in response to the timeless Word.

I have written this book in gratitude for the theology of the COF. While I must and will accept personal responsibility for mistakes, errors, fuzzy and unclear thinking and writing, and here and there maybe being entirely wrong, this book is a church work. It would not have been possible except for the fact that I have been a Cumberland Presbyterian pastor for more than forty years. Almost everything in this book has been "road-tested" in, with, and among living Cumberland Presbyterian congregations. I have written because it has been a blessed adventure to live out my life and faith with them. I also have written because I am hoping that the 21st century might become a broadly-based "theological century" for Cumberland Presbyterians throughout the world. The 19th was such a century for Cumberland Presbyterians. Why not the 21st? We are blessed that the technology is in place for this to happen with relative ease. Why do I have this hope? I have it because I believe that our *COF* is an inspired resource for helping all of us to "proclaim Christ," and for forming disciples who will follow him in ministry and service both locally and throughout the world.

All writing about theology, of course, is contextual. It is written and lived by people in particular contexts that shape, to some extent, their particular theological reflections. I am writing as a Cumberland Presbyterian who has lived his entire life in the context of the United States and, more particularly, in the American South. This will limit, to some degree, what I have to say. But this is not a bad thing. Dr. William Ingram, former President of Memphis Theological Seminary and of blessed memory, used to tell those of us who were in his classes: "When you make a theological statement, do not put a period at the end. Put a semi-colon. You can almost always say more, and you, or someone else, will probably be able to say it better." The fact that all of our theology is contextual and provisional should not stop us from theological work and theological sharing. When we say one thing, someone else can improve on it by saying more, less, or something entirely different. This is the way communal (church) theology works.

I would like to state one of my conclusions and, deepest beliefs, about the *COF* of 1984. Several of the historic Reformed confessions seem to have been written with an emphasis on what God has "saved us from." I think a strong case can be made that the Cumberland Presbyterian Church's (and CPCA's) *COF* of 1984, while not ignoring what God has saved us *from*, places the major emphasis on what God has "saved us *for*." Although I will take the liberty to point out a few ways in which I think the *COF* might be strengthened, I regard it as a theological "triumph of grace." Its guiding text is, "For God so loved the world, that he gave his only begotten Son, that whoever believes in him should not perish, but have eternal life" (Jn. 3:16).

My intention in this volume is to share an example of an effort at pastoral theology. It results from the putting together of notes, lectures, sermons, and conversations from the past thirty years. I have come to believe, as do the authors of *The Teaching Minister*, "of all the challenges facing Protestant churches today, none is as critical as that of teaching the Christian faith."[1] This work includes numbers of quotations, some rather lengthy. I have included them because they somehow helped me in the ministry of teaching, preaching, and pastoring, and because they may be of help to others now engaged in this same ministry.

Matthew, our eldest son, has worked for many years in the construction of hospitals. A few years ago I visited him at a job site in Scottsdale, Arizona. We stood on a windswept hillside observing his crew working below. The crew was stretching lines and digging trenches. The project was in its beginning stage. As we watched, he suddenly said to me, "Dad, if we don't get this right, nothing else will go right." Such is the critical importance of foundations. I have written this book because I am deeply grateful for the solid and reliable theological foundation of the Cumberland Presbyterian Church (1 Cor. 3:10-11). This foundation has served as the bulwark of my own life and ministry as well as the life and faith of many of those with whom I have served.

I would like to express gratitude to Dr. Barry Anderson of Memphis Theological Seminary who read portions of the manuscript and made several valuable suggestions for its improvement. I would also like to thank Susan Knight Gore, archivist of the Historical Foundation of the Cumberland Presbyterian Church and the Cumberland Presbyterian Church in America, for accepting the manuscript and watching over its publication. Finally, I am supremely grateful for the Cumberland Presbyterian congregations I was blessed and privileged to serve as pastor over the past four decades and more. Special gratitude is in order to the members of the congregations in Helena, Alabama, Elliottsville/Alabaster in Alabama, Whitehaven in Memphis, Tennessee, Rocky Ridge in Birmingham, Alabama, Milan in Tennessee, and Scottsboro in Alabama. I am especially grateful to the Tuesday morning Bible study group in Milan, Tennessee and the Wednesday morning Bible study group in Scottsboro, Alabama. It was in these groups, in particular, that many subjects in this book were first considered in depth.

Many are, and were, the people in these congregations who constantly encouraged me to remain concerned for and about theological reflection. I believe they encouraged me because they regarded such work as integral to the office of pastor. They valued that the pastor is a minister of the Word and Sacrament. But they also valued the fact that the pastor is called to be a teacher. Over the past many years, we have lived together, sometimes suffered and cried together, but nearly always rejoiced together that Cumberland Presbyterians have a really good theology. By God's grace, may this theology have generations who yet are to be born: "Whosoever will may come."

GOD SPEAKS TO THE HUMAN FAMILY

(1.01 -1.22 in the Confession of Faith)

Chapter One

THE LIVING GOD

A Preliminary Word: Beliefs and Faith

This book is a study of the theological statements ("beliefs") in the Confession of Faith of the Cumberland Presbyterian Church and the Cumberland Presbyterian Church in America. These beliefs are of fundamental importance to us. They contribute significantly to the understanding of our theological identity. They help us to discern who we are and what we are to do as a people who are in relationship to the God revealed in Jesus Christ and the power of the Holy Spirit. But it must be said that they are of penultimate rather than ultimate importance. There is something more important than beliefs. It is the lived and living faith of Cumberland Presbyterians. There is an important sense in which faith trumps belief.

These statements, of course, require elaboration. Especially concerning what is meant, in turn, by beliefs and faith. In scripture, especially in the New Testament, the words "belief" and "faith" are closely related. They are even used interchangeably. Believing in the Lord Jesus Christ and having faith in the Lord Jesus Christ ordinarily amounts to the same thing. But here by belief/beliefs is meant holding certain ideas in the mind, the brain. It is learning about, and even mentally assenting to, certain claims, statements, propositions, truths, and ideas. As such, all sorts of beliefs may be held without their resulting in a re-orientation in life, not to mention a radical re-orientation. For example, one may believe that the earth is facing an ecological crisis without this belief changing one's behavior or lifestyle in any really major way. Such a belief, even if weakly and ineffectually held, is certainly possible. Polls of the America people regularly report that over ninety percent of those polled believe in God. But it is altogether uncertain that such belief influences, to any significant degree, the way in which many (most?) persons actually live. We quite naturally hold many kinds of beliefs that do not grasp us at the center of our lives and result in radically re-arranging our priorities, commitments, and actions.

But here something different is meant by faith. As Christians, we have many important theological beliefs (and we will consider those of Cumberland Presbyterians in this volume). But learning about and having these beliefs in our minds, while important, is not the same as faith. It has been said, "In distinction from theology, which is reflection on God and our relationship to God, faith is consciously living in that relationship."[1] Faith, then, is more than beliefs about the God we know as Father, Son, and Holy Spirit. It is not believing in God, but believing God. It is not believing in Jesus, but believing Jesus. It is not believing in the Holy Spirit, but believing the Holy Spirit. Faith is the total response of the total person, or groups of persons, to the God revealed in Jesus Christ and the power of the Holy Spirit. Faith is the act of trusting God, and serving God, even though we may, perhaps are even likely to, struggle to grasp and understand many of the beliefs we have about God.

The *COF* sets before us the shared beliefs of Cumberland Presbyterians. As has already been said, these beliefs are very important to us, essential to us. They constitute "our particular theology." They give us our theological identity. But, at bottom, they are important because they are reflections on our faith - the trusting relationship we have to God and to one another as a result of what God has done and is doing for us in Christ. And it is this faith - this living and lived relationship to and with God —that is the main thing. Richard Norris puts it this way: "Christian theology . . . is the church's continuing effort to articulate, explain, and communicate the character and meaning of the relationship it has to God in Christ. What is settled and given, therefore, is not what Christians have to say about this relationship, but the structure of the relationship itself, the mystery into which theology peers."[2] Put another way, the study of theology does not have the power to redeem us (only God in Christ has this power), but theology can help liberate us "from the tyranny and bitter falseness of redemptive claims that have no power to redeem."[3]

The *COF* is what we, as CP's, "have to say" at this present moment in history (being in the Reformed tradition means that we are open to saying things in different, and perhaps better, ways as a result of new light from the Holy Spirit) about the relationship we have to God in Christ, and its various dimensions of meaning. But it is the relationship— the awesome mystery that is this relationship— that counts the most. In my opinion, the *COF* is a truly reliable and trustworthy statement of the essentials of the Christian belief-system. It is based on close and careful readings of the Bible. I offer this volume in hope that it will be of help to Cumberland Presbyterians, and perhaps others, in studying what it is that we believe. But I also offer it in thanksgiving to God for the lived and living relationship to God in Christ that is the faith of Cumberland Presbyterians throughout the world.

The Living God

We believe in the only true and living God, Father, Son, and Holy Spirit; who is holy love, eternal, unchangeable in being, wisdom, power, holiness, justice, goodness, and truth (1.01). It is beyond dispute that the universe, the earth, and all life and matter, originated and developed as a result of a mysterious and marvelous creativity; a creativity that is ongoing. If this were not true, we would not be here to write and read these sentences. But what or who is this creativity? Can it be known? Can it be named? The Christian faith and the Hebrew faith from which it sprang both believe that this awesome, mysterious, transcendent, and wonderful creativity has a name—God. We claim to know this because God freely and graciously has chosen to be revealed in the life and history of Israel, in the life and history of Jesus Christ, and is continuing to be revealed in the life and history of the Holy Spirit. Cumberland Presbyterians believe in this revelatory God— the one and only living God.

Knowing who this God is begins with the ancient Hebrew people. In their Bible (called the Old Testament or the Hebrew Scriptures) many different authors tell the story (and stories) of their people's experience of and relationship to *their* particular God. Why speak of *their particular God*? In their early history, the Hebrew people thought their God was only one God among many. The first commandment (Ex. 20:1-3) emphasized that the people would have (worship and serve) no gods before their God (Yahweh). At this point, it was not that they believed there were no other gods. In fact, the religious belief systems of the ancient world were populated by an incredibly wide assortment of divinities. Israel knew, as a matter of course, that her tribal neighbors and various surrounding nations had their own gods and goddesses. However, it was the religious genius of the Hebrew people that, over-time, they came to believe their God was indeed the only God. The other gods and goddesses frankly were not real—they were only empty idols (Isa. 44:9-20). Thus the Hebrew people appear to have been the first in the ancient world to have given us a true "monotheism"—belief in only one God. For them, the awesome, transcendent and unseen reality that formed the context and meaning of their existence was a singularity. And it was this single God who graciously had made a covenant with them.

It perhaps is understandable that Israel's neighbors (who were also often enemies) considered this claim to be an arrogant insult. What right did Israel have to claim that their God was the only God? Have you ever wondered why there was so much warfare in Israel's earliest days, as recorded in the Bible? This warfare was over who had the strongest, most creative and capable god, or gods. So warfare—of the most primitive and brutal type—occupies a considerable space in the biblical stories about Israel's earliest years. But the real genius of the Hebrew faith was the fact that they eventually came to understand and affirm that their God was also the God of all peoples (this was the case by the time of the eighth century prophets). The later prophets inveigh against the idea that Israel should consider herself to be in a relationship to God that was not also intended for and open to all other people. Israel struggled to remain faithful to this insight. There is a tendency to want God to be "your God only." But, in her best moments, Israel was faithful to the fact that her God had initiated a relationship to them so that they might be a blessing to the other peoples of the world. They were to bear witness to theses peoples, for the sake of these peoples, that the one God was just, righteous, merciful, compassionate, and impartial to all.

Our present concern is with the way in which the Hebrew people spoke about, wrote about, and experienced God. What was this God like? What did this God do? What did this God want? In the Bible, many different answers are given to these questions. It turned out, though, that two concepts were foundational to their efforts at describing who God was to and for them. They understood God to be both (1) "personal" and (2) "historical."

By personal, they did not mean that God was some really big, huge, over-sized person residing somewhere in the sky. God was not a really big person over against human beings as really small persons. Actually they were concerned to avoid thinking and speaking of God in too personal a way (see below). By personal, they meant that God could be encountered, and that God offered encounter, in the way that human persons can and do encounter one another. They meant that God is communicative. They meant that God "exists" the way persons know themselves to exist. This is to say that God is "alive"—is a living God. They meant that God thinks, wills, chooses, purposes, speaks, responds, feels, knows, reveals, loves, rejoices, regrets, is capable of anger, is compassionate, jealous, merciful, and judges. The variety of imagery for God used throughout the Bible (Father, King, Judge, Shepherd, Mother, husband, etc.) is intended to stress that God is personal. God is not a force or merely the energy of the universe. God is not an "it" or "thing" or "what." God is not an object but a subject. God is not something but someone.

But what about what is called "anthropomorphism" (picturing God in terms of human characteristics)? Many skeptics have charged that the Bible's authors have simply created God in their own image (rather than the other way around). God, thus, is claimed to be merely a projection of human longing—a wish fulfillment. We can admit that in the Bible God is made to sound like a human being, albeit a rather exalted one! God is said to have a mouth, arms, hands, eyes, and ears. God can behave like human beings. God can get really angry and act out, so to speak. God, alternately, can regret his emotions and actions, repent, and act differently. So, anthropomorphic language about God is used regularly by the writers of the Bible. But what other language was available to them? What language would have made it possible to communicate the important belief that God is personal?

It is noteworthy that they employed measures against making images of God. They didn't want anyone to think of God as being a person in the way that human beings are persons. “To say that God is a person, as though that description meant *exactly* what it means when it is used of an ordinary human being, is to miss the point entirely. God is *not* a person (in this exact sense). God is the ultimate mystery of existence—but a mystery which, in and through such events as the Exodus and Resurrection of Christ, we learn to trust, to obey, and to love. And in such a relationship, *person* becomes the only adequate way to model this mystery. We are not related to God as we are to an idea, an object in the world, or an ideal. We are related to God as we are to *persons*; and accordingly we model (as does scripture) God that way in our thinking.”[4]

The God Who Speaks

The *COF*, then, affirms belief in the “*personality*” of God. The title of the very first section is “God Speaks to the Human Family.” There could hardly be a better place to begin than by pausing to ponder the first two words of this title: “God speaks.” God, for Cumberland Presbyterians, is a communicative God. We are able to know, respond to, worship, and serve God only because God first has spoken to us. So, in its first two words, the *COF* begins at square one of our theology. It begins with an affirmation about the self-revealing, self-giving, self-communicating God (“revelation” is the biblical and theological word for God’s self-disclosure—the deliberate manifestation of God’s plans, character, and self). It is about a God who speaks and creation happens (Gen. 1-3). Thus God’s word is a powerfully creative word. God's word is also a saving, redemptive word (Col. 1:13-20; 2:8-10; Heb. 1:1-4). God is a God of gracious and saving speech. In the Hebraic thought-world, a word (*dabar*) is normally considered to have the same force as a deed or act. It can be said, then, that God's speech is God's act and God's act is God's speech.

When I was a student at Bethel College (now University), Miss Naomi Blanks, a wonderful person and equally wonderful professor of English, one morning casually said to our class, "One way you might think of God is as a poet." I must admit that at eight o'clock in the morning her remark hardly registered on me. But, of course, I have remembered it. And I eventually came to understand that Miss Blanks was absolutely right. She had said something profoundly biblical. Like a poet, God works with words. When God decided to create a universe, a place for us to live and something to preoccupy Einstein's brain, God did it with a word, with speaking. God offers several well chosen words and the result is everything from quarks to sharks, rodents to rainbows.

Consider God's choice of Moses and sending him to pharaoh with the message, "Tell him to let my people go." I can imagine Moses replying, "Tell him? Look, he's got all the chariots, horses, spears, swords, and soldiers." But God says, "OK, I can see that, but no problem. You have my word. So just go tell him." It's the same with Abraham and Sarah. God tells them they will have a baby. Sarah has a laughing fit, but then runs to the store to pick up some diapers. After all, God has said it will happen. This theme of the God who speaks, creatively and savingly, reverberates throughout both the Hebrew and Christian Scriptures. As for the idea of God as poet, there is good warrant for pastors and other Christians to understand themselves as minor poets who work with words, spoken and acted, in the service of the speaking-acting God. I was reminded of this recently when visiting in the hospital. I was making small talk with a family while their loved one awaited surgery. We talked about most of the normal things—the weather, sports, and the new industry that had come to town—that people talk about in these situations. A nurse came into the room and gave her, the patient, the so-called "don't care" shot. But there was still one thing she cared about. It was very important to her. She told me that it was time for me to do my job. She wanted me to read something from the Bible and then to pray. She wanted to hear something more than a human word. She wanted to hear from the God who speaks.

I once heard William Willimon, formerly Bishop of the North Alabama Conference of the United Methodist Church, give a talk in which he said he had asked a professor of education what it is that makes for a really good teacher? The professor answered simply, "Every good teacher talks a lot." Several of the congregations I have served have included very good teachers. A visit to any one of their classrooms would likely result in overhearing comments like the following: "Now children, let's all turn to page ten." Or, "Wow, Jenny, you got the correct answer right away." Or, "Denver, that is a nice picture. Tell me what it means to you." A good teacher is talkative, communicative, and interactive.

As Cumberland Presbyterians, our preaching, teaching, and life of faith, is about a God who has a history of conversation with the human family. One of our most fundamental affirmations about God is that God is present to us in and through God's speech. God is not a remote, abstract, removed, deistic or silent God. Rather, God is interactive, communicative, and talkative. The *COF* puts it this way: **The one living God, who is Father, Son, and Holy Spirit, the Holy Trinity, speaks through the holy scriptures, the events of nature and history, apostles, prophets, evangelists, pastors, teachers, but uniquely in Jesus Christ, the Word made flesh** (1.02). The following are among the texts the *COF* references in support of this statement: for the God who speaks through the holy scriptures— see Acts 7, 2 Timothy 3:14-17, 2 Peter 1: 10-21; through the events of nature and history—see Exodus 3:1-6, Psalm 19:1-6, Romans 1:18-20; through apostles, prophets, evangelists, pastors, and teachers—see Ephesians 4:11-13; but uniquely in Jesus Christ, the Word made flesh—see John 1:1-18, Philippians 2:5-11, Colossians 1:13-20, 2:8-10, and Hebrews 1:1-4.

Much is meant when affirming that God is a God who speaks, in word and deed, and speaks most fully in and through Jesus Christ. Sometimes one person will say about another person, "I will never speak to her again." This is a decision to cut off another person entirely. It is a decision that another person will become, in effect, a non-person. It represents, if carried out, a total and final rupture between persons. This is something that Cumberland Presbyterians believe the God of the Bible will not say. God is a God who has refused to stop speaking to the human family. This is an important aspect of what it means to say that the living God is long-suffering, merciful, and a God of grace. As long as creation stands, God remains a God who has spoken and is speaking to the human family. The theme of the God who speaks has a special meaning for our own time. Never before in the history of the world have human beings been able to communicate with one another, aided by quite fantastical technologies, using so many words in so many ways. But Cumberland Presbyterians believe that there is a word that seeks to be heard, aims to be heard, needs to be heard, and can be heard, that has not been spoken by us. The meaning and purpose of our life together comes from hearing this Word.

The God Who Acts

The second fundamental characteristic of God, as witnessed to in the scriptures, is God as *historical*. By this, the

Hebrew people, and later the earliest Christians, meant that God was revealed to and known by them not only in and through speech or through liturgy (worship) and ritual, but also, and especially, in and through concrete historical acts. They did not "find" God by philosophical reflection or speculation or through self-exploration. Rather, God found them in those events through which they understood God to be encountering and redeeming them. So, saying that God is historical means that God acts, does things, in the real space-time world of human beings. Consequently, and of very of great importance to our faith, Israel and the church believed the meaning of all history, the entire history of the universe and of human beings within it, is only made intelligible in light of and by to reference God's historical actions. The foundational historical acts of God on behalf of God's people, and the entire world of people, were the Exodus and the Resurrection of Christ.

Faith understands the history of the world primarily as the history of the actions of God. All other ways of considering, understanding, and explaining history are considered relative and subordinate to the unfolding actions of God in history. These actions have been summarized in the statements that 1) God is Creator (initiator of all history), and (2) God is Redeemer (will bring all history, including the fallen history of humankind, to its proper and just conclusion). Speaking of God as historical is saying God is not just an idea, or a "being" entirely remote from the world. Rather, God is an Agent acting in the world (while at the same time existing beyond it). One thing it may mean that we are created in the "image of God" is we also act in history. We are also agents. We, too, have purposes, make decisions, and carry out actions. Thus we also create history (history is made with every passing second). We certainly have a hand in creating our personal and familial histories. And we also join with others in ways that may impact the history of our community, our county, our state, our country, or even the entire world. But, for faith, our history-making, and the entirety of human history-making, happens within and is made possible only by the fact that God is the primary and over-all actor in history. Our own history-making as human beings will either serve God's purposes or militate against them. But the God Cumberland Presbyterians believe in is the sovereign Lord of all history. We believe this because God has acted in the special history of Israel and of Jesus Christ.

Langdon Gilkey speaks of the Christian faith's basic understanding of history: "In the Christian tradition . . . the locus or the clue to the ultimate meaning and power of history lies neither in nature or in general history, nor again in any particular cultural tradition. Rather, it lies in the special history or sequence of events culminating in a person, in and through which special sequence God is believed to have given a definite manifestation of God's power, purposes, and will. That special history is constituted by the events through which God established, preserved, judged, and reestablished Israel as a people. The person was, of course, Jesus of Nazareth who was formed by that Hebrew communal tradition, who, in Christian eyes, both completed and refashioned that tradition, and who provided in his person, his words, his destiny, his fate, and his response to that destiny, definitive manifestation of that same God's being and will . . . Thus a sequence of objective historical events and a person are, for Christian belief, the culminating media or vehicles for revelation. Through them the being, power, intentions or will of God are manifest."[5]

In the biblical world-view, the history of Israel, the history of Jesus Christ, and the history of the Holy Spirit are not smaller merely localized stories within the much larger and more impressive story of world history. Rather world history is the smaller story that has its existence and meaning only within the larger and much more impressive story of God's creative and redemptive historical actions. This is an amazing claim, but precisely the one that the scriptures make. The Christian understanding of history is that God has revealed, in and through the history of Israel, that he is and who he is, and that at the right time (Heb. 1:1-2) God made known to us "in all wisdom and insight the mystery of his will, according to his purpose which he set forth in Christ" (Eph. 1:9). These historical actions by God are, for faith, the key to understanding all of history.

These are especially significant times for Cumberland Presbyterians to preach, teach, and live their faith; the faith that God is a living God and Lord of history. There can be little doubt that in recent centuries there has been a steady erosion of belief/faith in a living, personal, speaking God who has acted, and continues to act, in human history. In his book *Thus Spake Zarathustra*, Friedrich Nietzsche's central character, Zarathustra, has spent many years dwelling in a mountain cave and reflecting on the meaning of life. He then decides the time has come to return to society. Descending the mountain, he encounters an old man who is a hermit. Zarathustra tells the man that he is returning to the world of people. The hermit is incredulous at this idea and asks why the stranger would do such a thing? Zarathustra replies, "I love people." The hermit replies, "I once loved people but they ruined my life. Now I only love God." They finish their talk and go their separate ways. Later, when reflecting on this encounter, Zarathustra says to himself, "Who would have believed it? This good old man has not heard—God is dead."[6]

In the 19th century, Nietzsche offered the world his famous pronouncement: "God is dead." He believed that God, in effect, "had died" in the consciousness of the European masses. His famous proclamation was really about God being "functionally dead." People might profess belief in God but this belief appeared to have little relevance to or significance for the lives they were actually living. God was no longer a "lively" reality. People could conduct their own lives and affairs as if God hardly mattered in any real or significant way. Nietzsche thought this was true even among the many people who still regularly attended religious services. God was far removed from their real lives. God had become a religious relic. Cumberland Presbyterians live in a world in which God often appears to be functionally dead in the lives of millions of people. Sadly, this may be true among some of us who regularly sit in pews or stand in pulpits. It can become true for any of us in given moments of our lives.

The single most common conception of God in the United States (and Western world) appears to be deistic. Historic deistic belief can be illustrated by the following kind of remark: "I believe in God but, as far as I can tell, this God appears to have little, if anything, to do with this real world or my real life. God got the world started and then took a leave of absence." If deistic style belief and functional atheism are widespread at the turn of the third millennium, as they appear to be, the future for the Cumberland Presbyterian Churches should be a promising one. The promise does not reside in us, our institutions, or even in our theology. It resides in God, the living God who has not stopped speaking and acting. The good news that Cumberland Presbyterians have to share with the people of the 21st century is that God is a living, speaking, active God; a God who remains present and involved in the life and affairs of the world, the church, and in the lives of individual persons. We, as Cumberland Presbyterians, are to communicate this belief to the world around us primarily through a way of life in community (the church) that would make no sense unless God is the living, speaking, acting God revealed in Jesus Christ. The truth of this living God is a fundamental affirmation of the *COF*.

The Attributes of God

In its first statement, the *COF* includes what in traditional theology are called the attributes, or perfections, of God. God is said to be **holy love, eternal, unchangeable in being, wisdom, power, holiness, justice, goodness, truth** (1.01). These attributes refer to the character of God. They are not, however, based on intellectual speculation about God. They come from the scriptural record of God's actions in the history of Israel and the history of Jesus Christ. We know who God/Christ/Spirit is by what God/Christ/Spirit has done. The attributes are worthy of sustained study. The most that can be done here is to offer brief, and therefore limited, comments on each of them.

God is "holy love." We human beings have experiences of love. Can we, however, imagine a perfection of love; a love that has never been, nor can be, tainted by egoism or any other of the human characteristics that often diminish our own giving and receiving of love? Yes we can. We can because scripture informs us of and about a "holy love." The word "holy" here means "different." God's love is different from our love in that God's is a perfection of love; a perfect love. The full revelation of God's love in Jesus Christ was so profound as to lead the writer of 1 John, and the John community, to make the remarkable assertion, "God *is* love" (I John 4:7-10; see also John 3:16-17; Ro. 5:5-11).

God is "eternal." We human beings are fully acquainted with and bound by temporality. That is we know something about time and its passing. As one writer observes, "Time is (for human beings) a strange experience of double-directionality. The future comes at us and becomes, far too fast, the present. The present (especially a summer vacation, one's youth, or when one's children are young) slips by and out, and like a train rushing through a station, soon vanishes, out of sight and out of touch, into the past."[7] As human beings, we are able to "transcend temporality with our minds and wills in the very condition of being immersed in it."[8] We human beings, perhaps alone in the universe, can rationally reflect on the idea of timelessness, but we cannot escape time. Our time eventually runs out. But God is not bound by time or space. God's freedom from the constraints of time and space is the fundamental meaning of the affirmation that God is eternal.

God is "unchangeable in being" (Ps. 102:25-27). Unchangeable means that God does not change in God's innermost purposes. God's purposes, as revealed in the history of Israel and of Jesus Christ, are to love and to redeem all of creation. God cannot and will not change with respect to these purposes. In classical theology, the question of God's being is spoken of as God's *aseity*. God is a *se* (from himself). God depends on nothing outside himself in order "to be." God is unchangeable in "wisdom" (1. Cor. 2:7; James 3:17). God is not ignorant of anything God must know in order to govern the universe and bring to fullness and completeness God's objectives. God is unchangeable in "power" (Ps. 145:8-11); an attribute that is related to God's *aseity*. The decisive thing about God's power is God's power to exist—to be. "No creature has this power; existence is a gift which the creature receives from beyond itself, from the source of all, that is, from God. But God is the self-existent being, the one who, unlike all others, is sufficient unto himself for existence."[12] Also, and most importantly, God's power is revealed in scripture as being the power to love. The power of God is to freely give God's self in love to and for the sake of humanity.

God is unchangeable in "holiness" (Isa. 6:1-3). The world "holiness" points to the contrast between everything human and God. This is especially true in the realm of the moral. God is morally different from human beings. God is separated from sin and is committed to seeking his own honor. God is unchangeable in "justice" (Ps. 111; and see all of the eighth century prophets; Rev. 15:3-4). God is God not only in terms of what exists, what *is*, but on the level of what is *right*. God alone, in his revelatory actions in the history of Israel and the history of Jesus, is the standard by which what is right is to be judged. God is unchangeable in "goodness" (Ps. 86:5; Mk. 10:18; Rom. 11:22). God is the source and foundation of all goodness, and the ultimate and final standard of what is good. And God is unchangeable in "truth" (Dt. 32:4; Ps. 33:4; Ps. 57:10; Jn. 17:17). God is without contradiction in himself. God's knowledge and communication of himself are both true and the final standard of truth. Therefore, it is God who reveals both the truth of who God is, the truth of who human beings are, and the truth concerning the meaning of all existence and the entirety of history.

The God Who is Trinity

Cumberland Presbyterians believe in **the one living God who is Father, Son, and Holy Spirit, the Holy Trinity** (1.02). Belief in the Trinity flows directly from a reading of the scriptures. The Trinity arose among early Christians as a result of a necessary way of speaking. Richard Norris writes, "From the earliest times, a 'trinitarian' way of talking sprang up as a means of explaining the character and structure of Christian existence. People's relationship to God, their experience of redemption, was a complex unity. It was not three separate relationships—one to the Father, another to Christ, another to the Spirit. It was a single, unified reality, a single relationship to the one God as Father, established and revealed in Christ, and brought home to people *through* the Spirit. God's presence for believers, and their resulting openness to him, took place in just this three-fold way."[9] Norris adds, "Christian identity appears, then, at the point when, through the Spirit, people enter into Christ's relation to God. For example, as the First Letter of Peter states it, Christians are 'chosen and destined by God the Father and sanctified by the Spirit for obedience to Christ' (1:2)."[10] This three-fold way of speaking and writing about God occurs throughout the post Easter and post Pentecost writings of the New Testament. The "experience" of God as Trinity is deeply embedded in the witness of the New Testament.

A formal "doctrine of the Trinity" came some centuries after the witness of the earliest Christians recorded in the Bible. It came through the efforts of the early church councils of Nicea (325 AD and 381 AD). If our purpose was to acquire a comprehensive grasp of the *history* of the doctrine of the Trinity, we would need to spend time researching these councils, the issues involved, the people involved, and the lines of discussion leading to their result. This would be well worth our time and the effort involved. These councils provided a unified and unifying doctrine of the Trinity (formalized in the Nicene Creed). They hammered out, using highly spun and complex theological, philosophical, metaphysical, and metaphorical language what has become the orthodox teaching about the Trinity in the churches of the Western world.

Why the complex language? They were seeking to state, in the language of their time and for the people of their time, what they understood the Bible to mean when speaking of God the Father, God the Son, and God the Holy Spirit. People back then had many of the same questions people have today. What is meant by three-in-one? What is meant by God in three persons? Are we talking about one God or three Gods? In what sense is Jesus God? How can Jesus be both God and a human being? How can God become flesh? And so on. These are not unimportant questions. But, as one scholar has cleverly written, "The problem the doctrine of the Trinity seeks to resolve, the normativity of Jesus as he relates to the uniqueness of God, is a problem Christians will always face if they are Christians. The doctrine of the Trinity is a test of whether your commitments to Jesus are biblical enough that you have the problem the doctrine of the Trinity solves."[11]

Another approach to the Trinity is to simply read the Bible. Doing so will help us see that before it was a doctrine promulgated by later church councils, it was simply the experience of the earliest Christians; those whom God used to give us the Bible. There is no particular passage, or passages, in the Bible to which we can turn for a fully orbed treatment of the Trinity. In fact, the word Trinity does not appear in the

Bible. It is not there explicitly but it is there implicitly. And what is there, and what the later church theologians expounded upon, was the experience of those who were originally closest to Jesus and the Jesus story. Shirley Guthrie provides one summary of what we find when reading the New Testament:

"The first Christians could not talk about the God of Israel who was their God too without talking about a man named Jesus. They did not speak of Jesus' 'deity' or 'divinity,' nor did they speculate theoretically about his 'divine nature' or 'essence.' They thought about what Jesus *did*. Here is a man who acts like God, does what only God can do. He speaks with the absolute authority that belongs only to God—even to the extent of calling into question the ethical teachings the people believed to be the will of God made known to Moses. He heals and raises the dead with the life-giving power that belongs only to God. He dares to forgive sin as only God has the right to do. He speaks and acts as if his coming means that the kingdom of God is breaking into the world. He speaks and acts as Judge, Reconciler, Redeemer, Liberator, and Lord over life and death. It is not surprising that religious people of his day accused him of blasphemy; he claimed that in what he said and did God was speaking and acting. During Jesus' life, the disciples were confused and uncertain about what all this meant. After his death and resurrection, it became clearer to them. They still did not try to explain it, but they now confess that the risen Jesus is 'Lord' and 'Savior' who is 'far above all rule and authority and power and dominion and above every name that is named' (Eph. 1:21). That is, they now give to Jesus the same names, the same authority, the same saving power that they had reserved for God."[12] And, of course, the earliest Christians also understood the Holy Spirit to be the Spirit of Jesus and, therefore, the Spirit of God.

Guthrie adds: "Christians do not 'believe in' the doctrine of the Trinity (or any other doctrine). We believe in a living God. But the God we believe in is the God this doctrine confesses, the one living and true God who is Father, Son, and Holy Spirit. Faith in this God—and lives shaped by faith in this God—is what distinguishes Christians from people who do not believe in God at all and from other religious people whose life and faith is shaped by other views of God. Moreover, within the Christian circle itself it is faithfulness to the will and word and work of the one 'triune' God that distinguishes authentic Christian faith and life from misunderstandings and distortions of it."[13]

Cumberland Presbyterians affirm that the God in whom we believe is Father, Son, and Holy Spirit. This is our faith. We, too, experience the one God who is present to us in three ways. I would like to add that all authentic Christian preaching and teaching is Trinitarian. This, of course, does not mean that every sermon or study will be about the formal doctrine of the Trinity. But it does mean that every sermon and study will presuppose that all speaking about God is indeed speaking about and in the name of the God who is Trinity. There is no other God about whom Cumberland Presbyterians can or will preach and teach. To keep this Trinitarian confession before the congregation and before myself, I long have chosen to end every sermon with the final words being: "In the name of God the Father, God the Son, and God the Holy Spirit."

The God Who Makes Covenant

By word and action God invites persons into a covenant relationship. God promises to be faithful to the covenant and to make all who believe his people. All who respond with trust and commitment to God's invitation find the promise sure and rejoice in being members of God's people, the covenant community (1.03). Cumberland Presbyterians preach and teach that God is a God who makes covenant with God's people. The Bible records a series of such covenants. God made a covenant with Noah (Gen 9:8-17). God made a covenant with Abraham and Sarah (Gen 17). God made a covenant with Israel at Sinai (Exodus 19-31). God engaged the people in covenant renewal (Joshua 24). God promised Jeremiah that there would be a new covenant (Jer. 31:31-34). And God's ultimate act of covenant is made in and through Jesus Christ. He is the mediator of the new (renewed) covenant (Heb. 9:11-28).

Covenant is a special word to Cumberland Presbyterians as well as others in the Reformed and Presbyterian tradition.

When the Reformers of the 16th century including John Calvin—the "Father" of the Presbyterian tradition—began to read the Bible anew (no longer under the aegis of the Roman Catholic Church) they came to regard "covenant" as the spine of the story that the Bible tells. They used other metaphors such as calling it the "golden thread that runs through scripture." For them, God is the God who, above all, makes covenant. God chose Israel for a covenant relationship. And God fulfilled and extended this covenant in and through Jesus the Christ. The people of God, both as Israel and as the church, are the people who are bound in covenant relationship to God. They are the covenant community of God. This covenant relationship is not for privilege but for witness and service. The covenant community is to be a blessing to all nations (Gen. 12:3). In the New Testament, it is said of the covenant community—the church— "But you are a chosen race, a royal priesthood, a holy nation, God's own people, in order that you may proclaim the mighty acts of him who called you out of darkness into his marvelous light" (1 Pt. 2:9).

For Cumberland Presbyterians, the importance of the word covenant, and the realities to which it points, can hardly be overstated. Often a single word, or set of words, becomes indicative of a particular Christian tradition. For example, if you say Roman Catholics, the word is likely to be Eucharist or Mass. If you say Methodists, it is holiness or sanctification. If you say Lutherans, it is justification by faith. If you say Episcopalians, the word is liturgy. If you say Pentecostals, it is Spirit baptism. If you say Baptists, it is believer's baptism. But when you say Presbyterians, the word is covenant. Some Cumberland Presbyterians will remember that in the mid 20th century the church engaged with other Reformed bodies to produce a new Christian Education curriculum. The end product was called *Covenant Life Curriculum*. It is likely that "covenant" remains the name most frequently given when establishing new congregations in the Reformed and Presbyterian tradition. So covenant is much more than merely a word to Cumberland Presbyterians. It is a very special and important identifier. Chapter nine will include a discussion of the theological significance that covenant has for Cumberland Presbyterians and the compelling interpretation given to it in the *COF* of 1984.

Chapter Two

THE HOLY SCRIPTURES

It is a well known remark that, "History is written by the winners." However, this is not the case with respect to the Bible. It was written, for the most part, by the "losers" in terms of world history and power. It was written by people who were on the political bottom. Some scholars maintain that it is the only such literature surviving from the ancient world. Israel, of course, did experience a brief period of being near the top of the then world pile. This was during the reign of David and later Solomon (ca. the 10th century BCE). But the Hebrew Bible primarily is the product of a people who knew what it was to be oppressed, enslaved, subjugated and otherwise dominated by this-worldly powers. The New Testament, likewise, is certainly not the record of a "worldly winner" and his followers. Rather it is a testimony to the one rejected and crucified as a common criminal who, nevertheless, was vindicated by God. It is the testimony of those who formed communities of worship, witness and service in his name.

However, in the third century AD the Bible did become something of a "winner's book." It happened when the Roman Emperor Constantine was converted to the Christian faith (312). Constantine's Edict of Milan, in February 313, declared that Christians would be treated benevolently throughout the Empire. These events led to the Christian faith eventually becoming the official religion of the Roman Empire. It remains highly questionable whether this was an entirely good development. The church, in many ways, seems to have lost theological and moral ground as a result. It often didn't do all that well, in terms of its faithfulness to the charter given it by Christ, given its new position as one of history's winners. It has been far too easy for the church, throughout the centuries, to accommodate to the reigning powers, the dominant culture, and to tame and domesticate the message of its original loser—the rejected, crucified but risen Christ.

I mention this history because we are in a time when the church, certainly in America, is progressively losing its cultural prestige, position, and privilege. Until the middle of the 20th century, the Christian church and ethos was dominant in, and in some ways over, the culture. The church is now only one more minority sub-group among a whole multitude of other minority sub-groups. The age of Christendom (of enjoying the support and endorsement of the surrounding culture which began long ago with Constantine) is over. How are we to react to this development? One way is to see ourselves as positioned to read and hear the scriptures anew. And to hear them as about a Lord whose reign and power and kingdom do not derive their legitimacy or authority from existing in the favor of the dominant power arrangements of this world (Jn. 18:36). I regard it as a wonderfully exciting time for Cumberland Presbyterians. During Christendom, the entire Christian church had, so to speak "gained the world, but lost our soul." But listening afresh to the scriptures, in our greatly changed cultural circumstances, can and might lead to a profound renewal of the church. Scripture reveals the Word of God has this power. If there is a renewal, the church likely will not look exactly like the church of establishment—the church of Christendom. But that is OK. The trappings of wide-spread cultural approval and support in the 20th century may have been to and for the church more like barnacles than blessings on the ship of faith.

Cumberland Presbyterians regard the Bible as God's gift to the church. N. T. Wright comments on what the gift is for. He does this as a part of his reflection on 2 Timothy 3:16-17: "The Bible is 'breathed-out' by God (the word for 'inspired' is *theopnuestos*—literally 'God-breathed') so that it can fashion and form God's people to do God's work in the world. In other words, the Bible isn't there simply to be an accurate reference point for people who want to look things up and be sure they've got them right. It is there to equip God's people to carry forward the purposes of *new covenant* and *new creation*. . . .The Bible isn't like an accurate description of how a car is made. It is more like the mechanic who helps you fix it, the garage attendant who helps you fuel it, and the guide who tells you how to get where you are going. And where you are going is *to make God's new creation happen in this world,* not simply find your way unscathed through the old creation. . . .The Bible is there to enable God's people to be equipped to do God's work in God's world, not to give them an excuse to sit back smugly, knowing they possess all God's truth."[1] G. Kaufmann adds these words about the function of the scriptures in the church: "The Bible is used in many ways in the church but the justification of them all is the same: it is the medium through which the church is able to apprehend again and again, and to reconstruct, the history which has produced her and the events which provide her norms by which to order her life."[2] These remarks by Wright and Kaufmann could have been written by any number of Cumberland Presbyterians.

God Inspired the Scriptures

√ **God inspired persons of the covenant community to write the scriptures** (1.05). Cumberland Presbyterians believe to an absolute certainty that God inspired the writing of the scriptures. This affirmation is a cardinal point of our faith. However Cumberland Presbyterians, unlike some in other Christian traditions, have never felt it necessary to subscribe to a particular "theory of inspiration." We have been content to affirm our belief in the inspiration of scripture based solely on its own internal testimony (See Ex. 24:3-4; Dt. 31:9-13; Joshua 8:30-35; Jn. 20:30-31; 2 Tim. 3:14-17; 2 Pt. 1:19-21, 3:18).

Perhaps it will be helpful to discuss when, why, and how the church (here meaning the Reformed church of about three centuries ago) went beyond simply affirming that God inspired the scriptures and developed theories to explain what is meant by this affirmation. This subject is a difficult one to summarize with brevity, but the following is an attempt to do so:

1) To repeat, that God inspired the writing of the scriptures is the internal testimony of the scriptures themselves (Again, 2 Tim. 3:14-17; 2 Pt. 1:19-21, 3:18).

2) That this was regarded as being true was the presupposition of the church as a whole up to the 17th and 18th centuries. These centuries saw the rise of what is known as Protestant Scholasticism (more to be said about this shortly). Before this period, the reformers of the 16th century Reformation, such as Luther, Calvin, and Zwingli, shared the simple presupposition. Their writings take for granted that the scripture writers were inspired by God. They, however, did not put forward theories to explain the nature of this inspiration, or how the inspiration was to be understood as occurring. It was simply so. It is worth noting that the Roman Catholic Church of that era, and still, shared the same simple assumption about inspiration.

3) The Protestant Reformation brought about disagreements among Christians over the interpretation of

scripture. No longer tethered to the Roman Catholic Church as the sole interpreter of scripture, the reformers found it impossible to achieve consensus for their own interpretations. Thus the Reformation issued in several new traditions, such as Lutherans, Presbyterians, followers of Zwingli, Anabaptists, and more. This Protestant development eventually led, of course, to the proliferation of denominations that we presently have. The point here is while they argued over many things none of the reformers argued among themselves about the fact that scripture was inspired by God. There was no need for this. They all agreed, by presupposition, that the scriptures were inspired by God. How one should interpret the meaning of these scriptures at some points was the rub (to take one example, how to understand the meaning of the Lord's Supper).

4) The rise of the European Enlightenment or Age of Reason (roughly 1650-1780) introduced an altogether new situation. The Enlightenment included skepticism about all forms of authority including those of religion. Suddenly, the churches found themselves debating not merely with one another but also with the surrounding world. The debate was no longer only among Christians over issues of biblical interpretation but also with the champions of human reason (as opposed to revelation), growing skepticism, unbelief, and with various philoso-

phies of doubt. According to Enlightenment thinking, the religious truth claims, and the documents on which they were based, could no longer be accepted at face value. Everything had to withstand the scrutiny of human reason and reasonableness. In other words, only human reason could determine what is true and worthy of belief.

5) One of the church's responses to this new situation was the rise, in the 17th and 18th centuries, of the movement known as Protestant (sometimes called Reformed) Scholasticism. It was a rise in academic theology. It was marked by a method of doing theology that set out to achieve theological precision through the exegesis of scripture, examination of how doctrine has been historically defined through church history, and how doctrine is to be expounded in contemporary debate. There seems to have been two main objectives of these academics: 1) explaining and defending the several newly written Protestant confessions of faith, and 2) engaging the Enlightenment world on its own terms by using rigorous reason applied to explain and defend the truth claims of scripture and church doctrine.

6) It was the Protestant Scholastics who gave us the first fully articulated theories of inspiration. They introduced ideas such as the following: the verbal, plenary inspira-

tion of scripture, that is, every single word in the Bible was inspired by God; that the writers of the Bible were to be understood in some fashion as stenographers who took down the words of God verbatim; that the Bible is infallible and without error (inerrant) as applied not only to saving knowledge but in terms of all knowledge ("Whatever the Bible says is true even when challenged by others fields of knowledge"); that not only the texts of the Bible were inspired, but God inspired and supervised the collection of the books to be included, and the process leading to canonization (which books belonged in the Bible and which didn't). Scholasticism was, at many points, an attempt to "out-do the Enlightenment" with respect to the employment of the faculty of human reasoning.

7) One result of Scholasticism was that belief in the theories of inspiration became almost as important as belief in the Bible itself. The theories themselves became "articles of faith." Believing in the theories meant believing the Bible. Not believing in them meant not believing the Bible. Not believing might even mean that you were not a Christian.

Where does this leave us with respect to our present *COF*'s affirmation that **God inspired persons of the covenant community to write the scriptures** (1.05)? We can say that

Cumberland Presbyterians share the faith of the early church and the church up to and through the Reformation and until the era of Protestant Scholasticism. We believe whole-heartedly that God truly inspired the writing of the scriptures. But we hold to no particular theory, or theories, that seek to define exactly how this inspiration took place.

For those interested in this subject, Dr. Joe Ben Irby, longtime Cumberland Presbyterian theologian, provides a substantial treatment of what several Cumberland Presbyterian theologians have said and believed about the inspiration of scripture (see Irby's book *This They Believed*). His careful study reveals something important about each of the Confessions under which Cumberland Presbyterians have lived (The Westminster Confession of 1647, The CP Confessions of 1813, 1883, and 1984). He writes, "While all these Confessions clearly affirm the inspiration of scripture, neither of the words 'verbal,' 'plenary,' nor 'inerrant' appear in any of them."[3] Dr. Irby's observation essentially underlines the point that has been being made. While Cumberland Presbyterians believe in God's inspiration of scripture, we do so without the necessity of espousing a particular view of the manner of inspiration. In taking this approach, Cumberland Presbyterians have remained consistent with the Reformers of the Protestant Reformation. About this and many other highly speculative points of theological interpretation, it can be said of Cumberland Presbyterians what is sometimes said about the act of preaching—namely, the purpose of preaching is to proclaim rather than to explain. Cumberland Presbyterians vigorously proclaim that God inspired the scriptures. They stop short of seeking to explain how God did so.

Infallible and Authoritative

The scriptures are the infallible rule of faith and practice, the authoritative guide for Christian living (1.05) . . . . **The authority of the scriptures is founded on the truth contained in them and the voice of God speaking through them** (1.06). That the scriptures are the "the infallible rule of faith and practice" and the "authoritative guide for Christian living," are important affirmations for Cumberland Presbyterians. We need to flesh out what is meant by the two operative words in these statements: "infallible" and "authoritative."

If we searched for the meaning of infallibility as it is found in the work of the above mentioned Protestant Scholastics of the 17th and 18th centuries, we would discover that they developed a "doctrine of infallibility." As with the theories of inspiration, the doctrine was a response to the empiricism, rationalism, and skepticism being newly encountered by the church as a result of the intellectual climate brought about by the European Enlightenment. In Enlightenment thought, everything human beings claimed to know was up for grabs. Everything was re-examined in the light of human reason alone without reference to or belief in divine revelation. "How do you know what you believe is true to the facts?" This was an important Enlightenment question. Maybe, it was thought, some things we think we now know are in conflict with things that are written in the Bible. For one thing, according to Enlightenment presuppositions, human reason would suggest that the kind of miracles recorded in the Bible do not happen. What is the proof that they did? What is the proof that the man Jesus was raised from the dead? And so on.

The response given by the Reformed Scholastics was not proof, for no such proof could or can be given. The response was in the form of theories: "Here is how you can know that the Bible is infallible. It happened in this way." As with the issue of inspiration, it is important to note that the church had never been put in a position to make this claim before. Formerly, it was simply believed that the scriptures revealed who God was and what God had done for the salvation of humankind and the world. There was no reason to defend every "fact" in the Bible because up until this time there had few challenges. The world was fundamentally a "believing world." But as a result of the Enlightenment it was felt that more needed to be claimed for the Bible than ever before. Now it was claimed that everything that the Bible says "on every subject" is factually or infallibly true. In other words, the Bible does not err on any subject on which it speaks.

While acknowledging the valiant effort of Scholasticism to "defend" the Bible (and God?), we can conclude that Scholasticism over-reacted. There was little, if any, reason for the church to defend the Bible (or God) against the challenges that comes from human reason. The church, after all, believes in God's revelation and therefore inspiration on the basis of faith and not on the basis of human reason. There is no proof that can be offered for these beliefs. It is God alone who inspires faith in his people. He does this by revelation (Mt. 16:16-17). The faith that God inspires includes enabling us to affirm that the Bible is trustworthy, true, and, yes, infallible. But it is infallible with regard to its own intention and purpose. It is infallible with respect to being the record of inspired witnesses to God's saving work in Israel and in Jesus Christ. Neither the Hebrew people nor early Christians would have contended that God had inspired something like a scientific textbook. This would not have occurred to them.

Our understanding of infallibility is that the scriptures will not fail to bring us into an encounter with the living God—the Father, the Son, and the Holy Spirit. The scriptures will not fail to tell us of Jesus Christ, his life, death, and resurrection, of his lordship, of the giving of the Holy Spirit, of the reality of the kingdom of God, of the faith and life of the earliest Christians, the meaning of discipleship, and of God's judging, reconciling work on behalf of humankind and all of creation. As was true concerning theories of inspiration, the

COF sets forth no particular doctrine of infallibility. It simply affirms that the scriptures are, in fact, the infallible rule of faith and practice for the church, the covenant community. The scriptures will not lie or deceive us when it comes to who God is and what God has done for the salvation of the world. There is no reason to demand that everything that human beings can know or discover be reconciled factually to everything that is said in the Bible (unless you have a doctrine that demands it).

The other important word is "authoritative" or "authority." The *COF* says that **scripture is the authoritative guide for Christian living** (1.05) and, **The authority of scripture is founded on the truth contained in them and the voice of God speaking through them** (1.06). If we were doing a historical study, we would find that the question of the "authority of the Bible," once involved an important point at which the Reformed theologians (Zwingli, Calvin, Luther and others) disagreed with the Roman Catholic Church. The Roman Catholic position was that the church maintained authority over scripture. It was the Roman Catholic view that the church had collected the scriptures, canonized them, preserved them, and therefore reserved the right to interpret them. The reformers roundly rejected this view. For them, scripture's authority came not from the church but from God. Therefore the church was not positioned above the scriptures. The scriptures were positioned above the church. Thus, in the Reformed view, the final appeal in matters of life and faith is not the church but the scriptures. The church does not tell us what the scripture is, but the scripture tells us what the church is. It was this kind of historical debate that led to the words "authority" and "authoritative" first entering into the various Reformed Confessions.

There is also, of course, a common sense meaning to these words. We can all name a book or books by certain authors who are said to be authorities, or the authority, on the subjects about which they have written. If you want to know something about a particular subject, you consult the authoritative writers and their writings. The church has always said, because we believe the Bible itself says it, that the real author of scripture is God. God brought forth this book. It is a book (or collection of books) that is read in order to hear what God is saying. God's truth can be heard in and through these writings because the very voice of God is speaking through them. Cumberland Presbyterians do not require a "doctrine of authority." We prefer instead to simply read and hear what the Bible says. The fundamental Cumberland Presbyterian attitude toward scripture is expressed well by Morrow: "Nowhere else {except in scripture} can one find the true account of how the miracle of faith occurs. Nowhere else but in scripture can one find Good News that God in Christ forgives and accepts the sinner and sets the sinner free from bondage to the sin and death of self-centeredness. Nowhere else but in scripture does one find both the good news of the grace of God, and the good news of the gift of faith by which one becomes able to respond to God's grace."[4] The scriptures, without failing, are used by God to bring us to faith.

God Speaks in and through Scripture

In and through the scriptures, God speaks about creation, sin, judgment, salvation, the church, and the growth of believers (1.05). Cumberland Presbyterians believe that God speaks to us in and through the scriptures of the Hebrew and Christian Testaments. Cumberland Presbyterians are a "People of the Book." However, in these opening years of the 21st century, Cumberland Presbyterians have become aware that there is a woeful lack of serious familiarity with the Bible among the American people, including many of those in our own congregations. Overcoming this condition is a serious, present, and future challenge for Cumberland Presbyterians.

Eugene Peterson makes use of a metaphor taken from Ezekiel 3:3 and Revelation 10:1-10 to speak about the importance of the Bible to Christian faith.[5] The metaphor is found in the instruction given both to the ancient prophet and to the seer of the Bible's final book: "Eat this scroll." As God's people, we are to devour and digest the scripture. It is unlikely that there can be a thoroughgoing renewal of the church, or of individual Christian life, or of the church's preaching and teaching without fresh, attentive and responsive listening to the voice of God in and through scripture.

As a pastor of and preacher for Cumberland Presbyterian congregations, nothing has been more vitally important than spending time with scripture. In my earliest years of pastoral ministry, the responsibility of preaching from the Bible was an extremely daunting task. It is painful to admit but in the earliest years of my ministry, in the early 1970s, I bought a book called **The Minister's Manual**. This book was published annually and included sermons and sermon suggestions for the fifty-two Sundays of the year. It also had a section of stock funeral and marriage sermons. It had a section of illustrations. And it had a section of "inspired poetry"—presumably for the pastor who organized the sermon with three points and a poem!

I bought this book because I was desperate when it came to preaching. However, after a couple of years, I realized that it depending on this book, and others like it, simply was not going to work. It became clear to me that I was going to have to do what I was told I would have to do at my ordination as a minister of Word and Sacrament. And, I should add, what I had promised to do. I was going to have to sit down regularly, take knife and fork in hand so to speak, and proceed to eat the book! There were no shortcuts. I had to listen to what the original witnesses were saying and to what the living God was saying to and through them. And so it was that I began seriously to enter into what Karl Barth once called, "The strangely wonderful world within the Bible." By strange, he meant, among other things, that the Bible is utterly fascinating and captivating as it invites us to consider a world, and world-view, that is alien to all other conventional world-views.

Persons who unite with a Cumberland Presbyterian congregation ordinarily answer, among others, the following question: “Do you believe the Scriptures of the Old and New Testaments to be the inspired Word of God, the source of authority for faith and practice, and will you read and study them for guidance in living the Christian life?” There it stands for every Cumberland Presbyterian. We all promise to eat the book!

An Interpretive Principle

God’s word spoken in and through the scriptures should be understood in the light of the birth, life, death, and resurrection of Jesus of Nazareth (1.06) Cumberland Presbyterians have a strong and clear interpretive principle when it comes to reading, preaching and teaching from the Bible. It is the Word made flesh in Jesus Christ as the pledge of God’s love. In the strictest sense, we do not preach the Bible but we preach Christ. The Bible is given to us so we may preach Christ. This interpretive principle does not mean that we are not to seek to understand various biblical texts in their own settings and circumstances and according to the intentions of the various authors. It does mean that finally we understand all that we read in the light of the person and work of Christ. Among the Reformers, it was commonly said that scripture pointed beyond itself to Jesus Christ as *rex scripturae*—King of Scripture.[6] Cumberland Presbyterians regard Christ as the center and circumference of God's revelation in and through scripture. All texts, therefore, are to be heard and evaluated according to the standard of the fullness of God's revelation in Jesus Christ.

Let's consider a couple of example of how the Christological interpretive principle might work and has worked in the history of the church. There are texts, for example, that appear to take for granted the practice of human slavery in the ancient world. These texts cannot be said to endorse the practice of slavery. The New Testament even elevates the slave as being an equal in the body of Christ (Gal. 3:28). But abolishing the practice of slavery was not a project that the New Testament era church seems to have thought possible. That this was the case, and that there are texts that call on the slave to obey his or her master, lead some Christians to claim, especially in the 19th century, that the Bible endorses or accepts slavery as a God-ordained human institution, such as the institutions of government and family. Who would argue this today? Who would deny that the Christological interpretive principle forbids the idea or practice of slavery?

There are scripture texts that appear to call for the subordination of women. Such texts clearly contributed to the male domination of women in almost all departments of life up until the most recent of times. We might consider the striking historical fact that it was not until the 1920s, still less than a hundred years ago, that American women were granted the right to vote! There were Christians who appealed to biblical texts to argue against women's suffrage. But we can be grateful that other Christians argued on the basis of the Christological interpretive principle, and the egalitarian Spirit of Christ, that the church had been wrong, throughout history, in continuing support for the subjugation of women. Many other examples of the importance of the Christological interpretive principle could be given.

Understanding Scripture

In order to understand God's word spoken in and through the scriptures, persons must have the illumination of God's own Spirit (1.07). Cumberland Presbyterians believe that it is God alone who makes possible the hearing and understanding of what God is saying in and through scripture. And that this is a primary work of the Holy Spirit.

I often have shared the following story when preaching about the Bible and the illumination of the Spirit. A friend, who told me the story, said he heard it from one of his professors in seminary. The professor said we often approach the texts of scripture as if they are ancient mummies lying before us on an examining table. We take our tools in hand (Biblical languages, commentaries, word studies, etc.) and begin to un-wrap the old mummy in order to see what secrets it may contain. We wonder if we will find anything that might be of interest to us. It appears, of course, that we are in charge of this process. After all, we are alive and the mummy is dead! But the professor said when the Holy Spirit is at work in our praying and reading of Scripture something truly startling happens. The mummy suddenly jumps up from the table! It proceeds to grab us by the lapels and begins to unwrap and expose us, layer by layer! Cumberland Presbyterians believe that the Spirit of God makes known to us the voice of God speaking in and through scripture. This voice confronts us in both judgment and grace. Following the metaphor, Cumberland Presbyterians believe that without the illumination of God's own Spirit the texts of scripture will appear to us only as ancient dusty mummies. Apart from the illumination of the Holy Spirit, we will be unable to understand what is being said to us by the voice of God speaking to us in and through scripture.

The classic Reformers spoke of the Holy Spirit's work of illumination as being "the testimony of the Holy Spirit." John Howard Yoder offers a contemporary image of what was meant by the Spirit's testimony. He does this by employing the metaphor of "resonance." "Resonance is the capacity of a string or tube, like an organ pipe, to sort out from a great number of frequencies the particular frequency for which it is set, thereby losing the other frequencies of vibration while reinforcing the one it chooses. The wind across the top of an organ pipe creates sounds of many frequencies, but the pipe resounds only to one wavelength, and therefore produces one tone. So the size and shape of the pipe determines which of the vibratory frequencies will be reinforced and heard and which (all the others) will go away as the windiness of the organ pipe. It is something like that in the heart of the believer. You read through the Bible and some things resonate. Some things echo. Some things provoke regular vibration. That is the message of Christ."[7] The classic Reformed position has been stated in these words, "Scripture's believability is not based on the authority of the church but on the Spirit's external witness in Scripture itself, and in the Spirit's internal witness in Christians."[8] And as Jack Rogers writes, "While many arguments for the truth of scripture may be produced, only the witness of the Holy Spirit in the human heart can finally persuade a person that scripture is the Word of God."[9]

Studying Scripture

Moreover (Cumberland Presbyterians) **should study the writings of the Bible in their historical settings, compare scripture with scripture, listen to the witness of the church throughout the centuries, and share insights with others in the covenant community** (1.07). Cumberland Presbyterians have a definite methodology for the study of scripture. First, we are cautious concerning private interpretations of the scriptures (1 Pt. 1:2-21). We take seriously the truth and reality of covenant community. Therefore, we prefer to be guided and informed by the Bible as it has been heard and interpreted by the church as a whole. The readings and hearings of the covenant community, both now and throughout history, take precedence over private interpretations. When private interpretations are put forward they are to be tested in light of the corporate interpretations of the church. The preacher or teacher must always keep this in mind. She or he preaches or teaches the faith of the church and not privatized versions of the faith.

Cumberland Presbyterians are also indisposed to proof-texting. We seek a comprehensive familiarity with the scriptures in order to be able to properly compare scripture to scripture as a means toward clarity of insight and understanding. Cumberland Presbyterians also seek to listen to the church throughout the centuries. We especially find it helpful to listen to those interpreters who share a history with Cumberland Presbyterians from within the Reformed and Presbyterian tradition. Cumberland Presbyterians are also free, of course, to listen to voices from within other traditions that may provide valuable insights into the understanding of scripture.

Of profound importance, Cumberland Presbyterians gather with others in their own congregations to share insights and understandings. We regard the study of scripture primarily as a "we/us" exercise rather than an "I/me" exercise. It is certainly true that Cumberland Presbyterians will and do value and practice private individual readings of scripture, often done with a devotional intent. But it is to be remembered that the scriptures have been given to the entire church and, therefore, corporate readings are vital to the church's life, witness, and service in the world. If congregations are to do theology, that is if they are to properly attend to the Bible's words about and from God, gathering for corporate listening and response is essential.

Cumberland Presbyterians believe in studying the scripture in light of **their historical settings** (1.07). "To understand them we have to enter their world, and not pretend they belong to ours. When we do enter it, we discover a rich panorama of literature: legal texts and poems; legend and history; myth and theological argument; letters, and epics, and sermons. We find changes of outlook, theological debate and disagreement, and constant reinterpretation of older beliefs and ideas. In short, we find the intellectual and spiritual product of the history of an entire religious tradition—but one which has, for all its variety, a clear thread of unity. This literature has one central theme: God in his relation to a people whom he has called, to whom he has spoken. And since the relation of the present day church to God belongs to the same story, God's calling and speaking as it is encountered through the Bible is the source of the Christian community's self-understanding today. There is no need to pay the scriptures superfluous compliments. It is enough that in them, in and through all their human variety, we learn to recognize and respond to the God and Father of Jesus Christ."[10]

Cumberland Presbyterians have the highest possible regard for the scriptures. They are the blessed God-given spiritual and ethical fountain from which we may continually drink. The following prayer, or one similar to it, is offered on Sunday mornings in many Cumberland Presbyterian congregations prior to the reading of scripture and the act of preaching: "Blessed Lord, who caused all holy Scriptures to be written for our learning; Grant us so to hear them, read, mark, learn, and inwardly digest them, that we may embrace and ever hold fast the blessed hope of everlasting life, which you have given us in our Savior Jesus Christ. Amen."

Chapter Three

GOD'S WILL

God's will for people and all creation is altogether wise and good. Although revealed in scriptures and in the events of nature and history, God's will is made known supremely in the person of Jesus Christ, who did God's will even to death. God's will is sufficiently disclosed for persons to respond to it in worship, love, and service, yet they should hold in reverence and wonder the mystery of divine ways. (1.08—1.09)

God's will is important to Cumberland Presbyterians. Many people (perhaps ourselves) often seek to know the will of God in quite personal terms and circumstances. We wonder if it is God's will for us to make this or that decision, or take this or that action. Although this is understandable, there are certain red flags that should be considered when thinking about God's will in personal terms. For example, one Christian, who has thought a great deal about what the Bible says on this subject, writes: "When we seek 'to find' God's will, we are attempting to discover hidden knowledge by supernatural activity. If we are going to find God's will on one specific choice, we will have to penetrate the divine mind to get God's decision. 'Finding' in this sense is really a form of divination. This idea was common in pagan religions. As a matter of fact, it was a preoccupation of pagan kings. Most of our texts from the ancient Near East pertain to divination. The king would never act in something important as going into battle until he had the mind of the god as to whether he should or should not go to war. Many Christians follow this same path in seeking the divine mind in decisions. I have talked with people who perform certain rituals before going to God with an important request as though they could make themselves more acceptable to God and therefore more likely to get an answer. But that sort of pagan behavior is what Christ saved us out of."[1]

Furthermore, "The New Testament gives no explicit command to 'find God's will.' Nor can you find any particular instructions on how to go about finding God's will. There isn't a magic formula offered to Christians that will open up some mysterious door of wonder, allowing us to get a glimpse of the mind of the Almighty. The Bible forbids pagan divination (Dt. 18:10) and invokes severe penalties for those who resort to magic for determining the will of God in this way. Simon Magus was severely rebuked in Acts 8 for seeking supernatural powers, and Christ criticized the perverse generation that always asks for a sign from God."[2] And, perhaps most importantly, "When we talk about finding the will of God we generally want divine guidance on specific choices, but it should be noted that this specific term is never used after the Holy Spirit came upon the church at Pentecost. The apostles, upon whom the church is founded, did not teach that we are to seek God's will in this way. Instead, the New Testament offers a program of the Father's guidance that is based upon *having a close relationship with Jesus Christ through the Holy Spirit* (italics mine and added for emphasis).[3]

I once made what I have long since considered to be a terrible mistake with respect to speaking of the will of God for my own life. When leaving one congregation and preparing to go to another, I spoke of being sure that it was God's will for me to make this decision. Perhaps it was God's will. But I had effectively disempowered the members of the congregation from openly disagreeing with me, and some were quite sure, I later learned, that it was not God's will! I subsequently came to believe that it was God's will to call me into ordained ministry. But, beyond that, God left where I lived out that calling to the process of my free choice based on prayer and prayerful conversations with many others. The point is that we should be careful when we use the language of knowing God's will about this or that personal matter, especially when it may impact the life, faith and concerns of others.

Cumberland Presbyterians have a cautious and wise hesitancy about professing to know God's will. Take the arena of politics as an example. Abraham Lincoln said that people from the South declared to him they knew God's will and people from the North declared they knew God's will, but he despaired that he did not know it although he was the one who most needed to know it! William Sloan Coffin once said, "The prophet said 'Let righteousness roll down live a river, and justice like a mighty stream.' But, unfortunately, the prophet did not tell us the details of the irrigation system."[4] Cumberland Presbyterians know that there will be broad areas of concern in human life about which Christians will disagree. This does not mean that Cumberland Presbyterians will avoid speaking and acting in the political realm. Being faithful to God sometimes will mean that Cumberland Presbyterians must speak and act in this realm. But they will seek to avoid sanctifying their own beliefs and perspectives, or preferred political parties, as if they are identical to God's will. We often simply do not have the details needed to claim we know for certain what is and is not God's will. The counsel of humility is important. As the Confession says, **God's will is sufficiently disclosed for persons to respond to it in worship, love, and service, yet they should hold in reverence and wonder the mystery of divine ways.** (1.09)

This being said, there is one thing about God's will of which we Cumberland Presbyterians are absolutely certain. God's will is Jesus Christ. God's will is fully made known in the being and action of Jesus Christ. "To say Jesus was the servant of God . . . is to declare that here a piece of finite reality, a man, has become transparent, as it were, so that when we look at him we no longer simply see him and his will; we see the *divine will* and the *divine being* whose will is carried out through his acts."[5] The Apostle Paul reflects on this in the opening chapter of Ephesians (1:1-14). He preaches that in Christ God has "made known to us the mystery of his will" (Eph. 1:9). According to Paul, we Christians now have the privilege of being in on God's purposes. The will of God is who Jesus is and what Jesus does. The will of God is to break down the barriers between Jew and Gentile. The will of God is to redeem the world in Jesus Christ. The one certain thing, then, that Cumberland Presbyterians know about God's will is that God is at work in Jesus Christ "to gather up all things in him, things in heaven and things on earth" (Eph. 1:10). In this sense, Cumberland Presbyterians can be absolutely confident that they know the will of God. The will of God is to seek to be faithfully obedient to Jesus. It is to follow Jesus in a life of discipleship. It is to seek to be in and for the world as Jesus was in and for the world. The will of God is to live in openness to the already present but still coming kingdom of God. The will of God is important to Cumberland Presbyterians. We regularly pray the prayer taught to us by Jesus that includes the petition, "Your kingdom come, your will be done, on earth as it is in heaven" (Mt. 6:9-13).

Chapter Four

CREATION

The Creator

It appears to be the consensus of modern scientific thought that the universe, as we know it, had its beginning approximately thirteen billion years ago in a physical event that is popularly called the Big Bang. It is an impressive, mysterious, and even beautiful account of the origin of the material world. Science, of course, has been spectacularly effective when it comes to the *"what"* of the universe's beginning. But science can tell us nothing about the *"why"* of this beginning. Nor can it tell us whether a *"who"* was, or might have been, involved in this beginning. Science can tell us that the universe is here, that it exists, but it cannot tell us whether it has a *purpose* or *meaning.* Over the past forty years, I often have had many discussions with people, often young people, who have wondered if what science tells us and what our faith tells us can be reconciled, or even if they are in need of being reconciled. I am of the opinion that faith is not an enemy of science, and that science is not an enemy of faith.

What is at odds, however, is the matter of world-views. If one has a purely naturalistic world-view (nature is all there is, hence there is no God), then the possibility of a "who" being responsible for creation is simply ruled out. If, on the other hand, one has a theistic world-view (God is, and therefore is responsible for creation), then the possibility of a "who" is not in question. It is quite beyond the capability of adherents of either the naturalistic or theistic world-views to prove their world-view is the true one. This, it should be noted, is not the same as saying there are no evidences that can be marshaled in favor of each. Through the experimental method, science has developed a body of knowledge about the natural world which has led many scientists, and lay observers, to choose a naturalistic world view. Theistic believers also have evidences for their own world-view including many of a highly rational and reasonable character (it is not naturalists alone who are reasonable). Whether or not one holds a naturalistic or a theistic world-view is, in the end, not a matter of unquestionable proof or proofs. In both instances it is a matter of faith. Christian faith cannot prove that God exists. Only God can prove that God exists. If there were proof (scientific kind of proof) that God exists, then faith would become meaningless. But neither can science prove that God does not exist. So denying the existence of God, in favor of a naturalistic world-view, is also a matter of choice and faith.

It is the faith of Cumberland Presbyterians that **God is ✓the creator of all that is known and unknown** (1.10). "In the beginning God created the heavens and the earth." (Gen. 1:1). Why does the universe exist? Faith's answer is it exists because

God causes it to be! We are able to grasp something of what is meant by God as the creator by inquiring into what it means to say human beings are capable of creativity. "Creativity is a power distinguishing human beings from other finite beings. We can clarify our meaning here most easily, perhaps, by contrasting 'creating' with 'making' or 'building . . . To create is not simply to make or build. 'Making' (coming from a root meaning 'to fit together') and 'building' connote a mere assembling of materials which are already available. Moreover, however intricate the structure, the assembling may be accomplished almost unconsciously and by instinct. Thus we say that birds build nests and beavers, dams; but we do not say they 'create' them. 'Creation' suggests a much more radical beginning than making or building. It is not simply 'a putting together;' rather it involves *a bringing into existence of something that did not exist before.* In this sense creation is unrepeatable and also unpredictable; it is therefore in a certain respect, always awe-inspiring, as with a beautiful work of art."[1] Faith apprehends the creation of God, the natural world, as a source of awe-inspiring wonder.

The analogy of human creativity, however, is inadequate to explain fully what is meant by God the creator. This is true because, "a human creator must always begin his (or her) work with materials which are already available to him and which he has not himself made. Thus, the artist has pigments and canvas, traditions regarding aesthetic form, and techniques and methods of work all presented to him by others who have gone before; in this respect he is limited in many ways by other realities. Doubtless he adds something new to all these from the depths of his own spirit, but this is only a tiny achievement in comparison with what he presupposes. God's creativity, however, as understood in Christian faith, is of a radically different order. For God begins with *nothing*; his creation is *ex nihilo*. All that exists – materials, techniques, forms, meanings, and purposes – all are given their being by him."[2]

The creation accounts in the Bible point out the uniqueness of Israel's faith in God. This can be seen when contrasting the biblical accounts with other ancient accounts of creation by Israel's neighbors. "Non-biblical creation stories pictured God as struggling with an adversary to produce and maintain harmony and order. Sometimes that adversary was positively malignant—a chaos monster; at other times it was simply recalcitrant 'stuff' or material with which, like any artist or artisan, God had to work as he 'fashioned' or 'molded' the world. In biblical thinking, however, imagery of this sort tended to be subordinated to another image . . . according to this latter image, the world sprang into being at God's mere word. There was no molding or forming; there was no adversary, active or inert. There was just God. And the point in such language is clear. It says, in effect, that God's power is final and unique. It is not limited by any opposition; it requires no tools, materials, or other sorts of helpers to be effective. What God says is so (Ps. 33:6)."[3]

Two important and inter-related theological points are derived from the *COF*'s statements about God the creator. 1) "Creation as a symbol expresses the unconditioned reality and power of God as the source of all beings, the power grounding all power, the life from which all life springs, and the eternity from which time itself originates"[4] and 2) "because the world—and ourselves—which this unconditioned power has created, have a real if relative autonomy, self-direction, and self-constitution—the symbol of creation *also* points to the mysterious self-limitation of God in producing a creation and creatures with freedom 'over-against' himself and thus relatively autonomous."[5] The second point, the freedom with which God endowed human beings, is the subject taken up at some length in chapter seven.

Creation Tells Us Something about God (But as a Matter of Faith)

Cumberland Presbyterians believe that the one and only living God communicates (is disclosed) in and through the observable, and non-observable, matter and elements of the natural world (earth and the entire cosmos including what is invisible to us). In classic Reformed theology, this belief has been called *general revelation* (also called natural theology). It refers to what is available to be intuited about God from the natural world. Scripture reports that the creation is telling us something about God: "The heavens and the earth are telling the glory of God" (Ps. 19:1; see also Acts 14:16-18; 17:22-23; Rom. 1:18-23; 2:12-16). Faith recognizes the hand of God at work in the many mysteries of creation, in the laws by which it operates, and in the boundless expanses of both the visible macro-world and the invisible sub-atomic micro-world. As the beloved hymn has it, "all nature sings and around me rings the music of the spheres." We, as CPs, firmly believe that God discloses something of God in and through nature. We believe this not because nature tells us, or that we can deduce it from nature, but *because* we believe in the one and only living God. It is this prior faith in God that enables us to see nature as the handiwork of God, and therefore affirm that **all creation discloses God's glory, power, wisdom, beauty, goodness, and love.** (1.10) As the poet, Gerald Manley Hopkins, wrote: "Earth is charged with the grandeur of God."

But our perspective concerning nature raises an important pastoral concern. It is sometimes asked, "How can anyone look at nature and not believe in God?" It is late spring as I write and this sentiment can be understood and appreciated, especially in light of the natural beauty that is the distant greening mountains that are presently in my view. The beauty of nature is real but it is also true that nature is not benign toward human beings or any other forms of life. As the poet said, "Nature is red in tooth and claw." A tornado recently ripped through the neighboring town of Rainsville, Alabama and thirty three persons lost their lives. In my last pastorate, two three year old children simultaneously were afflicted with cancer. Mudslides, tsunamis, hurricanes, and other violent natural events regularly kill thousands on planet earth. These facts constitute the great problem of what theologians call *natural evil* (evil that comes from the violence of nature rather than that of human beings). Therefore Cumberland Presbyterians know that nature is also paradoxical. It is not now what God intended that it be. Nature is good, but it is also fallen.

The problem of nature was not lost on the authors of scripture. Some clearly express the view that nature is fallen and in need of redemption (Rom. 8:22-23). The writer of Revelation envisioned the coming of a new heaven and new earth in which God's just and beneficent rule would finally be established, and evil and demonic forms of power overthrown and dismissed (Rev. 21). Scripture, on the one hand, reports that creation is orderly, coherent, and dependable. But, on the other hand, it reports that nature is also enigmatic, capricious, chaotic and morally disinterested. Pastoral sensitivity is required in knowing when to affirm the original goodness of God's creation, elements of this goodness which continue to exist and of which we remain gratefully aware. But there are also circumstances in the lives of people when it needs to be said that nature itself is in need of God's redemption and transformation. As the *COF* says, **the alienation of persons from God affects the rest of creation, so that the whole of creation stands in need of God's redemption** (2.06—See Gen. 3:17-18; Rom. 8:18-23; Eph. 1:9-10; Col. 1:19-20). Cumberland Presbyterians affirm that our faith is in God and not in nature.

One thing nature, or general revelation, cannot do is reveal the Gospel to us. It is possible for the human family to know the saving word and work of God only because God has revealed this word and work to us. We could not, and cannot, discover this knowledge from or through the creation itself, including that of our own created human nature—either by reason, deduction, intuition, reflection, or by any other form of searching. The saving word and work of God is something the human family can know only because God has graciously revealed it.

God the creator, then, is also God the revealer. John Lennox (Professor of Mathematics at Oxford University) employs a homely illustration, called Aunt Matilda's Cake, to illustrate the fundamental meaning of God's *special revelation*:

"Let us imagine that my Aunt Matilda has baked a beautiful cake and we take it along to be analyzed by a group of the world's top scientists. I, as master of ceremonies, ask them for an explanation of the cake and they go to work. The nutrition scientists will tell us about the number of calories in the cake and its nutritional effect; the biochemists will inform us about the structure of the proteins, fats, etc. in the cake; the chemists about the elements involved and their bonding; the physicists will be able to analyze the cake in terms of fundamental particles; and the mathematicians no doubt will offer us a set of elegant equations to describe the behavior of those particles. Now that these experts, each in terms of his or her scientific discipline, have given us an exhaustive description of the cake, can we say that the cake is completely explained? We certainly have been given a description of *how* the cake was made and *how* its various constituent elements relate to each other, but suppose I now ask the assembled group of experts a final question: *Why* was the cake made? The grin on Aunt Matilda's face shows she knows the answer, for she made the cake, and she made it for a purpose. But all the nutrition scientists, biochemists, chemists, physicists, and mathematicians in the world will not be able to answer the question—and it is no insult to their disciplines to state their incapacity to answer it. Their disciplines, which can cope with questions about the nature and structure of the cake, that is, answering the 'how' questions, cannot answer the 'why' question connected to the purpose for which the cake was made. In fact, the only way we will ever get an answer is if Aunt Matilda reveals it to us."[6]

We are able to make and affirm the *COF*'s various statements about creation because God has revealed, in the history of Israel and in the history of Jesus Christ, the answer to the 'why' question. "Revelation means . . . the self-manifestation of the divine power and meaning on which all depends and in and through which all is fulfilled . . .at its most fundamental level, revelation means the communication of divine *power* (being, life, health, and eternal life), of divine *truth* (order, illumination, insight, and meaning), and divine *love* (mercy, forgiveness, and renewing, reuniting love)."[7] Furthermore, "The objective event of divine revelation creates a new community with a new center of loyalty, new modes of understanding, new styles of action, new forms of relationship to one another and the world, and a new message—a community whose ultimate goal and norm is the Kingdom. A tradition thus begins, a new community is formed, and new ways of being human in history become possible."[8]

Human Beings Are Created in God's Image

Who are human beings? What is the purpose of human beings? What is their relationship to God and the creation of which they are a part? The ancient psalmist raised these questions: "When I look at your heavens, the work of your fingers, the moon and stars that you have established; what are human beings that you are mindful of them, mortals that you care for them? (Ps. 8:3-4). The biblical, and therefore Cumberland Presbyterian, answer to the fundamental identity of human beings is they are made in the "image of God" (*imago*

Dei- Gn. 1:26—27). **Among all forms of life, only human beings are created in the image of God** (1.11).

What does it mean that human beings are created in the image of God? The scriptures state but never offer an explanation of this affirmation. It has been suggested the origin of the concept may lie in the ancient view of the king as physically resembling the god and thus bearing a bodily stamp of his authority to rule.[9] This is consistent with the fact that God gives the first persons authority to rule over the fish, birds, animals and the earth (Gn. 1:24-30). Theologically, it has been suggested that the divine image connotes human beings as sharing *historicity* with God. That is, like God, human beings have the freedom to create history (obviously on a smaller scale!) through their decisions and choices. Morrow suggests that divine image surely includes that the first parents existed in the freedom and responsibility of personal relationship to God.[10] Just as God is personal and free for relationships, so also were those God created. They enjoyed fellowship with God based on their freedom to respond to God in loving obedience. Perhaps the important point with respect to the divine image is that human beings can only truly know who they are—their meaning, purpose, and destiny—through recognizing and responding to the fact of their having been created by God for fellowship with God. This recognition and response is made possible on the basis of the revelation of God made to faith.

It is, of course, not self-evident in our world that human beings are created in the divine image. There have been, and are, many other, and rival, accounts of human identity. Some people, certainly those with a purely naturalistic belief-system, will maintain that persons are *bio-historical* beings. This means that human beings, just as are other life forms, are the result of the evolutionary processes of nature, and the idea of God as creator is ruled out in *a priori* fashion. Life (bios) is a product of the long and complex march of nature. Even those who hold to this view, however, admit that human beings are a quite exceptional product of the natural processes. They have consciousness in a manner, as far as is known, that does not belong to other life forms. They are able to think, will, act, make decisions and so on. Thus they are also historical. This means that they are influenced and shaped not only by their biology (e.g. their DNA, genes) but by their familial and social histories—the histories of family, tribe, nation, culture, religion, etc. That human beings possess such a highly developed consciousness is in the naturalistic point of view merely a feature, if an extraordinary one, of the mysterious creativity of nature.

There are other challenges to the Christian understanding of human identity. As Kenneth Carder writes, "Our identity as made in God's image is denied by much of the contemporary world . . . we are bombarded with messages that we are our biological needs, drives, and characteristics; therefore, fulfillment comes from satisfying our biological impulses and preserving and/or enhancing our biological assets. The temptation to root our identity and destiny in our national and ethnic origins or our ideological or religious affiliations is pervasive and persuasive. Being an American or a United Methodist becomes more important than celebrating and living our identity as children of God. The exchange logic of consumerism promises self-fulfillment in having, accumulating, consuming. Everything, including our relationship to God, becomes a commodity to be used to fulfill our self-defined goals."[11] In short, denying we are created in the image of God creates a vacuum within us, and within whole societies. This vacuum will be filled by defining ourselves by some other image or set of images. CP's, however, believe **to reflect the divine image is to worship, love, and serve God** (1.11). To deny we are created in the divine image is to end up, ultimately, worshiping and serving only ourselves and/or the things we can make.

The *COF* also says **in the sight of God male and female are created equal and complementary** (1.11). In the Genesis story, there is no doubt that the woman (Eve) is created secondarily from man. This corresponds to the position of the male in a patriarchal society such as was Israel's, and nearly all other societies in the ancient Near East. Yet the scriptural story does stress the unity of the sexes and their mutual complementary need. In the history of the church, "the 'image of God' has been interpreted in different ways. Some interpretations have been destructive to humanity. They have resulted in the distortion of the divine image. For example, it has been contended that the divine image has to do primarily with dominion over the rest of creation. One consequence has been the frequent exploitation of the creation by human beings. Or, some have used 'made in God's image' as a statement about gender, implying male superiority and dominance. Both distortions pervert the meaning of the doctrine and provide a theological rationale for actions and relationships that are contrary to the nature of God.[12]

The Natural World is God's

German theologian J. Moltmann has written, "The earth is not unclaimed property, and nature is not ownerless. It is God's beloved creation."[13] Cumberland Presbyterians will heartily agree with these statements. As the *COF* says, **The natural world is God's. Its resources, beauty, and order are given in trust to all peoples, to care for, conserve, to enjoy, and to use for the welfare of all, and thereby to glorify God** (1.12). In these sentences, there are embryonic resources, along with the rich witness of the scriptures, for the development of a profound theology of nature/creation. The need and impetus for such a theology is based upon two contemporary realities: 1) the wide-spread concern for the environment, including the possible impact of human activity and behavior on the environment (widely viewed as being negative) coupled with the issue of the continued sustainability of the earth and its resources; and 2) frequent criticism of the Christian tradition (often called the "ecological complaint") for its alleged theological weakness with respect to the role of nature/creation in God's creative and redemptive purposes. About the latter, it is charged the Christian tradition usually has viewed nature/creation *only* as an instrument (a backdrop) for God's purposes with human beings. Therefore, the critics of the Christian tradition (and some within the tradition) claim that nature/creation has been ignored by the tradition at least and at worst devalued, even abused.

It seems to me these criticisms are not entirely groundless. Reducing the biblical witness of salvation to God's concern for human beings *alone* (as has been true in parts of the Christian tradition) fails to appreciate that God's redemptive concern and action is directed not only to human beings but also to the entirety of creation. A more biblical theology will move from an excessive human centeredness to recognizing God's concern for all living things —including the habitat which all living things share and on which they depend. It will remember that God is not only concerned to save people but also is at work saving nature. God's promise includes "new heavens and a new earth" (Isa. 65:17; Rev. 21:1) which is to say that the coming of God's kingdom is not the abolition of nature but the healing of nature. If God is concerned only to save human beings (often meant providing them with a future and other-earthly home), it is easy to see how this might lead to a failure to appreciate, honor, and properly care for God's gift of the present creation.

A more biblical theology will re-evaluate how human beings relate to nature/creation. In the first creation story, God gives Adam and Eve *dominion* over the rest of creation (Gn.1:26-28). The word *dominion* passed into English translations of the Bible by way of the earliest Latin translations. The word translated as "dominion" was taken, in the Latin, from the world of Roman politics. It meant "power over or domination of." The original Hebrew word, however, was taken from the world of agriculture. The pictorial setting, after all, was a garden. The Hebrew word meant "to tend, nurture, and care for" as a good gardener would for his plants and the soil which supported them. It has been unfortunate that, historically, a great deal of humankind has thought and acted in terms of "power over or domination of" nature rather than "tending, nurturing, and taking care of" nature. The most tragic aspect of this view has been regarding nature as being there for human beings to dominate, exploit, and use for human gratification alone. The negative and often destructive consequences of this view remain with us still. Turning creation into an arena for the human drive toward self-exaltation and self-aggrandizement is to take part in the sinful desecration of nature.

Fortunately, for those who may feel called to work toward a more complete theology of nature/creation (an eco-theology), the Christian tradition is hardly bereft of Christian voices that can serve as resources for such an undertaking. Both Calvin and Luther, major 16th century reformers, encouraged self-conscious theological reflection on the natural world. Both affirmed the immediacy of God in nature. Luther often said God "is with, in, and under" the whole created world. In his commentary on Genesis, Luther imagined Adam and Eve before the fall enjoying a common table with the animals. From the Roman Catholic tradition, the life and work of Francis of Assissi and that of 20th century priest, theologian and paleontologist Teilhard de Chardin have much to teach us about both respect for nature and how nature can and should inform our theology and practice. Anyone working in this area especially will want to consult the work of 20th century Lutheran theologian Joseph Sittler. It was his work, in the 1960s, which brought ecological concern to the forefront in many Protestant circles. Sittler called for a theology of God's grace that included rather than excluded nature. His sermon entitled "Care of the Earth" provides valuable insight into what it means for human beings "to use" nature rather than dominate and exploit it. Finally, there is an ever burgeoning contemporary literature devoted to eco-theology.[14] One recent example, from the evangelical community, is the book *Introducing Evangelical Ecotheology* by Brunner, Butler, and Swoboda (published in 2014). In the coming years, it is likely that Cumberland Presbyterians will understand God's call to mean that in addition to being theologians we are also "geologians." New attention will be given to what historically has been called "The Book of Nature."

As a final thought on creation, or nature, consider these words: "When we speak of our being as communal, we naturally think at once only of communities of people: of family, tribe, local community, small town, and so on. Interestingly, neither primitive people nor the most recent scientific understanding of ourselves would start there. As both primitive life and modern biology would tell us, our *first* community is the community of nature, the natural communal process of mineral existence, of vegetable and animal life out of which we arise, on which we depend, and with which we are and must be in continual interaction in each moment. This sense of *community* with nature, our participation in nature as one of its children, has long been forgotten in the West and we are paying dearly for the lapse . . . . (Yet) we are dependent through nature for our being. Our ultimate dependence on God the Parent is mediated to us from moment to moment through nature and our embeddedness in nature. Unless we participate in, respect and nurture nature's systematic order of interrelations, we vanish."[15]

Chapter Five

PROVIDENCE

God exercises providential care over all creatures, peoples, nations and things. The manner in which this care is provided is revealed in the scriptures (1.13). A good place to begin this chapter is with a couple of definitions of what is meant by God's providence. 1) "The doctrine of providence is an extension of the doctrine of creation. It says that the loving, just, and powerful God who first made heaven and earth continues to uphold, protect, rule over, take care of—provide for—God's good creation and each one of us."[1] 2) "In every moment and in every event God is working in and with his creation, creating his kingdom through time; and we live in the midst of this process. This continuous active presence of God working through time is precisely what is meant by his providence. Providence is not restricted to the happenings of human history; it refers to God's active working toward his ultimate objectives in any and every time and place. During the billions of years before mankind, or even life, had appeared, God was preparing the conditions which would make possible the emergence of free and creative spirits who could enter into community with him. . .the providential care of God overarches the whole course of history and moves it toward its ultimate goal."[2]

The experience of the covenant people of God is one of God's active care and concern for them (Ps. 103). Belief in the providence of the living God is belief that God did not create the world and persons and then abandon them. God is not an absentee landlord. The psalmist wrote "The Lord is my shepherd," (Ps. 23:1) and "he leads me in the right paths for his name's sake" (Ps. 23:3). Many other psalms express Israel's faith that God is actively involved in the care and guidance of his covenant people; as well as being sovereign over the affairs of all peoples and nations (Ps. 34, 37, 90-91, 105, 107, 121). The cycle of Joseph stories (Gen. 39-50) strongly emphasizes the providence of God as well as those, say, of the prophet Elijah (1 and 2 Kings). Jesus spoke of his Abba as one who cares for his own even more than "the lilies of the fields and the birds of the air" (Mt. 6:25-34). God is involved with his world, with his people, and with all people. The *COF* says, **God never leaves or forsakes his people. All who trust in God find this truth confirmed in awareness of his love, which includes judgment upon sin, and which leads to repentance and greater dependence upon divine grace. All who do not trust God are, nevertheless, under that same providence, even when they ignore or reject it. It is designed to lead them also to repentance and trust in divine grace** (1.16).

The era of modern science (especially in the form of scientism) has brought a challenge to many with respect to belief in God's providence. This is true because of that segment of scientific thought which regards the creation as a "closed system" which operates according to its own internal laws and therefore without outside (meaning divine) influence. Cumberland Presbyterians do not share this view. They believe that scripture clearly affirms the creation is not a closed system. Morrow writes: "Scripture knows nothing of a static world, something finished and running on its own, like a clock, which simply exists to be observed by persons. God's revelation in nature comes when persons encounter the living God everywhere doing and saying things through natural events . . . Both nature and history are arenas in which God is doing and saying things . . . That God is speaking and acting in all events of history, both good and bad, is one of the most important claims in scripture."[3]

The *COF* affirms this belief forcefully when saying, **God ordinarily exercises providence through the events of nature and history, using such instruments as persons, laws, and the scriptures, yet remains free to work with them or above them. The whole creation remains open to God's direct activity** (1.14). The key idea in this statement is a theological one—the freedom of God. God is not bound by creation and is free to continue to interact with it and to act upon it. The truly good news about the freedom of God, as attested in the scriptures, is pointed out when the *COF* says, **The purpose of God's providence is that the whole creation be set free from**

its bondage to sin and death, and be renewed in Jesus Christ (1.15).

Cumberland Presbyterians believe that providence does not mean that God's covenant people are exempted from the variety of ills that other persons, or groups of persons, may and do experience in this world. Persons, including Christians, suffer from moral evil and natural evil. Persons, including Christians, suffer from their bondage to sin. The *COF* says: **God's providence is sufficiently displayed to be known and experienced, but, at the same time, it partakes of divine mystery, and is the occasion for wonder, praise and thanksgiving. Thus even in illness, pain, sorrow, tragedy, social upheaval, or natural disaster, persons may be sure of God's presence and discover his grace to be sufficient** (1.18). At times such as the latter, many Cumberland Presbyterians can and do affirm the following words which I have frequently quoted when preaching: "God offers us a minimum of protection, but a maximum of support."[4]

Wendell Berry of Kentucky authored the novel *Jayber Crow*. He places into the mouth of his central character, Jayber, words that I think many Cumberland Presbyterians can and will affirm with respect to their own experiences of God's providence. Jayber is a young man when, in the 1930s, he returns to his small hometown of Port William, Kentucky. He settles there after several years of wandering in the world and trying to find himself and his place. At home again, he becomes the town barber, grave-digger, church custodian, and confidante to most of the people in the town. Central to the story is his love for Mattie Keith. Jayber is quietly devastated when Mattie marries someone else. He tells his story from the perspective of being an older man, now in his 70s. At one point, he offers the following reflections on the twists and turns of his life:

"If you could do it, I suppose, it would be a good idea to live your life in a straight line—starting, say, in the Dark Wood of Error and proceeding by logical steps through Hell and Purgatory and into Heaven. Or you could take the King's Highway past appropriately named dangers, toils, and snares and finally cross the River of Death and enter the Celestial City. But that is not the way that I have done it, so far. I am a pilgrim. But my pilgrimage has been wandering and unmarked. Often what has looked like a straight line to me has been a circling or doubling back. I have been in the Dark Wood of Error many times. I have known something of Hell, Purgatory and Heaven but not always in that order. The names of many snares and dangers have been made known to me, but I have known them only in looking back. Often I have not known where I was going until I was already there. I have had my share of desires and goals, but my life has come to meet me or I have gone to it mainly by way of mistakes and surprises. Often I have received better than I have deserved. Often my fairest hopes have rested on bad mistakes. I am an ignorant pilgrim crossing a dark valley. And yet, for a long time, looking back, I have been unable to shake the feeling that *I have been led*—make of it what you will."[5] Perhaps many, probably most, Cumberland Presbyterians can and will identify with these words. Through all the twists and turns of their lives, they believe themselves to have been led. This is one of the important meanings of belief in God's providence.

Chapter Six

THE LAW OF GOD

God gives the moral law to govern human actions and relations. It is the principle of justice woven into the fabric of the universe and is binding upon all persons (1.19). Cumberland Presbyterians believe, preach, and teach that the scriptures clearly show that the living God has given to the human family standards for relationship that are intended for human flourishing. These standards have been called the moral law. Cumberland Presbyterians believe that conducting life and community according to God's moral law is to go with rather than against the grain of the universe. Paul contended that all persons, even those outside Israel, had been given, by virtue of God having created them, at least a minimal consciousness of the way in which their lives could best be lived (Rom. 1:18-23).

The Ten Commandments, or Ten Words as the Jewish people traditionally have called them, are the paramount expression of the moral law in the Hebrew scripture. The religious and social vision revealed in the commandments embraces three realms of obligation: 1)"proper piety towards God, 2) due respect to one's neighbor and everything that is an extension of one's neighbor, and 3) a generous and ungrudging attitude towards others."[1] When reflecting upon the context in which the commandments were given to Israel, it becomes possible to understand why the *COF* says: **The moral law is a gift of God's grace** (1.20).

The Book of Exodus opens with the Hebrew people languishing in slavery in Egypt. They have endured this condition for several generations. But God hears their cries for deliverance and calls Moses to face down the Egyptian pharaoh and demand the release of God's people. The Book of Exodus records the back and forth struggle between Moses and pharaoh, the ten plagues that were inflicted upon Egypt, and finally the release of the people to go into the wilderness to worship their God.

But what do you do when you are free? And free for the first time that you can remember? How are you supposed to behave when you are free? It is somewhat like the young person who goes away to college for the first time. What is he or she supposed to do with the experience of a newly acquired freedom? For Israel, it included how a group of former slaves were to be transformed into a free and viable community. This is the historical context for God's gracious gift of the Ten Commandments to his covenant people. God gives them credible and enduring norms for their life together and their life with God. God gives them boundaries for behavior. The best of parents always provide certain boundaries and limits for their children and do so as an act of love. It helps enable their children to arrive at a creative and responsible use of their freedom. The Ten Commandments were just such a gracious expression of God's boundless love for his covenant people.

That Cumberland Presbyterians understand the law as a gift of God's grace becomes an opportunity to say something about an often heard, but quite mistaken, view of the relationship between law and gospel. A popular belief among many Christians is that the Hebrew scriptures present right relationship to God—saving relationship—in terms of keeping the law; whereas the Christian scripture present right relationship to God—saving relationship—in terms of grace through faith in Jesus Christ. This view is seriously mistaken in its view of the Hebrew scripture and the relationship God had with his covenant people. Cumberland Presbyterians are sure that the people of Israel were saved by the grace of God as truly as those who later came to faith in Jesus Christ.

The grace of God came first in his relationship to his people and the law came later. The grace of God is always prior to law. In the Hebrew scripture, God related to his covenant people on the basis of his free grace. God saved the Israelites by grace as truly as God saves persons by his free grace in and through Jesus Christ. The Apostle Paul, in his writings, makes this abundantly clear. He especially makes this case when arguing that Abraham was saved by faith—by trusting in the gracious promises of God—rather than by keeping the law

(Rom. 4:14-16). Cumberland Presbyterians do not want to perpetuate the view that the Hebrew people merited or received salvation by the keeping of the law. This is a misreading of scripture and an affront to the history and faith of the Jewish people (an affront to God?). The Hebrew motive for keeping the law was not salvation. Rather, it was profound gratitude for the grace and goodness of the God who had made covenant with his people. For the Jewish people, the law was and is God's gift that "enables one to know who one is, what God will have in the world, and where lies the course of life that leads to joy, peace and blessedness."[2] The law was a path toward abundant personal and community life, and *not* a system of and for salvation.

The Hebrew motive for observing the moral law as gratitude rather than for salvation brings us to Jesus and to the ✓ *COF*'s statement: **The moral law is fulfilled in the gospel** (1.21). No one was ever more grateful to God than Jesus. He is the perfect embodiment of the faithful and true Israelite. His keeping of the law was an act of gratitude for his relationship to his Abba. It is clear that he did not always keep the ceremonial law of Judaism, that having to do with the ancient worship of Israel; nor did he always keep the judicial or regulatory law, that appropriate for a desert people living as wanderers many hundreds of years before his time. But Jesus kept the moral law perfectly. It was this moral law—the keeping of which was a matter of gratitude to a gracious God—that Jesus said he came to fulfill rather than abolish (Mt. 5:17). It was the moral law which he summarized when saying, "You shall love the Lord your God with all your heart and with all your soul and with all your mind. . .and you shall love your neighbor as yourself" (Mt. 22:37-39; Dt. 6:5). That Jesus kept the moral law to perfection is at the root of the Christian scripture's claim that Jesus was without sin.

The *COF* says: **The purpose of the moral law is to create wholeness or health in human life—spiritually, mentally, physically, and socially** (1.22). In the next chapter, we will see that human sin and rebellion works to destroy the wholeness and integrity of life as God intended. It is the view of the Christian scripture that the law opens the eyes of the one who knows the law. A person's knowledge of the law enables him or her to recognize the depths of sin. If God had not given the law, Israel would not have known what sin is. The Torah (law) was the instrument by which persons could know that sin was not just moral wrongdoing, but also rebellion against God's holiness, justice, love, and grace.

Cumberland Presbyterians believe, preach and teach that all God intended for Israel in his gift of the law to them was perfectly present, expressed, and fulfilled in the person and life of Jesus Christ. He is *the* person who is the perfect image of God and without sin. To use the words of the *COF*, Jesus is spiritually, mentally, physically, and socially whole. All the forces that create integrity of life as God intended were fully and perfectly present in him. The law given by God to the Hebrew people was and is an expression of God's grace toward them and the human family. The Gospel of God's grace was in the law. But Jesus Christ is the full expression God's grace to and for the human family. Jesus himself is the incomparable revelation and fulfillment of the moral law of God.

The Human Family Breaks Relationship with God

(2.01—2.06 in the Confession of Faith)

Chapter Seven

HUMAN FREEDOM

The first section of the *COF* treats the doctrine of God, the living God who speaks to the human family. This section (chapters 7-8) will deal with the human family. Positively, it is concerned with the question of who we were created to be. Negatively, it addresses the problem of what has gone wrong with us. We can get at what the *COF* has to say about these questions by paying attention to its use of three words: *freedom*, *responsibility*, and *abuse* of freedom. Before considering the first two words (the third is dealt with in chapter 8), I would like to offer a few introductory paragraphs as background for the entire section—a section which is called "The Human Family Breaks Relationship with God."

The biblical view of the human family, of persons, is illuminatingly and importantly paradoxical. As created by God and in the image of God, each human being has an exalted status (Gen. 1-3; Ps. 8). The founding word about us, then, is that it is good to be human beings. But by having broken relationship with the living God, each of us is also fallen or sinful (Eph. 5:5-6; Rom. 1:18-32). This paradoxical view of who we are has been and remains of profound importance in the history of the Western world (and in much of the rest of the world). When we, and our various political documents, speak of the dignity of individual persons, the inherent worth of persons, and the fundamental rights of persons, we are doing so largely on the basis and foundation of the Jewish-Christian scriptural view of persons as exalted by reason of their having been created in the image of God. Therefore persons are to be honored. And they are to be protected from the power and abuse of others, including kings, emperors, states, governments, and other people. The dignity and valued status of human beings comes from God.

But the biblical view of persons is that we are also are fallen. We are sinful. We have been corrupted by the abuse of the freedom given to us by God. Although our abuse of our God-given freedom has had and continues to have tragic consequences, it also has had certain beneficent consequences. It means that persons, because they are sinful, are not to claim for themselves the right to unlimited and unrestrained power. Persons are not to claim for themselves, or behave as if they have, divine status or prerogatives. There is a need for a certain cautious suspicion of persons. They have mixed motives. In their fallen state, they do not fully know themselves. They often do not know what is good for them or for others. They are limited in their perception and apprehension of truth and reality. They also are capable of moral darkness and unspeakable evil. Persons are in need of redemption by God.

A rival (and relatively modern and secular) view of the human family advocates for the autonomy of persons; that is, for understanding ourselves without reference or appeal to God and the story, or theology, of human beings as having been created in the image of God. According to this view, we are simply what we, together with the various influences upon us and opportunities afforded us (or not afforded), are able to make of ourselves. The Cumberland Presbyterian *COF*, however, understands persons, and the entire human family, in the light of the God who in love has created us in God's image and with whom we have broken relationship. This truth forms an important part of the good news that Cumberland Presbyterians have to share with the world in the 21st century. We believe that scripture provides an accurate understanding of who we are as human beings, and the good news of the healing of our fallen natures—our tragic brokenness and estrangement from God, one another, and the world.

Human Freedom

God, in creating persons, gives them the capacity and freedom to respond to divine grace in loving obedience (2.01). Here the *COF* affirms that God who is love created the first persons and endowed them with freedom. In the creation stories of Genesis, Adam and Eve are created in freedom for a communal relationship with God. It was the freedom to love and obey God. It was the freedom to enjoy fellowship with God. It was the freedom, if we put it negatively, not to sin; not to abuse their freedom by breaking fellowship with God. This freedom was a real freedom. They were not created by God as puppets on a divine string, or as robots controlled from on high Their being created with freedom included the issue of what to do with this precious gift. Freedom of decision necessarily implies and includes responsibility. We know from the Bible that Adam and Eve were irresponsible with respect to their freedom. And we will discuss this more in the next chapter. But decisions and choices, by individuals and/or groups, are always followed by consequences. So the *COF* says: **Because of their God-given nature, persons are responsible for their choices and actions toward God, each other, and the world** (2.02). True freedom is responsible freedom.

The *COF* says, in light of God's gift of freedom: **therefore whoever will may be saved** (2.01). In this statement, we are able to hear echoes from a major theological disagreement within 18th and 19th century Presbyterianism. It is the disagreement which, at least partially, led to the founding of the Cumberland Presbyterian Church. The disagreement had to do with the way some Presbyterians interpreted the biblical word *predestination*. They considered it as meaning God chose/elected/predestined some persons for salvation "before the foundation of the world." Others were, in the mystery of God's ways (called "eternal decrees"), simply passed over. It was also believed that Jesus did not live and die for those who were passed over but only for the chosen (this whole idea is called "limited atonement").

Leading Presbyterian theologian Shirley Guthrie writes about the classic Calvinist understanding of predestination to salvation: "According to scripture (see Rom. 8:28-30 and Eph. 1:3-11), predestination has to do with the question of salvation: Whom does God choose (or not choose) to love and care for in the bad as well as the good things that happen to us? To whom does God choose (or not choose) to give the gift of faith that enables people to trust, count on, and live by God's love in sickness and health, in life and in death? Who is chosen (or not chosen) to be included among those to whom 'the saving grace' of God is not only promised but actually given so that, whatever happens, they find wholeness of life now and forever in loving the God whom loves them and loving others as they have been loved? Who, in short, does God choose to save—or not save? That is the question the doctrine of predestination seeks to answer. In traditional theology, it is called the doctrine of election: who does God 'elect' to save or not save?"[1]

Early Cumberland Presbyterians rejected this interpretation of predestination. For them, predestination did not mean

God saves some people and passes over others. Rather, it meant God's overall determination to have a covenant people (this is what was predestined) through whom God's saving grace in Christ could and would be made available to all people. The early Cumberland Presbyterians refused to think of God as choosing some for salvation and passing over others. They refused to conceive of the life and death of Christ as having saving meaning only for some (the elect) and not for all. In fairness, it should be noted that Presbyterians, in the history of their confession-making, have modified the classic understanding of predestination. They have done so in the direction of the Cumberland Presbyterian view on the matter.

Cumberland Presbyterians readily acknowledge that we are no longer free in the original sense. Our freedom has been severely diminished, but not destroyed. "What we will and how we live is determined to a large extent by where and when we were born. We think and act with the limited point of view and biases of our particular race, cultural environment, and national heritage; with the fears and prejudices of rural, suburban, or city people; with the narrow self-interest of people who are poor, middle-class, or rich; with the advantages of a healthy or crippling family background. Moreover, what we want and strive for is motivated to a large extent by anxiety, pride, envy, greed, and lust . . . Even when not always aware of it, we are driven and controlled by all kinds of social and psychological forces that determine our attitudes, decisions, and actions. And many of them alienate us both from God (who loves other kinds of people as much as our kind) and other people (especially those who are different from us)—so that our enslavement to all these external and internal 'powers' is what scripture calls our enslavement to *sin.*"[2]

Cumberland Presbyterians believe that, after the fall, all human beings now *are enslaved* to sin. This means that we, of ourselves, cannot choose God; we cannot of our own unaided volition return to a relationship to God. But we believe that the Holy Spirit seeks to awaken all human beings to their sinful and tragic condition and thus lead them to turn to God in order to receive the gift of faith in Christ for salvation. By the illumination of the Holy Spirit within, we can come to see our situation of enslavement and cry out to God for forgiveness, mercy, and freedom.

It is noteworthy that the *COF*'s initial statement in this section says "God" before it says that the first persons were given a "capacity for freedom." This is, in itself, a way of indicating something important about human freedom. True human freedom is *derivative*. True and authentic human freedom comes from God. Cumberland Presbyterians believe that it is only within the context of the truth and reality of who God is that we can grasp, comprehend, and appreciate the meaning of authentic human freedom. This meaning can be apprehended and realized only in, by, and through faith—and not faith as simply beliefs or ideas but faith as personal encounter with the living Triune God—the Father, the Son, and the Holy Spirit. Christian faith is not first believing that something may be true, but being encountered by Someone who is true.

It is this encounter that answers the great problem of human existence. "The problem of man's historical existence—sin—is his enslavement to powers and institutions and practices which control and ultimately work to destroy him. . .man's most fundamental problem is thus to gain the conditions of true freedom." [3] The possibility of the restoration of authentic human freedom is precisely the message of the Gospel. One of the most memorable books from my seminary years was simply titled *Jesus Means Freedom.* What we cannot do for ourselves, God in Christ has done and will do for us. As Jesus said, "You shall know the truth, and the truth will make you free." And, as the Apostle Paul wrote, "For freedom, Christ has set us free, stand fast, therefore, and do not submit again to a yoke of slavery" (Gal. 5:1). Cumberland Presbyterians, therefore, have been entrusted with good news concerning freedom for the people of the 21st century.

But what does the human family usually mean when thinking and speaking about freedom? That is, when persons think and speak about themselves? Perhaps most Americans will think of political freedom and the documents of the

American founding. They will think of the freedom of speech, of assembly, of religion, and of the press. Some rightfully and thankfully will point to Abraham Lincoln and the Emancipation Proclamation. Some will point, soberly, to military cemeteries and the sacrifices they represent. People in other nations around the world will celebrate their own histories that have resulted in political freedom.

There is also personal freedom with an indefinite number of expressions. Freedom for a child may mean going outside to play. Freedom for a sixteen year old may mean acquiring a driver's license. Freedom for an older teenager may mean going away to college. For a caregiver, it may be an hour or two of free time as a result of someone providing respite care to a loved one. For an incarcerated person, it may be the opening before him of prison gates. For a gay person, it may be that he or she has come out of the closet. For a soldier, it may mean the end of a tour of duty, or a return to duty. For a recovering alcoholic, it may be the support found at an AA meeting. Freedom to some people may mean not much more than the arrival of the weekend. It may mean being able to say, "No one tells me what to do." Freedom may be Janis Joplin singing, "Freedom is just another word for nothing left to lose." Freedom is good health. Freedom is having a job. Freedom is retirement. Freedom is a round of golf. Freedom may mean considering oneself to be a free-determining autonomous self. Freedom is the right to make up one's own mind. Freedom is the power of contrary choice. One writer observes, "Our market-oriented culture promotes the illusion of the autonomous individual. In that setting freedom is understood negatively, as liberation from commitments, burdens, identities or histories that would limit options. Freedom is un-curtailed choice, the ability to 'shop' for everything from mouthwashes to churches."[4]

But as important as any of these expressions of freedom may be, and some truly are, none even begins to approach what is meant in scripture or in the *COF* when they speak about freedom. Freedom there is the free and gracious gift of God that is life received from and lived in relationship to God. Freedom is hearing and responding to, answering, the living God who has spoken and acted in the history of Israel, the history of Jesus Christ, and the history of the Holy Spirit. Freedom is the restoration of life as being in the image of God. Above all, as H. Morrow writes in *The Covenant of Grace*, "The Confession defines the essential freedom that belongs to the image of God in persons as the freedom to love. It is the freedom of personal relationships. It was the freedom that Adam and Eve exercised as they daily walked and talked with God 'in the garden at the time of the evening breeze' (Gen. 3:8). It is this freedom that sin caused humanity to lose."[5] It is faith in Jesus Christ that constitutes the recovery of freedom. Jesus means freedom.

Chapter Eight

THE ABUSE OF FREEDOM

In rejecting their dependence on God and in willful disobedience, the first human parents disrupted community with God, for which they had been created (2.03). Cumberland Presbyterians take seriously, if not always literally, the story of Adam and Eve (Gen. 1-3). This story is a mirror into which we can look and recognize ourselves. The first human parents exchanged the freedom given to them by God for a lie. They forfeited the blessedness of their fellowship with God for the promise that they themselves could become as gods. This was an abuse of freedom with drastic consequences. The *COF* says: **They became inclined toward sin in all aspects of their being** (2.03). This is a way of saying that the center of their lives moved from God to self. Sin is the condition of self-centeredness. Human beings are now estranged from God, lost within themselves and their concerns.

Perhaps the following story can serve as an analogy of our predicament: "On a clear blue day the entire landscape is visible to the sailor in a small boat: familiar islands with their treasured landmarks dot foreground and horizon alike, and helpful buoys are evident a mile or two away. Thus is the *structure* of the scene visible to every eye; and since it is easy to find one's way, so to speak, 'by sight,' no special means are necessary or even thought of. Let us suppose, however, that now a fog covers the whole bay, shutting out everything except fifty yards of gray water around the small boat. The structure of the bay has quite vanished: islands, landmarks, buoys are as if they were not there at all, and a general direction, much less a particular course, is anything but evident. The structure, of course, is still there. But now it is unseen and unknown; its rocks and shoals can appear as a menace rather than a blessing. Special means of 'knowing' it come immediately into relevance, for only through those means—compass, radar, depth soundings, and so on—can that structure now be known at all. So it is apparently in our existence. The temporality and finitude characteristic of our existence and history is that of creative destiny, freedom, and new possibilities; it is 'good' and manifests a divine creative ground. However, there is a reality of estrangement or fallenness to that existence which has obscured not only the divine ground but also the creative nature of our creatureliness in time."[1]

Cumberland Presbyterians believe that the primal story of Adam and Eve's sin is about the fog that has enveloped us. The story accurately represents and portrays the situation of all persons in their relationship to God. Another way of speaking about our predicament is that human beings have become de-centered. They have become centered in themselves rather than centered in relationship to God. I once read a story about a professor of theology who played a recording of Mozart for his class. Together the class enjoyed the beautiful music. The next day the professor surprised the class by choosing to play the recording again. But, on the night before, he had bored a hole in the record slightly off center. This time the class heard only screeching noises that were nearly impossible to bear. The beautiful music was gone. The loss of a center in God means that life does not and cannot produce the music that God has intended for it. "Sin has affected that deep center of our being that shapes all we are and do, including any process of self-transformation we may embark upon. Our problem is not only that we continually make wrong choices, speak hostile words to others, do selfish deeds that hurt others, and so on. Our problem is that those explicit symptoms of our estrangement arise from a depth in our being that is itself falsely centered inordinately attached to itself, at odds or estranged from itself. In this sense, then, there is an 'original sin'—or a deeper level of estrangement—that generates our specific sins."[2]

The disobedience of Adam and Eve traditionally has been called *original sin, universal sin,* or *the fall.* While Cumberland Presbyterians believe this story of original disobedience is stunningly insightful and truthfully revealing as to the condition in which all persons find themselves, they do not believe that the story of Adam and Eve "explains" the origin of sin. This is so because the origin of sin is inexplicable. As one observer has put it, "The Bible reveals the historical beginning of sin and evil but not the behind the scenes origin."[3] Serene Jones writes, "What exactly is sin? The question is hard to answer because sin has been defined in a myriad of ways but also because at its heart sin does not make sense. It doesn't make sense that humanity would turn away from the wondrous offer of covenant relationship with God; in this sense, sin is inexplicable."[4]

Cumberland Presbyterians reject, as do all Reformed theologies, the charge that God is responsible for sin (1 Jn. 4:5). It can and has been said, however, that God's love (*agape*) from which the first persons and all persons were and are created with freedom and responsibility set the condition for the exercise of sin. One theologian asks how it could have been otherwise any different. He writes, "The problem of evil (sin) can be traced no further back than this: the possibility of disobedience is the sole condition for the reality of human freedom and personality. Why then did God take the risk when it would have been so much easier, so much simpler, not to create the problem? God could have run people through their paces and never needed to atone for them. Stated this way, the question is clearly out of order, if not sacrilegious. The only answer is that God is *agape* (love) and *agape* respects *the freedom of the beloved.* This last statement is the one solid point where no exceptions can be made. It is the starting point of theology, ethics, of history, of church order, and of every realm where *agape* matters. *Agape* respects the freedom of the beloved even to lose himself or herself. The first revelation of *agape* was thus the creation of human freedom, and no theology or ethics that denies this freedom can be true. . .God takes the risk of leaving people free; this is the definition of *agape* that lies at the bottom of all meaningful thought. That this lets the problem of evil (sin) in the back door is too bad, but there was no other way and God took that risk, precisely because of *agape*."[5]

Although the origin of sin remains a mystery (Why did we do we do it?), it is simply the case that persons *do* turn from a relationship to the living God. It is what we do. It is what groups of people do. It is what nations do. Sin is simply so. "Sin is a part of our *whatness.* It is simply what we are, regardless of our awareness of it. Just as we are beloved creatures of God, so we are sinful—all of us. But here is a difference. Unlike the universal features of our creaturely nature, this reality is not given to us by God. Humanity has collectively generated it over time. We have conjured it up, imposed it upon ourselves, spread it around, and passed it on to each new generation. . .our sinful nature lives off the features that constitute our primary creaturely reality, corrupting and twisting the functioning of our primary nature."[6] The *COF* affirms this when saying: **As did Adam and Eve, all persons rebel against God, lose the right relationship to God, and become slaves to sin and death. This condition becomes the source of all sinful attitudes and actions** (2.04). Cumberland Presbyterians affirm that this, as attested by scripture, is simply the way things truly are.

Attempts have been made to explain how the sin of the primal parents has been transmitted to persons down through the centuries. Some of these attempts come from the days of the early church. Some early Christian thinkers, such as the Pelagians, held that we are all sinners by imitation—we all simply imitate Adam and Eve. Calvinists in the 16th century spoke of Adam's sin being imputed to us. Adam acted representatively for us. Some contemporary Christians appeal to the theory of evolution, viewing sin and evil as remnants of a primitive stage in the development of human beings.

Perhaps the most unfortunate attempt to explain the transmission of sin was that of Augustine who, in the fourth century, suggested that original sin was passed on biologically through the pro-creational sexual act—sin is transmitted by heredity from generation to generation. Among other things, this view contributed to a perspective on human sexuality that, down through the centuries and even until today, has been tragic in its consequences. The sexual act became viewed as something "dirty" rather than the good gift of God to be exercised within proper safe-guarding boundaries. This has put generations of people at odds with the fact that they were created by God as sexual beings. In the history of theology it also has often led to a devaluing of the "human body" in favor of the "spiritual soul." This represented a move away from the Hebraic understanding of the created goodness of the human body and toward the Greek understanding of the body as a "prison" which the soul must hope to escape.

None of the attempts to explain the transmission of sin have full explanatory power. They were attempts to do what very likely cannot be done. That is, offer a satisfactory explanation of in what sense the sin of Adam and Eve is passed down to us. We do know that every person is raised in a world in which there already exist modes and patterns of being sinful. Sin is our environment as water is to the fish in the sea. Beyond this, Cumberland Presbyterians are simply content to say that all persons do what Adam and Eve did. In other words, their story is an accurate and truthful way of describing the reality of human experience. Cumberland Presbyterians are apt to subscribe to the words of the Puritan New England Primer: "In Adam's fall, we sinned all" and to do so without too much fuss over the origin and transmission of sin.

One important thing that Cumberland Presbyterians *do* believe about sin is that it did not belong to God's original and good creation. Persons were created in the image of God and in the freedom which was life in relationship to and fellowship with God. Sin is precisely what God did not create. Sin, rather, is an intruder into God's good creation. It was unnecessary. It does not belong. Sin is parasitic. It lives off of the goodness of

God's creation. Sin is a lie. The fact that sin did not belong to God's good creation led theologian Karl Barth to speak of sin as "nothingness." He didn't mean nothingness in terms of sin's devastating consequences in and for human life. Rather he meant that it is nothingness in terms of God's original creation. And Barth maintained, of course, that sin will be revealed as nothingness when God fully reclaims creation at the coming of the day of Jesus Christ. Sin will be exposed for the lie it is and without a place when God's kingdom is fully realized.

The doctrine of original sin is best viewed as a dark backdrop against which can be contrasted the brilliant redemption that was God's saving action in Jesus Christ the Lord. When I have sought to preach and teach about this doctrine, I have sometimes made use of the following quotation:

"A mother says to her-self at the breakfast table, 'I'm going to do better today. I won't be as impatient with the children as I was yesterday.' But when she goes to bed that night, she feels guilty knowing that despite her good intentions today was yesterday all over again. 'I'll be more understanding, forgiving and open, more courageous in standing up for what I know is right—more Christian.' Who of us has not decided that over and over again in dealing with members of our families, with friends and people we work with, with strangers who wait on us in stores—only to discover over and over again what we should do but can't or could do but don't? What we are up against is 'original sin.' The problem lies in two apparently contradictory truths. (1) Sin is universal and inevitable. All people, everywhere, always, have lived in self-contradiction to their true being in the image of God (Rom. 3:10-11). But if *all* are sinners, then *everyone* must be a sinner. There is no one who *cannot* sin. 2) Nevertheless, every person is responsible for his or her sinfulness. No one forces me not to love God and other people. It is *I* who sin and *I* know that *I* am guilty, even if I do not want to do it. All of us, in other words, are caught in the trap William Faulkner describes when he has a wise person in *Requiem for a Nun* say paradoxically about sin: 'You ain't got to. You can't help it."[7]

Sin means that human freedom has now been radically compromised. In the Bible, the devastating effects of sin are portrayed in the Genesis stories of Adam and Eve (who now hide from God), Cain and Abel, the Tower of Babel, and so on. And, of course, the Bible indicates throughout that since the fall all of life is now lived within the context of sin. Reformed theology has consistently pointed out the danger of sin as idolatry: serving and worshiping that which has only relative value, or no value, thus placing it above the worship and service of the true God (Ex. 20:1-15; Rom.1:25; Mt. 4:8-10; Ps. 115:4-8; Is. 46:6-10). "Now all human choosing occurs within the context of sin."[8] And sin is not only the context for our bad choices. It is also the context for our good or better choices. Sin is not just doing bad things. Sin may also be the doing of good things but in ways that come from now being centered in ourselves, or worshiping some idol of our making, rather than being centered in God.

Sin is about God

In willfully sinning all people become guilty before God and are under divine wrath and judgment, unless saved by God's grace through Jesus Christ (2.05). "To put the matter as plainly as possible, sin is a violation of God himself. It is not violation of a code of right and wrong which, for some obscure reason, happens to 'anger' God. It is closing oneself off from him . . . Adam and Eve's real problem was not that they ate a piece of fruit in contravention of law. It was that they refused to believe, trust, and obey God: they 'they hid themselves from the presence of the Lord God.' And that, at root, is what is meant by 'sin.'" [9] Sin, then, is about God. Just as we must first know who God is in order to know what true freedom is, we also must know who God is in order to truly know what sin is. Only by inhabiting the world of the Bible can we come to know what sin is; otherwise it will be called something else. A person may not know that he or she is in rebellion against God. He or she, for example, may think he or she is simply living the American dream or claiming what are his or her rights, or living according to what is conventional human wisdom. Sin is deceptive.

Cumberland Presbyterians believe that the scriptures and life in the covenant community train us to know what sin is. We learn first that sin is a theological word. It is a word about God. It especially is a word about persons in their defiance of God. Cumberland Presbyterians do not think it strange that almost the only place one hears about sin is in the church. Persons must know who God is in order to truly know that they are sinners. It is not the responsibility of the world, which does not know God, to communicate the reality of sin. It is most certainly the responsibility of the church. The church's proclamation includes the truth that persons not only commit mistakes, errors, or have lapses in judgment, but that they also rebel against God. The church does not receive some prurient or pious enjoyment from talking about sin. And it is not even the first thing that the church is called to say (the Gospel is the first thing). But it is only in light of the Gospel that we can truly understand what it means that we are sinful and sinners. The church believes that it must be said that we all are "sinners" because scripture attests that this is a truthful and accurate description of who we are. We are not sinners because we sin, but we sin because we are sinners.

The church is obligated to say that life is not only a matter of a horizontal relationship to our-selves and others but also a matter of a vertical relationship to God. Because persons ignore, turn from, and rebel against this vertical relationship with God means that persons do sin and are sinners. This we know because the Bible tells us so. Scripture enables us to name the situation that afflicts every person. Unless we know that we are sinners, we cannot, or will not, hear the good news of what God has done for us in Christ by which the enslaving power of sin in and over us has been broken.

Thomas Long writes about the importance of the word "sin:" "Like other key theological terms, 'sin' cannot be replaced with any other more accessible term. 'Immorality' is too tame, too attached to the human will and social codes. 'Estrangement and alienation,' existentialist favorites, are too small, focused upon the individual. 'Evil' paints too broadly and lacks personal bite, while concepts like 'co-dependent' and 'psychopathic' are located on a single floor of the human mansion. No other word gathers up in a single stitch the intra-psychic, the interpersonal, the moral, the social, the cosmological, the ecological, and the theological character of the brokenness of human life and all creation. To be able to use the word 'sin' is to be able to speak honestly about who we are with and to each other. Because it places us on common ground, it is the soil of compassion, forgiveness, and hope. An anthropology that lacks a vigorous doctrine of sin is headed for constant disillusionment, chronic and bitter disappointment, and ever deepening spirals of rage over the inability and unwillingness of human beings to act responsibly."[10]

Sin as Personal

Sin is personal. It is what persons do. Cumberland Presbyterians take this seriously. They will agree with the words of Eugene Kennedy, "Sin is not an imaginary phenomenon, nor some artifact from a civilization of long forgotten gods. It remains a lively possibility, with deadly consequences for all of us. Sin, by its very nature, is not outside of us; it exists in and through the deliberate actions of human beings. It is a special human power, the shattering capability that human beings alone possess."[11] It is a turning away from God. It is self-exaltation. When I was a child, I was told that the sin of Adam and Eve was pride. After more than sixty years of life experience (including personal sin!), this explanation still stands. Sin is exalting ourselves rather than accepting that our true exaltation comes from God. There is a great irony to sin. While sin is the act of self-glorification, the end result of sin is self-debasement. It is not the gain of the self, but the loss of the self. In the primal story, Adam and Eve must leave the garden paradise and now live east of Eden. Sin is not gain but loss.

Jesus told a parable about the danger of sin as self-exaltation (Luke 18:9-12). Two men went to the Temple to pray. One was a Pharisee and the other was a tax collector. The Pharisee gave thanks to God that he was not like other men, and especially not like the tax collector. The tax collector prayed, "Lord, be merciful to me a sinner." Jesus must have surprised persons when saying that it was the tax collector who went home justified, and when he added that "all who exalt themselves will be humbled and all who humble themselves will be exalted." I am reminded of an interviewer asking Tim Keller, the pastor of Redeemer Presbyterian Church in New York City, the following question: "Will being a homosexual cause a person to go to hell?" Keller replied, "Well, I am absolutely certain that being a heterosexual will not cause a person to go to heaven." And then he added, "I believe Jesus taught that the only thing that will cause a person to go to hell is self-righteousness." Personal sin is personal self-righteousness.

But personal sin also takes many other forms. The early church spoke of the seven deadly sins: pride, envy, anger, sloth, greed, gluttony, and lust. Persons and congregations would do well to become familiar with the nature of sin that these seven designate. I have sometimes suggested that persons listen to the music of the great blues singers such as Muddy Waters, John Lee Hooker, Bessie Smith, and others in order to reflect on the nature and consequences of personal sin. The lyrics of this powerful music ordinarily concern human brokenness, pain, betrayal, infidelity, abandonment, rejection, and many other, if not all, of the degrading and dehumanizing conditions that afflict people as a result of sin. There is little wonder that the word "mercy" is often heard in these songs which are so fundamentally honest about the human condition. Great literature can also serve as a mirror in which we can see more clearly the nature and consequences of personal sin. I know one person who says he first became more fully aware of his own personal sin by reading Herman Melville's great novel *Moby Dick*. Like the arrogant Captain Ahab who sought to subdue and conquer the great white whale, this person said he came to realize how the sin of self-centered arrogance was dominating his life and relationships.

That Jesus understood and realistically and relentlessly described personal sin and its consequences is revealed in his many stories:

- The unjust judge, needing to be plagued into doing his duty
- The churlish neighbor, impatient to a simple request
- The money-making farmer, with no thought above his barns
- The unfeeling glutton, ignoring the beggar at his door
- The ungrateful youth, rebelling against restraint
- The rascally steward, embezzling his master's capital
- The lazy servant, burying money entrusted for use
- The ruthless money-lender, mortgaging a widow's home
- The ostentatious Pharisee, parading his piety
- The flattery loving scribe, delighting in obsequious tributes

- The inconsistent debtor, forgiven but refusing to forgive
- The heartless priest, unconscious of social duty
- The indifferent Levite, ignoring the needy
- The crafty king, ruling by his cunning
- The envious farmer, sowing tares in a neighbor's crop
- The bargain hunting crowd, following for a feed
- The ruthless press-gang, compelling service for Rome
- The domineering foreman, beating and starving the servants
- The faithless servants, carousing in their master's absence
- The slave driving boss, demanding his supper at once
- The tyrant rulers, called great because over-bearing
- The treacherous disciples, who will betray and forsake
- The shallow friends, boasting but denying
- The slumbering spirits who miss festive opportunities
- The callous legalists, valuing ritual above suffering
- The misguided zealots, serving God by violence
- The trivial minded, offering childish excuses
- The vacillating governor, unequal to his responsibility
- The blasphemer against light, placing himself beyond forgiveness
- The corrupter of children, better never born[12]

Sin as Corporate and Systemic

Cumberland Presbyterians know from scripture and life in the world that sin is not only personal but also corporate and systemic. I grew up in Bessemer, Alabama, near Birmingham and not far from Selma, in the 1950-60s. These were the years of the great struggle to overcome the evil system of racial segregation in the South and elsewhere in the country. Coming of age when and where I did meant that I was an eye-witness to many of the signal events that marked this unhappy time. Thus I was an eye-witness to what is meant when saying sin is corporate and systemic. As such, it is sin and evil that is embodied in groups of people (often otherwise very good people—even church people!) and the systems in and by which they live. It is sin and evil that is embodied in the cultural and social worlds and institutions we invent and sanction, or ones which we may have inherited. Sin is personal, but it is much larger than the merely personal. It is also a collective reality. It often is institutionalized and called normative—simply the ways things are and, it is often thought, the way they should be and remain.

Cumberland Presbyterians look to Israel's great prophets (Isaiah, Jeremiah, Amos, Hosea and others) and, of course, especially to Jesus in order to understand the sense in which sin is more than simply what individual persons do or do not do. They recognize that Jesus challenged and exposed the corporate and systemic sin of his day—the taken for granted 'rightness' of the way things were. He challenged the corruption of religion including the way that this corruption reached even into the Temple. He challenged as illegitimate the social honor and shame system that exalted some and devalued others. He challenged commercial and political corruption. He challenged every reigning power system of the first century world including that of mighty Rome.

It was for these reasons that Jesus was charged with rebellion and finally crucified. It has been observed that if Jesus' message had only been one of 'love,' he might have lived to a ripe old age. But his core message was the arrival, the in-breaking, of the kingdom of God. Such talk was political speech. Human kings and emperors would not easily or patiently abide talk of rival kingdoms (consider the story of King Herod slaughtering the innocent children following the announcement of a child born to be a king). Jesus gathered followers to join him in his kingdom mission. He acted as a king when entering Jerusalem for the final time. When brought before Pontius Pilate, the Roman procurator's primary question was, "Are you a king?"

It is not to be missed that when Jesus was crucified he was "provided" with a kingly crown of thorns and a kingly robe. Pilate's final mockery was to have a sign printed, in three languages, that was placed above the head of the dying Jesus:

"The King of the Jews." It is clearly the case that Jesus was crucified primarily because of the challenge he presented to the corporate powers arrayed against him. He had announced, and embodied, the kingdom of God's love, righteousness, and justice and this was more than the reigning religious, social, commercial and political powers could or would tolerate. Cumberland Presbyterians acknowledge that the revelation of God attested in scripture and culminating in Jesus Christ is not about the problem of personal sin alone. It is also about corporate and systemic sin. It is about all forms of sin that oppose and resist the appearing among us of the kingdom of God. "The problem of sin is that it is profitable. There is money to be made in the marketing of cancer-causing cigarettes, of death-dealing instruments of war, in selling handguns, in slum housing, etc. . . . for the Bible and the greater part of the Christian tradition, sin is not only profoundly personal (persons are not unrelated individuals), but deeply structural." [13]

Sin as Embodied Evil

Noel Erskine writes of scripture's view of sin, "Sin is not merely seen as a state into which everyone is born, but it is understood as a destructive power that human beings cannot handle on their own. Seen as endemic and systemic, sin holds humanity in slavery."[14] Some human behavior, by persons or groups of persons, is so utterly evil that it seems as if something beyond or more than the merely human is being manifest. There are evils so sinister that they defy ordinary rational comprehension (Nazism remains the prime 20th century example). While persons and groups of persons remain accountable for participating in and carrying out such evil, it also appears that some incredibly dark, truly malignant force also must have been at work to have produced what is so completely inhuman and inhumane. In the New Testament, such evil is regarded as the work of the "Evil One" (Eph. 6:16; 1 John 2: 13-14) who is also known as "Satan," "the Adversary," or "Diabolos" (the devil). The Evil One is regarded as fomenting the dark and destructive evil that plagues the world (Mt. 17:14-18; Acts. 5:5; 2 Cor. 12:7). God's people are pictured as being involved in a struggle with the Evil One and his minions, known as evil spirits (Eph. 6:12). The evil spirits seek to crush the righteous (1 Pt. 5:8). They are seen as being able to manipulate the human heart (John 13:2). But the Evil One and the evil spirits are never presented as having a power that is commensurate with that of God. They are simply regarded as "being there" and without explanation. But they have no power over God. And, at the close of the age, the Evil One and all that is evil will be utterly eliminated (Rev. 19-21).[15]

What is clear to Cumberland Presbyterians is that sin and evil are not matters that should be trivialized. To speak of sin as demonic is not to exculpate persons of their responsibility in co-operating with evil. Rather it is to attempt to express the frightful, terrible, and incomprehensible nature of corporate sin. Somehow the whole adds up to being worse that the parts.

In his compelling book *Christ Crucified*, the late Lutheran theologian and missionary Mark W. Thomsen writes of sin as embodied evil: "Identifying the mission and death of Jesus with the reign of God means that faith experiences and acknowledges that sin as embodied evil has incredible power in the world. God's very best is pushed out of life and onto a cross. Past and contemporary history manifests this continuing power of evil, embodied in the historical antagonists to life, as the good, the true and the beautiful are crushed again and again. People of the cross will seek to identify and acknowledge the presence of the creative word of God within all creation and cultures and religions. They will also fearlessly name evil in all its forms . . . As sinful, yet forgiven, participants in the reign of God they will struggle against the forces of Satan in every context in order that life might be transformed. A contemporary theology of the cross will reclaim Luther's own acceptance of demonic reality and humanity's struggle with evil. The clash of the divine and demonic, however, can never be simply identified with ethnic, political, national, or international clashes within history. It is a conflict far deeper—*between the Abba and Spirit of Jesus and demonic powers that are destructive of God's gift of love and life*" (italics added for emphasis).[16]

Sin and Creation

The biblical authors see the effects of the abuse of human freedom as extending to the entire creation. Morrow writes, "The prophets had identified idolatry, war, disease, hunger, injustice , and even hostility among animals as evidences of the universal problem of sin and rebellion against God" (see Amos 8:1-14; Hos. 4:1-3; Isa, 24:1-20; Joel 3:9-15).[17] The *COF* asserts: **The alienation of persons from God affects the rest of creation, so that the whole world stands in the need of redemption** (2.06). Somehow sin has pervasive consequences for the entire created order. The Apostle Paul viewed the creation as being in bondage to decay and subjected to futility (Rom. 8:18-23). Thus the entire creation is in need of redemption and return to its original goodness (see the comments about creation and sin in chapter 4).

Sin as a Perversion of the Good

Earlier in this chapter it was mentioned that theologian Karl Barth spoke of sin as "nothingness." In this, he was influenced by Augustine (4th century) who viewed sin and evil in terms of "privation." Augustine's argument was that good exists, but when good is missing the result is evil. He did not regard evil as a force or entity in and of itself nor as a part of nature. Rather, it was a privation of, and therefore perversion of, the good. The English Christian apologist C.S. Lewis would follow this view and speak of evil as "good spoiled." Merwyn Johnson discusses the matter as follows: "sinners alone or in society cannot discern clearly which part is which, since the good and the bad are intermingled. Every action of the sinner is at least partially skewed no matter how well intentioned . . . sin perverts the good things God provides. The most notable items perverted are the God-given covenant, the sinner's own thinking-willing-acting capacities, and the larger world of nature. As a perversion of the good, sin lodges in certain focal points of human outlook, behavior, and relationship. Most often are pride (self-worth turned to ambition, power, fame); desire (becoming self-serving in sex, money, self-indulgence); truth (turned to ideology or unreality); freedom (independence without responsibility and relationship); obedience (turned into blind loyalty, disobedience), and faith (as an end in itself, unbelief, or religion)."[18]

It is especially important for Christians to grasp the sense in which sin is not only "doing bad things" but also a perversion of good things. It is important because the practice of religion itself can blind us to sin's deceptiveness. It is relevant at this point to recall that the temptations of Jesus were not that he engage in doing bad, "sinful," things, but that he engage in doing some very good things (e.g. turning stones to bread and feeding the hungry, see Matt. 4:1-11). It would have been a very good thing to turn stones into bread to feed the hungry. But not if the motive for this good deed was to be rewarded by the tempter—and to result in worshiping and serving the tempter! Jesus often warned of the danger of doing good things but for the wrong reasons (see Matt. 6:1-21). He was especially critical of "practicing piety" (a good thing) "before others in order to be seen by them" (a perversion of the good); of "sounding a trumpet at the giving of alms" (giving alms was a good thing) "so that they may be praised by others" (a perversion); "of standing in the synagogues or on street corners to pray (praying is a good thing) "so that they may be seen by others" (a perversion)

Jesus indicated, in his many disputes with the Pharisees (who mostly were very good people), that religion can be dangerous. It is dangerous when we fail to see that our religious beliefs and practices are insufficient, in themselves, to inoculate us against the deceptive nature of sin. The last congregation I served participated annually in a program called Christmas Charities. The program was designed to help "needy" families with food and toys at Christmas. For many years, some of our people would deliver the food and toys and would return to report their disappointment and amazement (and, yes, feelings bordering on anger) that many of the people served seemed ungrateful for the kindness that had been extended to them. One year, prior to the Christmas season, we made a study of the Latin words for "love." *Benevolentia* was interpreted to mean "love for others but from a position above them." The Latin Church fathers said this form of love is often met with resentment. *Concupiscentia* is love but from a position beneath others. It is needy love; that of a child for a neglectful parent; or of the person who has an abusive spouse. It is love that is often intermingled with hatred. Finally, the Latin church leaders spoke of *amicitia.*[19] They meant by this love that is side by side with others; that is neither being above them or beneath them. The Latin fathers said this is true love. It is the biblical *agape*. It is the love of God in Christ that descended into the world in order to be alongside of us. It is the love demonstrated by the incarnation.

This study enabled us to ask whether our good deeds at Christmas were primarily in the form of benevolence. If so, we could begin to understand why some people responded to us with what felt like resentment and lack of gratitude. We were, after all, approaching them from a situation located above them—socially, financially, and in many other ways. The study led us to see that authentic Christian love would mean finding ways the other 364 days of the year to be alongside the people we aimed to help. I wish I could say we were successful in this effort. But the point is even our good actions can be tainted by sin. Giving to others at Christmas was a good thing, but not if we expected a response that served to reward our own feelings or entitle us to pass judgment on others. "Perhaps the unique insight of a Christian interpretation of the human predicament is, first, only God is God, and, second, as a consequence, all else, even the most creative aspects of our human existence, are not absolutely good, good in themselves. But possess the possibility of the demonic if they are made self-sufficient and central."[20]

The Wages of Sin and the Gift of Life

The Apostle Paul is well known for having written, "The wages of sin is death" (Rom. 6:23). Death is not to be understood as a punishment by God, but as the inevitable consequence of sin. Sin leads to death. It is very important to note, however, that in scripture death is not simply biological death. It is that but it is more than that. Sin also is death in the sense of being separation from God who is life. It is alienation from God. Jesus' story of the Prodigal Son illustrates this meaning of sin as separation from God. When the younger son comes to his senses and finally comes home, the father says to the older brother, "But we had to celebrate and rejoice, for this brother of yours was *dead* and has come back to life; he was lost and has been found" (Lu. 15:32). Death, then, is not only a biological event. It is also a spiritual condition. Sin brings about a living death, a death in living. God is life and to be separated from God is death. Morrow observes, "The gravity of the human predicament is overwhelming. It is not the case that persons are liable to simply die and go to hell. Rather it is that all persons are already dead in trespasses and sins, already in bondage to sin and death—hell."[21]

Although the abuse of human freedom (and sin and death) is a big story in the scripture, it is by no means the biggest story. Paul said more, of course, than "For the wages of sin is death." Consider his complete statement in Romans 6:23, "For the wages of sin is death, but the free gift of God is eternal life in Christ Jesus our Lord." The latter affirmation is the biggest story in the scripture! "The law of death envelops everything we do and think and feel. But now a law of life breaks into all this dying, and it is the Lord Jesus himself. He is the one who lives forever, who rose from the dead, who keeps in touch with us from the world beyond, who sends us the Spirit, so that in the midst of our dying we may live and may ever again receive something fresh and living through his gift, through his presence, through his coming." [22] God in Christ overcomes death in all of its form and grants life in and through Jesus Christ. And just as death in the scripture is more than biological finality, eternal life is more than existence in a world to come. Eternal life is God's life in the here and now. It is abundant life now (John 10:10). If sin is the act of the human family turning from God in rebellion, grace is God coming toward the human family in redemptive and saving love. This is the primary story the scripture tells. And it is why the Cumberland Presbyterian *COF* has chosen John 3:16 as the verse which summarizes its entire theology.

Earlier in this chapter we read words about the "trap of sin" and William Faulkner's character who said about sinning, "You ain't got to. You can't help it." But has there ever been anyone who has not been caught in the trap of sin? Has there been anyone who did not disrupt fellowship with God? Is there anyone who is in the perfect image of God as were Adam and Eve originally? Cumberland Presbyterians affirm that there has been just such a person. He is Jesus the Christ.

The Apostle Paul was the first to refer to Jesus as the second Adam (Ro. 5:12-19; 1 Cor. 15:45-49). His argument is that what the human family lost through the sin of the first Adam is now being restored through the second Adam, Jesus Christ. **In willfully sinning all people become guilty before God and are under divine wrath and judgment, unless saved by God's grace through Jesus Christ** (2.05).Cumberland Presbyterians believe that being "under divine wrath and judgment" is the equivalent of saying that we are alienated from God, separated from God, in rebellion against God, and like Adam and Eve living east of Eden. We also know, and rejoice in the fact, that God was not willing to leave the human family in this situation of hopelessness and helplessness. God was not willing to leave his creation in a state of rebellion and in bondage to sin. The next section of the *COF* is devoted to God's act of redemption and reconciliation of sinful humanity in and through the life, death, and resurrection of Jesus Christ; so that **whoever will may be saved** (2.01).

God Acts Through Christ to Reconcile the World

(3.01—3.11 in the Confession of Faith)

Chapter Nine

GOD'S COVENANT

The third section of the *COF* is entitled "God Acts through Jesus Christ to Reconcile the World." If we were climbing a confessional and theological mountain, this section would bring us to the summit. When Jesus Christ comes into view, we are able to behold the entire panorama of the story that scripture is telling. Cumberland Presbyterians read all scriptures in the light of God's revelation in Jesus Christ. We are Christological people. Christ is at the center of our faith. It is through Christ that we know who the Triune God is and what the Triune God does. We will never know more about God than what is revealed to us in the person and life of the Christ. The following is among the important affirmations that the *COF* makes: **Jesus Christ, the eternal Word made flesh, is always the essence of the one covenant of grace** (3.04). Before it speaks of God's saving work in Jesus Christ, the *COF* begins this section with what is meant by God's one covenant of grace of which Jesus is "**always the essence**."

God acts to heal the brokenness and alienation caused by sin and to restore the human family to community through the reconciliation effected in Jesus Christ. God acts to restore sinful persons to a covenant relationship, the nature of which is that of a family. It is established through God's initiative and the human response of faith. God's covenant is a relationship of grace. It appears in various forms and manifestations in the scriptures but always as one of grace. The new covenant in Jesus Christ is its ultimate and supreme expression. Jesus Christ, the eternal Word made flesh, is always the essence of the one covenant of grace (3.01—3.04).

As mentioned in chapter one, covenant is a very important word to persons in the Reformed and Presbyterian tradition, including Cumberland Presbyterians. We understand ourselves as having a covenant theology and being members of a covenant community. We consider covenant to be at the heart of God's relationship to God's people in both testaments ("testament" is synonymous with "covenant"). God is a God who makes covenant. Anyone who wants to understand Cumberland Presbyterian theology, especially as it is set forth in the *COF* of 1984, will want to become familiar with the key phrase "God's one covenant of grace." This phrase, and what is meant by it, is basic to the theology of the entire Confession.

The significance of claiming that God's covenant has always been a covenant of grace is best understood by recalling that a "two-covenant theology" was characteristic of most Presbyterian theology throughout its history. This theology was clearly set forth and firmly established in the classic *Westminster Confession of Faith* of 1647. Consequently, it has influenced Presbyterian theology since that time (including the theology of some other Christian traditions). It was this theology under which the Cumberland Presbyterian Church began its life and ministry in 1810. However, the Cumberland Presbyterian Church soon authored its first confession (1813) which began to alter what it regarded as the misleading aspects of two-covenant theology.

A short-hand way to grasp the fundamental difference between the two-covenant theology and the Cumberland Presbyterian one covenant of grace theology is to ask how each understands the Bible's witness concerning God's relationship to the human family. In two-covenant theology, God is primarily thought of as a *Judge* with people being defendants in a courtroom. This is to say that God's relationship to people is thought of as a legal one, a matter of law with rewards for obedience and punishments for disobedience. But in one covenant of grace theology God is thought of as a *Parent* whose relationship to his or her people is that of a parent's relationship to his or her children (one here may think of Jesus' great story of the Prodigal Son in Luke 15:11-32). While a parent may and does reward obedience and discipline disobedience, the fundamental identity of a parent is not that of a judge; and the fundamental setting of a parent's relationship to his or her children is not that of a courtroom, but of a home and a family.

Another short-hand way to think of the difference in these two theologies is to consider what it means to sin against God, or be disobedient. In two covenant theology, sin is a matter of breaking God's law. Again, it is a legal matter. In one covenant of grace theology, sin is a matter of breaking relationship with God—it is, so to speak, the breaking of God's heart. In two-covenant theology, God's original relationship to the first human parents was a matter of works (law). If they were obedient, they were rewarded. The fact that they were disobedient led to punishment including the consequence of death. Two-covenant theology then maintains that when God's original covenant, the covenant of works, was breached by Adam and Eve, God instituted a covenant of grace *as a matter of expedience.* This covenant of grace with Israel culminated in God's gift of Jesus Christ to the human family. But *what is important to keep in mind* is that in two covenant theology God's original covenant with humankind was a covenant of works (law). Law in two covenant theology was the permanent covenant God made with his people while grace was an expedient and temporary covenant.

This view of matters has, of course, theological implications for interpreting the life and death of Jesus. Two-covenant theology maintains that Jesus came into the world fundamentally to satisfy the covenant of law. In this view, Jesus satisfied this requirement by virtue of the fact that he was a perfect human being. He was fully obedient to God. He was not a law-breaker. His death on the cross, therefore, satisfied the demand of punishment of sinners by God. This was a punishment that was necessary for all law-breakers in order to satisfy God's holiness and justice. Jesus, it is maintained, took this punishment on himself but as a necessity in order to satisfy the just anger of God toward sinners (law-breakers).

It is likely that two-covenant theology remains, in contemporary Christian belief, the most commonly held view of God's relationship to his people (a legal one) and the most common interpretation given to the death of Jesus (a punishment deserved by law-breakers). But the two-covenant theology breaks down significantly at least at two points. First, if Jesus' death satisfied the punishment for sin required of those who break God's law, then what about those who remain in sin, who remain lawbreakers? It must be the case, then, according to this theology, that Jesus did not die for them. This led two-covenant theology to claim that Jesus' death was not for all persons but only for "the elect"—those chosen by God for salvation. The un-elect were, in the mystery of God, simply but justifiably passed over for salvation. Jesus, then, cannot be said to have died for the non-elect. The view that Jesus did not die for all but only for a part of humankind gave rise to the concept of a limited atonement. Secondly, and of equally major concern, is that two-covenant theology's view of the atonement introduces a conflict within the very heart of the Holy Trinity. William Placher explains: "To think of the 'Son' appeasing the 'Father' would misunderstand the Trinity, whose Persons do not work in opposition, or have to win one another over, but operate in perfect unity. Therefore, any sense of conflict, of one Person paying a price to appease another Person, has the story wrong. The Triune God works together to achieve our salvation."[1]

But some will ask, and rightfully so, what is the place of God's anger (wrath) against sin in Cumberland Presbyterian one covenant of grace theology? After all, God's wrath is accounted for, rather expediently, in two-covenant theology. Jesus took God's wrath upon himself. Although Cumberland Presbyterian theology is fully aware that scripture speaks clearly and unambiguously when saying that God has justifiable anger or wrath against sin, and even that Jesus took it upon himself, it has a very different understanding of what it means when scripture speaks of God's wrath. One scholar observes that in the progression of the Old Testament, "More and more, wrath is seen as a process, a power, something less personal and more autonomous, and independent of God. Just as in the proverbs, *wisdom* was close to sharing the nature of God yet independent. So it is with wrath. Wrath takes on a character of its own, and is not simply a trait of God's personality. In fact, it is not personal at all. It is more mechanical, like a process. . .wrath and hell are the biblical words for the bindingness of our own historicity, to put it in contemporary speculative language."[2]

In other words, we become what we choose to become. God respects (out of love) our freedom to rebel, disobey, and go our own way, and so "gives us up" to go our way and the result is called living under wrath (see Rom. 1:18-32). Wrath is what happens to us when we refuse the love of God. God is not angry and vindictive and does not need to be appeased. And wrath is not a means God uses to educate us. "It is simply the outworking of the process that ensues when we turn against God."[3] We might look again to the story of the "Prodigal son" and suggest that the son, when reaching the pig pen, was now experiencing the wrath of his father. But it was not an active wrath on his father's part, but rather the sorry result of the son's own disobedience. It is what happened to him as a result of his own misguided choosing.

Cumberland Presbyterians believe that on the cross Jesus experienced and absorbed the judgment and wrath of God against sin. But what Jesus absorbed was not some angry passion from within God. Rather, Jesus absorbed what the world is capable of, what the world can do at its very worst, when it turns away from God who is love. So Cumberland Presbyterian theology does not say that Jesus' death was required as a way to appease or satisfy the just anger of God (a judicially imaged God). It claims, as already has been said, just the opposite. The death of Jesus is the ultimate expression of God's love (Jn. 3:16). That the world did not know what it was doing when crucifying the Lord of life, even though it thought it did, was, in that moment and in every moment when God is rejected, under the wrath of God; which is the Bible's way of speaking about the negative side of God's love—what happens when we refuse God's love.

Cumberland Presbyterian theology, in the *COF* of 1984, firmly rejected two-covenant theology. This rejection actually began with the founding of the Cumberland Presbyterian Church in 1810. The first Cumberland Presbyterians objected to and denied the doctrine of limited atonement, or that Jesus had died only for a part of humankind (the elect) and not for all. Fundamental to Cumberland Presbyterian theology is its belief, based on close and Christological reading of the Scriptures, that God's one and only covenant with his people was and always has been a covenant of grace offered to all. It was a wrong move, Cumberland Presbyterians believe, to have interpreted God's relationship to Adam and Eve in legal and judicial terms rather than in terms of grace (relationship). For Cumberland Presbyterians, God's grace always precedes law. Grace came first, then law (or command). God was in a grace-full relationship to the first human parents and not in a legal relationship with them.

The one covenant of grace theology also has special, and very important, implications for understanding the death of Jesus. Cumberland Presbyterians share the belief of two covenant theology that Jesus completely fulfilled the law. Jesus' life was one of utter obedience to his Father (Abba). But this obedience was not a matter of satisfying the legal requirements of a covenant of law. Jesus, rather, was obedient to his Father as a result of an intimate, personal relationship of love. Similarly, Jesus death on the cross was not to satisfy God's just punishment of law-breakers (i.e. sinners)—Jesus' death was not a legal transaction required by God—but it was the length to which God's grace was willingly to go to demonstrate God's love for humankind—for sinners (John 3:16). Cumberland Presbyterians, then, do not regard the death that Jesus willingly endured as being a payment made to God to satisfy God's justice and holiness. Cumberland Presbyterians do not believe that God exacted the death of Jesus so that God's anger at sin could be placated. In short, Cumberland Presbyterian theology does not espouse the "penal-substitutionary" theory of the atonement that is the centerpiece of two-covenant theology. We will consider the fact, in the next chapter, that the Cumberland Presbyterian Church has no official theory of the "how" of the atonement.

Substitution and *satisfaction* are key words used in two-covenant theology when discussing the death of Jesus; in the light or darkness) of the penal substitution theory of the cross. The key word for Cumberland Presbyterians, however, is *reconciliation* (note the number of times the word "reconciliation" appears throughout the *COF*). The life and death of Jesus is God's great act of reconciling the world to himself (2. Cor. 5:17-19; Col. 1:20). It is to be remembered that scripture makes it abundantly clear that God does not need to be reconciled to us. There is nothing in God needing reconciliation. Therefore, God does not need or require the death of Jesus in order to be reconciled to us. In fact, God loved us while we were still sinners (Rom. 5:8). The death of Jesus was not so that God *could* love us but because God *does* love us. Nothing in God had to be satisfied, appeased, or placated. We are the ones in need of reconciliation. Reconciliation is a *relational* word rather than a *legal* word. When preaching the cross, Cumberland Presbyterians do not think in terms of an angry God whose hatred of sin is appeased by the bloody death of his Son. They think, rather, in terms of God having gone to the utter limit in sacrificial, self-donating love in order to bring the human family back into right relationship with God. This is truly amazing grace. And it is the heart of the Cumberland Presbyterian understanding of God's one covenant of grace.

Before Christ's coming, it (the covenant of grace) **was made effective by promises, prophecies, sacrifices, circumci-**

sion, the Passover lamb, and other signs and ordinances delivered to the people of Israel. These were sufficient through the ministry of the Holy Spirit to instruct persons savingly in the knowledge of God and to lead them to believe God (3.04). Here is presented, in synopsis, the entire history of God's relationship to the people of Israel. **Since Christ's coming, the covenant of grace is made effective chiefly by the preaching of the word and the administration of the sacraments of baptism and the Lord's Supper. In these, together with other acts of worship and acts of love toward the neighbor, the gospel of the one covenant of grace is set forth simply and yet in fullness and with spiritual power** (3.05). Here is presented, in synopsis, the history of God's relationship to the church including in the present. **Children have always been included with their parents in the covenant of grace. Before Christ came, the appropriate sign and seal thereof was circumcision. Since the advent of Christ the sign and seal is baptism** (3.06). Here is presented, in synopsis, the fundamental ecclesiology (understanding of the nature of the church) of the Cumberland Presbyterian Churches. God's covenant was always one involving entire families. There was never a covenant that was made with or intended for a single, individual person. The covenant was always familial, or corporate, in design. God's original covenant with Abraham and Sarah was for the blessing of all the nations (families) of the earth. The new (or renewed) covenant of which Jesus is the mediator was always intended as a covenant for and with a family of people (the church). Thus, the Cumberland Presbyterian Churches understand the one covenant of grace to include "children with their parents." More will be said about this in the chapter on baptism.

Chapter Ten

CHRIST THE SAVIOR

I would like to begin this chapter, on Christ the Savior, with an account of a fictional telephone conversation. I receive a call from a longtime friend. We haven't talked in awhile so we exchange pleasantries, catch up on our families, and then the conversation becomes earnest. He begins by saying he is in a difficult place in his personal life. He is feeling overwhelmed by his responsibilities at work and his life at home is suffering. He says he thinks he may be severely depressed or becoming so. I listen for awhile and then I say, "Glad to hear from you. Sorry that you are having such a hard time. Tell you what, why don't you check out the Internet? Google Mayo Clinic, for example. They have some really good stuff on how to deal with depression. Call me again some time. Bye."

This would be a callous (and, of course, hopefully unlikely) response on my part. But my point about this brief fictional conversation is my friend had not called because he needed some information I could provide. He didn't need, nor was he asking for, guidance concerning a website. He called for one reason. He was hurting and reaching out to make contact with a *person*. Often what we need most in life is a person. We need someone who incarnates caring personhood. We need another ear, voice, another heart, and a sensitive and compassionate presence. Sometimes we may need another person to be frank with us, challenge us, and call us to accountability and responsibility. But we will experience many times in life when nothing else will do except another person.

The heart of the Christian message is that God has come to us in a *person*. Jesus is the incarnate one. In him, God comes to us in the flesh of our own personhood. As Edward Humphrey writes, "The gulf between God and man is personal rather than physical. Therefore the bridging of this gulf may occur only in a personal manner. Hence God willed to come to us in the only personal guise which we could receive—that of lowly human existence."[1] The incarnation of God in Jesus Christ is that great and decisive act by which God freely chooses to enter history and take up a place alongside us. God does not remain at a distance but enters fully into our situation. This is the great mystery of God's self-emptying and self-donating love in Jesus Christ (Phil. 2:5-11).

Before considering the *COF*'s theological statements about the person who is Christ the Savior, I would like to deal, briefly, with how the early followers of Jesus came to understand him and his message.

The Gospels make it clear that the first followers of Jesus, and other of his contemporaries, knew that he was a man, a fully human Jewish man. But he was also very different, utterly different, from any man they had ever known, or of whom they had ever heard. Colin Greene writes of the sense in which Jesus was an enigma to those who first knew him: "He did not seem to fit with previous patterns and expectations of what constituted a messenger of God, a prophet, or teacher of religion. He was not a priest; unlike his cousin John the Baptist, he did not come from a priestly family. Neither was he a bona fide prophet in the OT sense of the word, because his preaching was not couched in the idiom of a reiteration of the word of God. Nor was he simply an apocalyptic seer or visionary whose main concern was to interpret the signs of the times and proclaim God's judgment upon society in general. He was most definitely not a teacher of the law in the Pharisaical sense of the word; indeed, he was opposed to the casuistry that typified their profession. Nor was he merely a teacher of wisdom, although he did speak in aphorisms, parables, and proverbs. He was not a politically motivated Zealot, nor was he simply another itinerant magician, wonderworker, or charismatic miracle worker. In all respects, Jesus broke apart previous categories and expectations. As Eduard Schweizer observed, 'Jesus was the man who fits no one formula.'"[2]

This fact about Jesus, that he was a square peg for which no square hole could be found, helps account for the near absolute mystery of his identity as reflected throughout the Gospels. No one who follows him or meets him seems to understand him. The people of his hometown do not know who he is, and become terribly offended by his preaching. His own family does not know who he is. The religious leaders do not know who he is. The political leaders do not know who he is. His own disciples are bewildered by him and are slow on the uptake. Is he a prophet? Is he the Messiah? John the Baptist, when in prison, has questions about the latter. If he is the Messiah, why does he not fit commonly held messianic expectations? Even when Peter confesses him to be so, the lead disciple clearly fails to understand what being this particular Messiah will involve. Is he a revolutionary? He did speak of the destruction of the Temple. Is he a king? Pontius Pilate wanted to know this and questioned him about it. Who is this man? How can he be understood and explained? How are people to regard him? What is his significance? What is his agenda? When he enters Jerusalem on Palm Sunday, the crowd asks, "Who is this?"

The Gospels show that the first followers of Jesus knew, beyond any doubt, that he was a man. But eventually they came to believe more than this had to be said about him. What they began saying about him came as a complete surprise to them. As first century Jews, it must have been incomprehensible to them that they would begin to say what, in fact, they did. The only way to account for this claim, that a very Jewish man was something more than an ordinary man, was the *resurrection*. It is worth remembering that there would be no written Gospels, nor any of the remainder of the New Testament, were it not for the belief in the resurrection. The death of Jesus alone would not have produced this result. The New Testament did not arise as a story about Jesus to which a happy ending had to be supplied following his tragic death; a kind of Hollywood ending to a great tragedy. It was quite the opposite. The resurrection was the catalyst for the various accounts of the Jesus story. This singular event in the life of Jesus came first, and the documents of witness to and faith in him came later.

So, following the resurrection, what is the story the first witnesses tell in terms of who Jesus was and became to and for them? In short, the earliest witnesses came to believe that all that could be said about God could also be said about him. The following provides a useful summary of this development: "The very earliest Christians did not say directly that Jesus *is* God or that God *is* Jesus. First of all they said only that Jesus *does* what only God can do. Here is a man who *acts* like God, who does God's work. He speaks with authority—even more authority than Moses through whom the people believed that God had made known his will (Mt. 19:3-9). He forgives sin (Mt. 9:2). He dares to speak and to act as if *his* coming means that the kingdom of God has come (Mt. 12:28). He speaks and acts as Revealer, Reconciler, Redeemer, Lord and Liberator. It is not surprising that the Pharisees accuse him of blasphemy; he claimed to do what only God can do. During Jesus' life, his disciples were confused and uncertain about what all this meant. After his death and resurrection, it became clearer to them. But they still do not say it directly, or try to explain it. Now they confess Jesus as Lord—the Lord who is 'far above all rule and authority and power and dominion, and above every name that is named' (Eph. 1:21). That is, they now give him the name and the sovereignty they attributed to God himself. Still without explanation, they began to mention Jesus and God in one breath: 'for there is one God, the Father from whom are all things, and for whom we exist, and one Lord Jesus Christ, through whom are all things and through whom we exist' (1 Cor. 8:6). But finally it was said openly—still without explanation—Jesus *is* God. In the Gospel of John, we hear it most directly: 'The Word was with God and the Word was God' (Jn. 1:1). 'Thomas said to him, 'My Lord and my God' (Jn. 20:28). 'I and the Father are one' (Jn. 10:30). 'He who has seen me has seen the Father' (Jn. 14:9). In the first chapter of Hebrews, an Old Testament psalm originally written as a prayer to God is now addressed to Christ (Heb. 1:8). In Christ we have to do with God himself. Christ is not just a man sent from God, or a prophet or an angel. When we meet this man (a real man!) we meet God himself—the Lord. If you want to know who God is and what God is like, you must look at this man. He is Immanuel—God with us."[3]

The Message of Jesus

Earlier it was mentioned that Jesus was an enigma to all who attempted to fit him into a category understandable to them. The core message of Jesus, however, is not so enigmatic. He began his ministry by saying, "The time is fulfilled, and the kingdom of God has come near; repent, and believe in the good news" (Mk. 1:15; Mt. 4:12-17; Lk.4:14-15). Jesus proclaimed that God, the king of Israel, was once again taking charge. All through the centuries since the glorious kingdom of David and the terrible exile in Babylon, faithful Jews looked forward to God one day re-establishing God's kingdom on earth. Jesus proclaimed that this hope was now being fulfilled! It was happening. It was breaking in. This was the audacious and provocative message of the young man from Nazareth in Galilee. As one author observes, "Jesus is proclaiming a *kingdom that is at hand.* He is not merely instructing people in a body of ideas or doctrine (although ideas and doctrines will be implied and cannot be avoided). He is not inviting people primarily into a personal experience (although you cannot respond to his message without its being personal and an experience). What he is announcing is a whole new order of things. To describe it, he uses political language; his preferred term is 'kingdom.' It is a new set of *relationships.* It involves healing and other mighty works. It is a *movement* which includes drawing people away from their regular occupations to come with him. Some will even permanently leave their prior occupations to be part of his serving community."[4]

It is a mistake to think that the core message of Jesus was love. It was certainly an important aspect of his message, and loving God and neighbor as self was his summary of the law. But if the central message of Jesus had been love he might have lived to a ripe old age. If he had been merely a preacher and exemplar of love, he would not have gotten into so much trouble with his contemporaries. He would have been scoffed at by many religious folks for spending so much time with obvious sinners and telling them that God's love was available to *them*. He would have been considered idealistic and foolish by some for saying such things as "Love your enemies." He would have been dismissed as a dreamer of dreams. But his message of love would have hardly caused a stir among those who finally became his implacable enemies. To understand why Jesus met such resistance, and finally death, requires looking elsewhere than his message about and embodiment of God's love.

Kingdom talk was definitely political speech in the first century world of Jesus. When he spoke of God's kingdom becoming present here and now, and when he attracted followers to his cause, the rulers of this world took notice. This message of Jesus, and the many ways he enacted the message, was not met with indifference or amusement. Kings in authority, even puppet kings of the mighty Romans such as Herod, do not easily brook challenges to their power and rule. Politics really is a blood sport. The Temple authorities also braced against Jesus' kingdom talk, and especially the fact that he was gaining a following. It was their job to keep peace for the

Romans who would come down hard on them in the event of trouble-makers not being held in check. Religious leaders such as the Pharisee party objected fiercely to Jesus' kingdom speech since the implication was that they were getting and doing God wrong. Who was this backwoods boy from the Galilean hills to tell them about God? And yet Jesus went about doing precisely this. He spoke insistently of the kingdom of God that was becoming present day by day in his own life and ministry.

N. T. Wright attempts to help us get a sense of what this speech meant in the ears of those in political and religious power in Jesus' day: "Imagine what it would be like, in Britain or the United States today, if, without an election or any other official mechanism for changing the government, someone were to go on national radio and television and announce that there was now a new prime minister or president. 'From today onward,' says the announcer, 'we have a new ruler! We're under new government! It's all going to be different!' That's not only exciting talk. It's fighting talk. It's treason! It's sedition! By what right is this man saying this? How does he think he will get away with it? What exactly does he mean anyway? An announcement like this isn't simply a proclamation. *It's the start of a campaign.* When a regime is already in power and is simply transferring that power to the next person in line, you just announce that it is happening. But if you make that announcement while someone else appears to be in charge, you are saying, in effect, 'The campaign starts here.'"[5]

The Romans, of course, hardly would have had an interest in Jesus and his kingdom campaign. They could have cared less about his religious teaching. The Romans were interested only in collecting taxes and maintaining their form of peace by subjugation. And they had a method for dealing with serious trouble-makers—crucifixion. Crosses often lined the roads leading into and out of cities or towns where people had dared to raise the ire of the great Roman leviathan. The crosses dreadfully made the point: "We are in charge so don't make trouble." Jesus engaged in speech and actions (think of clearing the Temple) that led the religious and political powers of first century Judaism to bring him to the attention of the Romans.

When he appeared before the Roman procurator, Pontius Pilate, the governor's question was whether Jesus claimed to be a king. Jesus said to him, "My kingdom is not of this world." When saying this, Jesus did not mean that his kingdom was airy-fairy, ethereal, or merely a spiritual or mental exercise in interiority. He meant that the kingdom he represented was not authorized by the powers of this world, as was Pilate's. That Jesus' crucifixion was a politically induced death is made clear by the details provided by the Gospel writers. Pilate had an inscription placed at the head of the cross announcing, in three languages, that Jesus was king of the Jews. This was a joke to the Romans but must have been infuriating to the local religious leadership. Jesus is given a *crown* of thorns. Roman soldiers mockingly draped him in a royal robe. He was the man who would be king.

From the Gospels, it is impossible to miss that Jesus' core message was the proclamation of God's kingdom. His parables were kingdom parables. Every one of them is a story about what the kingdom is like, what it means, and how persons may enter it, resist it, or rejoice in it. Jesus' actions were kingdom actions. Healings, miracles, and exorcisms were all ways of demonstrating the presence of the kingdom. His proclamation of forgiveness was a sign that the messianic kingdom had come in his ministry. The messianic age expected by first century Jews was a time when Israel's long exile would be over and God's forgiveness of Israel's sin would be fully realized. Jesus' acts of forgiveness of sin announced that the messianic age had indeed come.

Jesus' table fellowship with sinners, and with others, was an enactment of the long awaited and hoped for messianic banquet in the kingdom of God. When Jesus entered Jerusalem on Palm Sunday, the Gospels understand that he was enacting the arrival of Jerusalem's king. The Gospel writers came to understand that Jesus' crucifixion was an enthronement. The cross was his throne. They regarded his resurrection as the exaltation of the king to the right hand of God. The gift of the Holy Spirit was the ongoing presence and power of the Triune God in the life of this God's kingdom people. In every way possible to the imagination, the New Testament writers creatively assert that in Jesus the saving rule (reign) of God has come to earth. He taught them to pray, "Your kingdom come, your will be done, on earth as it is in heaven" (Mt. 6:9-13).

If what has been said about the core message of Jesus is accurate, certain consequences follow for our understanding of Jesus' life and mission; and our understanding of what it means to be church. For one thing, it seems certain that Jesus' core message was not, "Believe in me so that you can go to heaven when you die." His call to his disciples, rather, was a call to join him in his kingdom project and kingdom life. When he said "Follow me" this certainly meant following him in the kingdom mission that was happening here and now. The call to discipleship was a call to participate in his kingdom work, which was, most definitely, this worldly work.

When Jesus told Nicodemus that he must be born again (or from above), this necessary new birth was in order that Nicodemus could "see" the kingdom of God (John 3). There is almost nothing in the Gospel accounts of the words and actions of Jesus which lend credence to a concept of the kingdom being an internal, private, spiritualized matter of the heart. There was, of course, and inward as well as outward dimension to the kingdom. "There is little doubt that the kingdom Jesus proclaims also comes inwardly, in the hearts and minds of women and men, as a radical qualification of their most personal and inward attitudes, commitments, and trust . . . the kingdom comes silently, hiddenly, in the response of men and women and in the total transformation of their lives that result."[6] Persons clearly were transformed in this way by their encounter with and response to Jesus. But it remains that the call of discipleship was a call for the forming of a people who would live together on the basis of kingdom energy and kingdom priorities in this world. For Jesus, the kingdom was a living, this worldly *social* reality. It was to be expressed in a community (church) in and through which it was being demonstrated that God was taking charge. The church emerged as a people who would embody the kingdom way of Jesus. The call to discipleship was not so that persons could go to heaven when they died, but so that the world might see the kingdom of God being lived out in the here and now.

It appears that this core message of Jesus has been misunderstood in much of American Christianity. Instead, the saving work of God in Christ has been almost entirely understood to be about the personal salvation of individual persons. There is a relatively long history behind this development. The 16th century European Enlightenment gave rise, in the western world, to the significance and importance of the individual person. This widespread and far-reaching intellectual, political, scientific, and social upheaval was regarded as liberating the individual from many of the oppressive shackles of the past—from religion, the church, historical myths, the superstitions of the masses and, on the political front, the divine right of kings and ruling elites. The individual and his or her powers of reason now took center stage. The theocentric (God-centered) world view of the Middle Ages gave way and was replaced by an anthropocentric (man-centered) world view.

Man (human beings) was now at the center and God (religion) was at the periphery of human concern. Man, not God or gods, became the truly interesting subject of inquiry and discussion. It is beyond serious questioning that the Enlightenment resulted in a giant step forward in the history of humankind. The modern achievements of humanity in almost every field of human endeavor have their roots in the Enlightenment world view. The rejection of medieval style top-down authoritarian political structures resulted in the spectacular rise of western democracies. Everyone, of course, is familiar with the astounding achievements and developments made possible by the rise of modern science. The beneficent fruits of the Enlightenment are to be appreciated. But for our purposes, and has often been observed, there is a straight line from the Enlightenment's exaltation of the individual to the free-standing, autonomous individual, or self, that is so exalted, in near absolute terms, in our contemporary world.

The 16th century Protestant Reformation preceded the Enlightenment and, perhaps unwittingly, had provided a religious legitimization for the new emphasis on the individual. The Reformers challenged and then denied the long-standing authority of the Roman Catholic Church and its popes, bishops and hierarchy. The Bible was translated into the vernacular meaning that individuals could now read it for themselves. The doctrine of the "priesthood of believers" replaced the theological idea and ecclesiastical practice of intermediaries (priests) between God and the individual. Individuals and groups of individuals were freed to form new churches according to their theological investigations and beliefs. There is much to appreciate, celebrate and give thanks to God for, when it comes to the Protestant Reformation from which the Cumberland Presbyterian Church itself sprang. But the point here is that after the Reformation and Enlightenment there was a new reality in the world and in the church. The individual person now occupied an altogether new place in the history of the world and of religion. Just as humankind became the focus of concern for the Enlightenment, so individuals became the focus of concern in religious life, especially in terms of interpreting the meaning of Jesus' message.

The person-centeredness of the Enlightenment and Reformation, not to mention the primacy of the autonomous person, or self, in most contemporary western democracies, has had certain negative consequences for the understanding and practice of church for Cumberland Presbyterians and most other of the Christian traditions of the West. Jesus' kingdom message and project, and the fact that salvation was to enter the kingdom and live in light of its reality, has suffered too often from a reduction in meaning—namely to that of salvation being about the individual's relationship to God. This is hardly unimportant, to say the least, but it may result, and often has, in turning Jesus' broad, this worldly, but also cosmic, message into being a matter of the individual and God. The practical result of this has been the individualization, privatization, personalization, and often near total interiorization of the meaning of Jesus' message and work. Jesus and the faith can become so personalized and spiritualized that little is left of the social reality and demand of his kingdom message.

There is a quite common tradition in which persons speak of Jesus as "my personal Lord and Savior." Many of those inside the culture and life of the church will understand and appreciate the meaning of these words. But is it possible that speaking in this way might represent, even if unintentionally, the personalization of the Christian faith about which we have been talking? And might it not fit rather easily and comfortably into the exaltation of the free-standing autonomous self that is a hallmark of our time. For example, it now is not uncommon to hear persons speak of "my personal trainer," "my personal computer;" "my personal diet;" "my personal portfolio;" and on it goes. It is quite easy to see how speaking of Jesus as "my personal Savior" (even when it is profoundly true) may sound like the triumph of the personalization of the faith; and behind it the triumph of the person-centered world view that is a bequeathal to us from the Enlightenment project. In this world view, everything is about the potential of humankind, with little consideration or room for God. If Jesus' kingdom message, and the broad meaning of salvation it involves (personal but so much more than personal), is narrowed down to the salvation of the individual as the primary thing, what keeps it from being the triumph, in the church, of the Enlightenment point of view that regards human beings as the center and measure of all things?

Lest this appear as an exercise in abstraction, I would like to point to what I believe are some of the negative consequences of the triumph of the almost total personalization of the message of Jesus. First, the primacy of the individual has resulted in a weakened understanding and practice of what it means to be the church. In the 1970s, when I was a young pastor, it was not uncommon to hear people say, "The church does not save you. Jesus saves you." This was still in the era when the church was culturally established, especially in the southern United States. This statement ordinarily was a way of expressing disdain about petty denominational squabbling over which was the "true church with the right doctrine." But it probably also expressed something more. It was the kind of statement made possible by the primacy of the "God and the individual" understanding (or misunderstanding) of the message of Jesus. It was the expression of the primacy of the person *over* the church. The church hardly mattered. A person might love his or her congregation and serve it but the truly important thing was his or her "personal relationship to Jesus Christ." The practical result was to strengthen the view that the individual, in her or his judgments and practices, matters to God in a way that the church does not matter.

Secondly, the primacy of the individual, even the religious individual, has made the communal nature (koinonia) of the church much more difficult to nurture and sustain. Since the dominant culture and also the church (to the degree that the individual is unduly exalted) tend to celebrate the autonomous, free-standing self, the individual maintains the right to choose the terms of his or her commitments, loyalties, and behaviors. Very often the personal takes precedence over the communal. Personal interests, desires, and attractions often trump the needs and concerns of the community, either secular or church. This has resulted in far too many people having only "a casual relationship to the church." People who are formed in their thinking, and in their cultural circumstances, to regard the person as paramount will often fail to grasp the biblical meaning and reality of community.

Thirdly, the near total emphasis on salvation being about "God and the individual" may dampen the church's understanding of how the Gospel, the kingdom of God, is about seeking justice and righteousness in this world. Ominously, a theology that fails to understand and live from Jesus' proclamation of the kingdom may result in the church failing to recognize its calling to challenge the evils and injustices of this world, including those that are structural and systemic. If the Gospel is understood only in terms of the individual's vertical relationship to God, the horizontal demands of Jesus and the kingdom may be missed, minimized, or even ignored. Finally, the primacy of the individual has made church discipline, in the positive sense of reproof, correction, and support, nearly non-existent. Persons in their autonomy, even persons who understand themselves to have surrendered their autonomy to Christ, often resist the idea of the church having communal standards, behaviors, and ethics that apply to them.

Unfortunately, it is possible to read the Cumberland Presbyterian *COF* and conclude that the Gospel is primarily about God and the individual. This is especially true in the sections entitled "God Works through Jesus Christ to Reconcile the World" and "God Acts through the Holy Spirit." This is because of the number of times that God's salvation in Christ is said to have to do with "persons," "sinners," and "believers." Once again, that God in Christ saves individual persons is not at issue. It is just that God's saving work, as attested in scripture and the core message of Jesus, is so much broader than this. I recommend, modestly, that in future revisions of the *COF* work be done to lift up the significance of the core message of Jesus concerning the kingdom of God. It is from within the context of this message that the salvation of individuals will find its proper and true New Testament meaning.

The COF's Theological Statements about Christ the Savior

God's mighty act of reconciling love was accomplished in Jesus Christ, the divine Son who became flesh to be the means by which the sins of the world are forgiven (3.07). As already mentioned, reconciliation is a key biblical word for Cumberland Presbyterian understanding of God's saving work in Jesus Christ. Imagine the following scene as taking place in one of the big box stores: A kindly looking young woman is holding the hand of a small child who appears bewildered and close to tears. They are standing near the customer service desk at the front of the store. An attendant at the desk speaks into a phone and her message is heard throughout the store. "Will Mr. and Mrs. Smith please come to customer service to pick up your daughter?" Shortly, the Smiths emerge from one of the aisles, looking frantic themselves, and run toward the desk. They embrace their child with hugs and kisses. They also turn and hug the kindly young woman who had found the child walking alone in one of the long aisles. This was a moment of reconciliation. The parents, who had been looking everywhere throughout the store, were brought back together with their daughter, and vice versa. She was no longer lost from them. The kindly young woman smiles and thinks she will do nothing more important on this day. She was the kind of person who, when coming upon the child, could not look the other way. She took the initiative to make this situation come out right.

The human predicament is that we are separated from God. One difference from our imaginary story is that we are willfully lost as a consequence of the abuse of our human freedom. We have turned away from God and toward ourselves. But, in what is true to the story, God in Jesus Christ *has taken the initiative* to bring us back into relationship with himself. The Gospels ordinarily present the act of reconciliation in narrative form. Numerous are the stories in which Jesus brings (and is) the good news of God's love and acceptance of sinners. Luke summarizes this ministry of Jesus when saying, "The Son of Man has come to seek and to save the lost" (19:10).

It was the Apostle Paul (and his disciples), however, who made theological use of the word reconciliation to set forth the meaning and consequences of God's saving action in Jesus Christ. Luke Timothy Johnson comments on the way in which reconciliation is at the heart of the message found in Ephesians (in this epistle human beings are regarded as being under the influence and in the grip of cosmic forces who oppose God and enslave human beings; we might, in our day, understand the cosmic forces in terms of something like the advertising industry that captures our attention and leads us to idolize our opportunities for consumption; or the sports industry; or racial prejudice; or any combination of worldly influences and powers that may addict us and distort and even destroy the possibility of authentic human freedom): "Human alienation from God is expressed (in Ephesians) as enslavement to forces fighting God, and manifested in hostility toward, and alienation from, fellow human beings. The prime example of this hostility is the division of humanity into 'two races,' the historical competition between Jew and Gentile. The 'good news' in Ephesians announces God's work as a reversal of this state of cosmic-historical reality. God has revealed his mysterious plan to reconcile all reality, bringing harmony between God and humans and therefore establishing the possibility of unity among humans themselves. The agent of this reconciliation is the Messiah, whose paradoxical death heals the rupture between God and humanity, eradicating the cosmic forces that have enslaved humans to captivity, and reveals the possibility of a new way of being human, one that is not divided by hostility but united in peace. The sign of this reconciliation is the unity of Jew and Greek in the church."[7]

It is worth asking, at this point, whether the potential unification of the Cumberland Presbyterian Church and the Cumberland Presbyterian Church in America might be a sign of God's reconciliation for and to our present time. It also is worth noting that for Paul God's reconciliation in Christ is not just a matter of the salvation of individual persons, but it is a profoundly social and communal reality. The mystery of salvation for Paul is the putting together of Jew and Greek, the breaking down of the barriers that had kept them separated. This was a new and altogether unheard of, and formerly impossible to conceive, social reality in the ancient world.

How is it that God's act of reconciliation is accomplished in Jesus Christ, in this one *person*? How is it that in him **the sins of the world are forgiven** (3.07)? That is, how is it that the barriers which separate human beings from God and one another have been overcome? Cumberland Presbyterians believe that it is the *entire life of Jesus Christ* that has accomplished the reconciliation. It was not the cross alone, or the resurrection alone, or the teachings alone, but the *totality* of the life and person of Jesus that *is* God's act of reconciliation. What was it about Jesus, who was he, that 2000 years ago, and in him alone, God brought about the great act of reconciliation? This is sometimes called "the scandal of particularity." What about this particular person's being and life was so unique that in him God acted so decisively to save the world? We have here raised questions that have given rise to an endless number of theological books. And, of course, these questions originally gave rise to the books that became the New Testament.

We can, I believe, be helped in our thinking about these questions by focusing on two words that can be applied to Jesus, words which are clearly indicated by a reading of the New Testament: *freedom* and *obedience.* G. Kaufman writes: "The claim that God was incarnated in Jesus Christ is the claim that the estrangement or separation between man and God was overcome in the person of Jesus Christ. Here a point in history was finally reached where God's will was perfectly done in and through the *free* response of a human being. Thus, the kingdom of God—God's full sovereignty over a history of free spirits—actually began to break into human history here and could now become an effective force *within* history. That is, at *this point,* in and through *this* obedience God was able to enter history and work within it in a way not possible before."[8] There is a sense, then, in which we can say God's act of reconciliation was accomplished in and through Jesus' perfect freedom and obedience to God—a freedom and obedience that led him all the way to the cross, and a freedom and obedience that was vindicated by God in the resurrection of Jesus. The Christian claim for the uniqueness of Jesus, that in him alone God acted decisively for the salvation of the world, is based on the conviction, witnessed to in the New Testament, that he was the only person who was or has been perfectly and freely obedient to God. It is this belief that is affirmed in the *COF* when it says **Jesus Christ . . . was tempted in every respect as every person is, yet he did not sin. While fully sharing human life, Christ**

continued to be holy, blameless, undefiled, and thoroughly fitted to be the savior of the world, the only hope of reconciliation between God and sinful persons" (3.08).

Truly Human, Truly Divine

The *COF* affirms the belief that Jesus Christ is **truly human and truly divine** (3.08). The meaning of this belief can be approached in two ways, or at two levels. The first, of course, is by listening to the testimony of the earliest followers of Jesus and those who produced the New Testament. The Gospels themselves do not use the words "truly human and truly divine," nor does the remainder of the New Testament (they appear, as we will consider below, in the later theological work of the church). But what is meant by them, and what the later theology seeks to elaborate, is clearly indicated in the writings that comprise the New Testament (especially the Gospel of John and the letters of Paul). Earlier in this chapter we referenced the progression in the original follower's understanding of who Jesus was for them (see footnote 2). In brief, we can say that at least by the time of the completion of what became the New Testament the earliest Christians (mostly Jewish) believed that their encounter with Jesus was at one and the same time an encounter with God. Another way to put it is that in Jesus they were confronted by both human nature and the nature of God; and in a way, in Jesus, that was indivisible. However, nowhere in the New Testament, do they attempt, or offer, what we might call a metaphysical explanation of how this was so. We also might say they were interested in proclaiming rather than explaining. But the impact of Jesus upon them, and the fact to them of his being raised by God and his giving of the Spirit, meant to them that in Jesus they had met not only a man at work but God at work. In Jesus, they experienced a very real human being but they also experienced God.

Consider, now, the second level. With the passing of time (by the third and fourth centuries), the church found itself pressed, from within and without, to explain more fully how it was that Jesus was considered to be both the nature of God and the nature of man in one person. Many attempts at such explanation were put forward by various church theologians, leading to various beliefs and factions within the church as a whole. Those who are interested in the various explanations can consider them by looking at resources (books, encyclopedias, websites, etc.) that deal with "heresies" in this early period of church history. The fact that there were so-called "heresies" implies that at some point what was considered to be an "orthodox" (right-thinking) position was developed. This occurred at the Council of Chalcedon (AD 451). It was this council that "settled" the question of the two natures for subsequent orthodox belief. It should be noted that rather than the language of Hebraic experience (that of the first believers and those close to them who wrote the New Testament) the council employed the language of Greek reason and philosophy. The philosophical methods and language of the Greeks reigned supreme in the intellectual world of the ancient Roman Empire. So it was not unusual, or to be unexpected, that the Christians at this point in time and place would use the same methods and language. The language of the New Testament, of course, was available to them, but not the *experience* of Jesus upon which the language of the New Testament was based. The latter language had affirmed that in meeting Jesus persons also were meeting God. Again, scripture proclaimed this but did not explain how it could be so. The church council's intention was to explain!

As Cumberland Presbyterians, we affirm that Jesus is truly human and truly divine. We do so, however, based upon the New Testament's witness concerning Jesus (among the texts are: Jn. 1:1-4, 14, 3:13-19, 36, 17:1-5; Acts 4:12; Ro. 1:1-6; Col. 2:9-10; 1 Tim. 3:16; He. 2:17-18, 4:15, 7:26-28; 1 Pet. 2:22-25; 1 Jn. 3:5). We acknowledge the history of church councils such as Chalcedon by employing the language "truly human and truly divine." But most Cumberland Presbyterians, at least I believe most, regard the "two natures of Christ" as an affirmation of faith (the faith of the writers of the New Testament upon which our own faith is based) rather than a subject for metaphysical or philosophical speculation. We also, as we read the Gospels and the remainder of the New Testament and seek to follow Jesus, discover that in meeting him and following him we are also meeting God. This is something that is beyond the power of language to fully explain.

Jesus Christ as Willing

About Jesus, the *COF* says **Jesus Christ willingly suffered sin and death for every person** (3.09). **Willingly** is a carefully chosen and important word for our understanding of Jesus. Here we once again are called to consider his *freedom*. A long quotation is in order since I have come across no more concise or impressive way of speaking about this matter. It begins with mentioning that Jesus' own fundamental self designation was as a *servant* of God. "A servant or slave is one who obeys the lord's commands. As one who fulfills the will of another, he is himself *under lordship*, and he is also the *instrument through which the lordship of the other is exercised* over other persons and things. It is important to note that no mere thing could be a servant; the term applies properly and directly only to a human being in a particular kind of relationship to another. A servant is never merely a puppet manipulated by his master: in some sense he freely submits to the will of his lord and to the exercise of lordship over himself. Of course, in most actual servitude there is a strong element of compulsion involved, usually of an economic or political or socio-psychological sort. But it is not compulsion *per se* which defines the lord-servant relationship: it is rather *submission of will*; for it is possible *freely* to become the servant of another.

The disciples remembered Jesus as one who thus freely took up the role of servant. 'I am among you as one who serves' (Lk. 22:27); 'the Son of Man came not to be served but to serve, and to give his life as a ransom for many' (Mt. 20:28). For Jesus, it was precisely service that defined greatness in God's kingdom (Mk. 10:35-45). Jesus, then, was remembered as one who freely and willingly gave up his own wishes and desires to serve God's will; he was one who sacrificed everything that was Jesus (i.e. finite, individual, particular) to the absolute demands of God upon him. And, thus, through making himself a servant in the first sense, through standing under God's lordship, he also became a servant in the second sense: he became the instrument of the divine will among men, and *through him* God's will was done . . . To say Jesus was the servant of God in a preeminent sense—and this is what it means to call him the 'Messiah,' or 'Christ,' or 'Son of God'—is to declare that here a piece of finite reality, a man, has become so transparent, as it were, so that when we look at him we no longer simply see him and his will; we see the *divine will* and the *divine being* whose will is carried out through his acts.

Moreover, this 'transparency' is not something foisted upon him from without, God forcing him to become a servant, predestining or determining him in such a way that he has no choice in the matter. Rather, Jesus himself freely wills to be God's servant. *He could in fact have decided otherwise*—certainly the temptation stories (Mt. 4:1-11, Lk. 4:1-13) and the final struggle in Gethsemane (Mk. 14:32-42) must signify at least this. But, though it involved a personal struggle to do so, he deliberately chose to align his will with God's. Since it was in the concluding days, and even hours, of Jesus' life that his supreme resolve to subordinate his own wishes and desires to God's will was most clearly apparent to his disciples, the passion story became the center and criterion of their memories of him: here he displayed most fully who he was; here he was most of all himself . . . 'nevertheless not what I will, but what thou will' (Mk. 14:36). Jesus was freely the servant of God."[9]

Death of Jesus

Jesus died on a Roman cross as a direct result of his proclamation, in word and deed, of the coming, even now present, kingdom of God. Rather than turn from or abandon this kingdom proclamation, Jesus freely accepted the consequences wrought by those who rejected both it and him. As the *COF* says about Jesus: **on the third day after being crucified** (3.09). Here the *COF* calls us to reflect on the event and meaning of Jesus' death. We can begin with the fact that the writers of the New Testament employed an imaginative array of metaphors, taken from ordinary first century life, to communicate the meaning and saving significance of Jesus' death. Most Cumberland Presbyterian preachers and teachers have drawn upon the following biblical metaphors or images as they have shared the good news of God's saving work in the life and death of Jesus.

- The Financial Image—The scene is a slave market. There sit slaves who have lost their freedom. A man steps up and pays the price (gives ransom money) to purchase their freedom. We are the slaves and Jesus is our redeemer. He pays the price for us to be free. The use of this image is found in Mark 10:45, Rom. 3:24, 1 Cor. 6:20, 7:23, Gal. 3:13, Titus 2:14, 1 Peter 1:18.

- The Military Image—The scene is a battlefield. God and the devil are at war for people whom the devil has stolen from the kingdom of God and carried off to the kingdom of darkness. A warrior from God invades the territory ruled by the devil to bring these people home again where they belong. Jesus is the Victor who delivers us from the realm of darkness and death and brings us into God's realm of light and life. See Col. 1:13, 2:15, 1 Cor.15:24-28.

- The Sacrificial Image—The scene is now a place of worship with a bloody altar where sacrifices are offered. There stand guilty people who deserve God's punishment. A priest comes forward who is a mediator between God and the people. He makes a sacrifice to atone for the people's sin. Blood is shed. And animal life is offered up. But Jesus has offered his own life's blood.

See Mark 12:22-14, John 1:29, Rom. 3:25, 1 Cor. 5:7, also the entire letter to the Hebrews.

- The Legal Image—The scene is now a courtroom. God, the just judge, sits on the bench and people who have broken the law stand before him. They hear the verdict: guilty! They receive the sentence: death! But a righteous man who has obeyed the law perfectly comes and stands by the accused, takes the death penalty on himself, and suffers the consequences of their guilt in their place. The legal imagery is especially important to the Apostle Paul. See Rom. 5:6-11, 2 Cor. 5:16-21, Col. 1:19-20.[10]

The fact that the New Testament witnesses employed these various images points to something important. Each is a metaphor. None can fully explain, and certainly not exhaustively explain, the saving significance of Jesus' death for humankind. No single metaphor could do it for the first witnesses. Satisfactorily explaining the saving significance of Jesus' life and death is like attempting to wrap a gift with a piece of paper that is too small for the job. Each metaphor expresses something important, but each also has limitations. Cumberland Presbyterian preachers and teachers employ each of the metaphors, as scripture does, but will raise no single one to the status of being fully explanatory. Cumberland Presbyterians are certain of the saving significance of Jesus life and death.[11] This fact is beyond question. But the exact "how" of this salvation remains a mystery within the heart of God.

But this leads us to the fact that in the history of the church various elaborate, and sometimes fanciful, theories of the atonement have been advanced. Our desire to explain what cannot be fully explained has been persistent. Four basic theories have exercised the greatest influence upon the thought and life of the church in the western world, and therefore upon the Cumberland Presbyterian Church. These four theories have been summarized as follows:

- The Ransom Theory—This theory originated in the early church and is particularly associated with Origen (182-253). The theory argues that the death of Christ was a ransom, usually said to have been made to Satan but in some views paid to God the Father. The payment was in satisfaction for the bondage and debt of the souls of humanity as a result of inherited sin. Adam and Eve, it was said, sold humanity over to the devil at the time of the Fall. Justice required that grace pay the devil a ransom to free us from the devil's clutches. God, however, tricked the devil into accepting the death of Christ as a ransom because the devil did not realize that Christ could not be held in the bonds of death. Once the devil accepted Christ's death as a ransom justice was satisfied and God was able to free us from the devil's grip.

- The Moral Influence Theory—This theory was formulated by Peter Abelard (1079-1142). He suggested the purpose and result of Christ's death was to influence mankind toward moral improvement. This theory denies that Christ died to satisfy any principle of divine justice, but instead that his death was designed to greatly impress mankind with a sense of god's love resulting in softening their hearts and leading them to repentance. Thus the atonement is not directed toward God with the purpose of maintaining his justice, but toward man with the purpose of persuading him toward right action.

- The Satisfaction Theory—This view was propounded by the great theologian Anselm of Canterbury (1033-1109). He said human beings cannot render to God more than is due to him. The satisfaction due to God was greater than what all created beings are capable of doing. Therefore, God had to make satisfaction for himself. Yet, if this satisfaction was going to avail for humans, it had to be made by a human. Therefore only a being that was both God and man could satisfy the honor that is due to God. Anselm regarded human sin as defrauding God of the honor that God deserved. Christ's death, the, ultimate act of obedience, gave God proper honor. As this was beyond the call of duty for Christ, it was more honor than he was obliged to give. Christ's surplus can therefore cover our deficit. Hence Christ's death is a substitution for us. He pays the honor to God that we could not.

- The Penal Substitution Theory—In the 16th century Protestant, Martin Luther and John Calvin were the leading exponents of this theory. The main point is that Christ died on the cross as a substitute for sinners. God imputed the guilt of our sins to Christ and he, in our place, bore the punishments we deserve. This was a full payment for sins which satisfied both the wrath of God and the righteousness of God. God can now forgive sinners without compromising his own holy standards. The Reformers believed that Anselm's theory of substitution was correct but insufficient. The especially believed it was not God's honor that had to be satisfied, but his holiness and righteousness. This view says that in Christ's death he took on himself the punishment that sinners rightly deserved. This set the sinner free from the penal demands of the law. The righteousness of the law and the holiness of God were satisfied by this substitution.[12]

The Penal Substitution Theory and the Confession of 1984

The Penal Substitution Theory was famously codified by and for Presbyterians in the *Westminster Confession* of 1647.

As such, it has exerted the greatest influence on the Presbyterian and Reformed traditions, but also very likely has been the dominant theory of the atonement in the Western world. It was the theology of atonement implicit in the previous Confessions of the Cumberland Presbyterian Church. However, as has already been discussed, it is not the theology of atonement expressed in the *COF* of 1984. This is because the penal substitution theory was part and parcel of the two covenant theology discussed in the previous chapter. The *COF* of 1984 rejected the two-covenant understanding in favor of embracing the one covenant of grace. This necessarily has had profound significance for Cumberland Presbyterian understanding Jesus' death on the cross and the manner in which it has saving power (Rom. 1:16).

Hubert Morrow comments on this as follows: "The interpretation of the death of Jesus as a legal satisfaction of the demands of the law belongs in a theology in which a covenant of law is primary, in which persons understand their relationship to God in a legal rather than a personal sense. Such a theology defines salvation as God's act of legal acquittal of persons under the penalty of death by accepting the death of Jesus the Christ as a substitute. This is a legalistic substitutionary theory of the atonement. A theology based wholly on a covenant of grace understands the meaning of the death of Christ in terms of grace rather than law......What God has done and does in the death of Jesus the Christ is not to exact a penalty required by law, but to seek reconciliation with sinful persons through suffering, sacrificial love. This is so because the covenant that binds God to the human family is a covenant of grace rather than law. Accordingly, the key word in the Confession is reconciliation not satisfaction. Salvation is the restoration of personal relationship, not the fulfillment of the requirements of the law (3.01, 3.02, 3.07, 3.08, 3.11)."[13]

For reasons set forth earlier, I would like to see more work done on a theory of the death of Jesus, the atonement, as being a proclamation of the kingdom of God. The Gospel writers may hint at this meaning in the report of the ironic decision by Pilate to have a sign placed above the head of Jesus announcing in three languages that he was the king of the Jews. But all theories are just that—theories. They are attempts to explore the meaning of the death of Jesus in terms of God's project to save the world. As with the images employed in the New Testament, none of the theories of the atonement have full explanatory power. Each points toward a truth of the atonement, but none fully explains it. The Cumberland Presbyterian Church, and its Confession, has no official theory of the meaning of the atonement.

I have found that many Cumberland Presbyterians have been grateful to learn that the penal substitution theory is just one theory, and that our *COF* does not endorse it. They have been relieved to be freed from thinking of the death of Jesus as being demanded by God in order to placate God's anger against sin. Others have been grateful that the Cumberland Presbyterian one covenant of grace theology takes the violence out of the atonement (that God "needed" or "required" a death to satisfy his righteousness). Others have come to see that the power of God revealed in the cross is the power to become vulnerable and to enter into solidarity with the suffering of the world. It has been easier for some to come to see that the cross is not only that which Christ endured for us, in his proclamation of the kingdom, but also a way for us to live, a way we must live, in the world as signs of God's kingdom. While the cross is uniquely something that Christ has done for us, it is also the pattern for the Christian's life in the world. In the end, many have seen the wisdom in affirming that we do not know exactly how the cross of Jesus has saving significance for ourselves, for all of humanity, and the entire cosmos, only that it does so! About this, Cumberland Presbyterians are absolutely certain.

I close this section with two quotes on the theological meaning of the death of Jesus. "Jesus . . . died not in the consequence of his own sin, but in consequence of the world's sin. The evil which afflicted him was not of his own making. Rather, his death was the point where the world's alienation from God came into focus and showed both its reality and power. Consequently, it is true to say, morally speaking, that in his passion and execution, Jesus carried the sin of the world. He was associated with his world in its alienation from God; and that sin is the inner meaning of his death. He dies the death of his world. But God raised him; and this news compels yet a further and more considered look at the Cross. Jesus bore the sin of his world; but that sin did not have its ultimate effect. It did not cut Jesus off from God, or frustrate God's design—the design which Jesus' ministry had proclaimed and expressed. On the contrary, the death of Jesus led to Resurrection. It brought about the opening of the new age in him. *If his death frustrated anything, then, what it frustrated was sin.* The dying of Jesus seems to have neutralized the effect and the power of his world's estrangement from God. In the light of the Resurrection, the execution of Jesus can only appear as God's way of bringing sin to nothing—of short-circuiting it . . . (The Cross) was not sin's victory over God. On the contrary it was God's victory over sin. Jesus' death was the way in which God drew off the power of sin to make way for the new life of the Resurrection. The Cross is, strangely and mysteriously, a scene of triumph."[14]

And, "The trans-valuating miracle which is so difficult for men to believe is that God's power is really 'made perfect in and through (human) weakness' (2 Cor. 12:9), that it is really through what is weak and lowly and despised in the world that God overcomes the strong and powerful (1 Cor. 1:27-28), that is, when one is weak he is really strong (2 Cor. 12:10). If such notions are true—and this is surely what it means to say that ultimate reality is manifest in that image of a helpless man dying on a cross—then man's contrary worldly wisdom is sheer foolishness (1 Cor. 1:20); and life should no longer be ordered by it. To be Christian one must bring whatever the world teaches, whether it call its teaching secular or garb it in the pious robes of the church, to the cross for evaluation. . .the ultimate standard of judgment and life is the historical event through which God has decisively manifested himself, and no traditions or interpretations of men must be allowed to displace it."[15]

The Resurrection

"Christ is risen! He is risen indeed!" On Easter Sunday mornings, these words express the faith of Cumberland Presbyterians. The *COF* says: **On the third day after being crucified, Christ was raised from the dead** (3.09). As already discussed, without the resurrection there would be no written Gospels (or *the* Gospel) or any of the remainder of the New Testament. The authors of the Gospels did not tell stories about Jesus, including his tragic death, and then proceed or feel compelled to invent a happy ending to a very sad story. It was the other way around. The resurrection gave rise to faith and the eventual recording of the story of Jesus. James Alison writes about the apostolic witness to the resurrection and makes a surprisingly important point: "Now, please note, that witness is not merely a witness to the fact of the resurrection, though it certainly is that. It is not merely saying: yes, we can affirm that on such and such a day, the dead man Jesus of Nazareth did in fact rise from the dead. They *are* saying that. Paul says that in 1 Corinthians 15:3-8: 'I handed on to you . . . . he was raised on the third day in accordance with the scriptures, and that he appeared to Cephas. . . .' But even more than bearing witness *to* an event, as you or I might witness a traffic accident, they are witnesses *from* the resurrection. That is to say that it was a happening which profoundly changed them, not only turning pusillanimous fisher-folk into international heroes and martyrs, but causing them to rethink the whole of their lives, their relationship with their homeland, their culture, its values, and radically altering their understanding of who God is."[16]

Since we have just considered the death of Jesus, it is important to remember that the resurrection is the resurrection of the crucified Christ. This means that the church is in the world as witness to the resurrected Christ who is also and always the crucified one. There is no warrant for the church to think, or believe, that since that Jesus has been raised from the dead the cross is behind him, or us, resulting in what has been called a "theology of glory." The resurrection does not mean that the church can leave the cross behind. After all, what God gives back to Jesus in the resurrection is the whole of his life, *including his death.* The authentic church, then, will live in the world by way of a "theology of the cross." The church will live the way of the sacrificial, suffering, self-donating love of its crucified but risen Lord. The church affirms that the resurrection was God's vindication of the life and way of Jesus and his embodiment and proclamation of the kingdom of God. As Mark Thomsen has written, "The resurrection confirms that the way and word of Jesus, which culminates in his resurrection, is God's way of being active and present in the world. God's identity is defined not out of a philosophical tradition but in Jesus' living and Jesus' dying."[17]

Resurrection Train—from a Sermon

On Wednesday I drove to Huntsville by way of Gurley. At Gurley, I had an experience that I have had on several occasions. The experience always startles me. I was driving along with cruise control set on fifty-five. I was playing soft music on the radio, but not really noticing it. I was having the last cup of *COF*fee for the day, and I was enjoying the beauty of spring time in the Tennessee Valley. I was lost in my thoughts. It was the kind quiet time that we introverts treasure, actually lust after. And then it happened!

Off to my right, there was the sudden blast of an oncoming freight train. The tracks run parallel to the road and the train is only about twenty yards away. It sounded as if the train would be the sudden end of me! I jump in my seat, the coffee goes flying from the cup, and I yell out. . .I am not going to tell you what I yelled out. Although I have had this experience a score or more of times, it always stuns me.

Here we are on Easter Sunday. It is the great festival of our Lord's resurrection. We have just read of the disciples' experience on that first Easter morning. They go to a quiet garden. It is the place of a tomb. It is one of the quietest places imaginable. They are lost in their thoughts. And their thoughts are sad ones, grief stricken ones. But, suddenly, right in the middle of that cemetery there is the blast of an oncoming train. It is God's glory train. It startled the first disciples, taking them completely by surprise. Maybe it is impossible to experience Easter if we are incapable of being surprised.

Easter in Buckhead—from a Sermon

When Linda, my wife, worked as a sales representative, she invited me to go with her to Atlanta to attend a training meeting. She would attend sessions in the day and I would read, loaf, and otherwise do nothing. It was an offer I could not refuse, and turned out to include an experience that I will never forget. The people who hosted the event invited the participants and their spouses, or companions, to a dinner. It was at a Greek restaurant located in Buckhead. It was a delightful evening, one of those rare slow, easy, two hour dinners. I had lamb for the first time.

There was after dinner entertainment. A band played Greek music for about fifteen minutes. Then an authentic Greek belly dancer appeared on stage. She performed an eye-popping routine that lasted for about thirty minutes. She then danced her way off the stage and down into the audience. She danced from table to table with a long chiffon scarf around her neck. She teased person after person with a request to join her in a belly dancing lesson. Then she came toward me! She placed the scarf around my neck and up I went. What else could I do? I was the lucky candidate who would be taught to belly dance. I remember having two random thoughts. First, I wondered what my seventy-five year old mother would think about what was about to happen? And, secondly, sometimes you are simply in the right place at the right time!

I shook parts of my body that I believe had never been shaken. And then there was more fun. The dancer invited everyone to join in forming a belly dancing train. I placed my hands on her hips. My wife placed her hands on my hips. And about twenty to thirty people joined in the train. For the next ten minutes, we danced around the restaurant in a mildly riotous manner.

I tell you this because this experience has become my personal gold standard metaphor for the resurrection of our Lord. It seems to me that Easter means that God, freely and graciously, has put the scarf of the resurrected Christ around our necks (hearts) and drawn us into the dance of God's life—the joyful dance of the Holy Trinity. The inner life of the Trinity has been described in just this way—a divine dance (perichoresis). But we, like the first disciples, were not expecting this. We were not prepared for it. We could never have imagined it. But now we are dancing. And we are being led in the dance by the Master Dancer. I am sure each of you has a metaphor for Easter. That night in Buckhead is mine.

The Ascension of Jesus

Christ was raised from the dead and **afterward ascended to God** (3.09). The ascension of Jesus is an event recorded in Luke 24 and Acts 1. As such, it is an event that is more assumed in the New Testament than described. As for the meaning of the ascension, it reveals Jesus' exaltation to the right hand of God (Acts. 2:33). Jesus is exalted because he is the righteous one (Jn. 16:10) and he is entitled to the restored glory that he had with the Father before the world was made (Jn. 17:5). The ascension declares Christ's enthronement as cosmic ruler. Using the language of Psalms 68 and 110, the apostle Paul announced Christ's victory over all the principalities and powers that had been vying for world dominion. Christ is enthroned at their expense (Eph. 1:20-23; 4:8-10). The enthronement is for the sake of the church of which Christ is the head (Eph. 1:22) and it is the source of abundant blessings because the enthroned king gives gifts to his people (Eph. 4:8ff). These gifts enable the church to attain 'to the measure of the stature of the fullness of Christ" (Eph. 4:13).[18]

From a Sermon on the Ascension—Psalm 96, Ephesians 1:15-23, Luke 24:44-53

Once a year, in May, I join seven or eight other Cumberland Presbyterian pastors for a week of trout fishing on the White River near Mountain Home, Arkansas. One year my absence was especially disconcerting to my then three year old granddaughter, Rose. Linda told me that on her days for visiting us she went through the house asking, "Where is Pop?" Then, on Sunday at the church, she went into my office and again asked, "Where is Pop?" She was especially disturbed when I was not in my normal place in the pulpit. My wife did her best to explain where I was but Rose was still troubled. Linda told me that on the night she usually stays with us, and right before falling asleep, she put her head on my pillow and said, "Pop, Pop." My wife told me these things only when I returned. Otherwise, my trip would have been considerably shortened that year!

The Gospels and other New Testament writings were written decades after the life of Jesus on earth. New generations of Christians would hear the wonderful story of Jesus and then would ask, "But where is he now?" The answer given was Jesus has ascended to the very throne of God. He brought God to earth in his incarnation and now he had taken humanity into heaven with his ascension. Jesus brought God to us and now Jesus has taken us to God. And now he is reigning at the right hand of his Father.

Psalm 96, that we have heard read this morning, is known as an enthronement psalm. When a new Jewish king came along, he would be enthroned in Jerusalem complete with festive liturgy and songs such as our psalm. The accounts of Jesus' ascension are intended to say that King Jesus has now been enthroned. His earthly throne had been a cross. His earthly crown had been made of thorns. But now his throne is eternal in the heavens. This is who Jesus is for us now and where Jesus is for us now.

In the epistle lesson for today (Ephesians 1:15-23), the author provides a theological reflection on the meaning of Jesus' ascension. He is now the cosmic Christ who reigns as Lord over all creation. This passage proclaims the lordship of Christ over the church and over all the powers of the created order. The following is taken from a commentary on this text: "Even though Christ may be seen as having cosmic dominion, his exalted lordship is most properly defined and experienced with reference to the church, here conceived as 'his body' (v. 23). Once again, our minds are being stretched to think of the 'body of Christ' in terms greater than his physical body, his crucified body, even his resurrected body. He now is seen to have a corporate existence large enough, expansive enough, to incorporate the existence and identity of hosts of others, those 'in Christ.' Obviously, the church is being conceived here in terms larger than the congregation, but also larger than the 'church universal' in the sense that the latter represents the sum of all living communities of faith on earth. It is rather a reality that extends into the 'heavenly places' (vs. 20) where Christ is. We are being summoned to think of Christ in the most comprehensive sense possible, as the One who encompasses all reality as we know it, as the One who brooks no rivals, as the One who has transcended both time and space and in doing so has redefined both."[11]

The Gospel lesson for today, Luke 24:44-53, is a narrative telling of the ascension of Jesus. Jesus lifts his hands in blessing upon those gathered near him and then ascends into heaven. Here we may find an expression of the church's true nature, an ecclesiological theology if you will. It is that as the church we exist on earth to lift our hands in blessing in the name of Christ. This world is a place in which there is a great deal of cursing. There is the cursing of life and the cursing of persons. But the church lives under the outstretched arms of her Lord. The church will fulfill the ancient promise to Abraham that God's people will be a blessing to the nations. This promise is brought to perfect expression in the life of Jesus. This promise continues to be fulfilled as the Spirit of the Christ enables and empowers the church to lift its arms in blessing upon others. It is not the blessing of the church so much as it is the blessing of the Lord of the church through the church. I remember reading somewhere the story of a young girl who was mesmerized as a pastor lifted his arms to pronounce a benediction at the end of worship. The girl turned and whispered, "See, Mommy, he is trying to look just like Jesus." So may it be for all of us who live under the blessing of the outstretched arms of the ascended Lord.

The Giving of the Spirit

The penultimate comment of the *COF* about Christ the Savior is . . . **through the Holy Spirit, people are able to acknowledge and repent of their sin, believe in Jesus Christ as Savior, and follow Christ as Lord. Believer's experience Christ's presence and guidance, which helps them to overcome the powers of evil in ways consistent with God's nature and will"** (3.10). This statement remembers that the *totality* of the life of Jesus included his promise and gift of the Holy Spirit. The saving work of God in and through the Holy Spirit is the subject of the next chapter.

James Alison beautifully summarizes the heart of what it means that, following his resurrection, Jesus gave the Holy Spirit to his followers, and to us: "In Luke (Acts 2) the Father sends the Holy Spirit from on high. In John (20:19-23), Jesus breathes the Holy Spirit upon his disciples, but in both cases the Holy Spirit is the Spirit of the risen Lord, the Spirit that was in Christ. The Spirit constantly makes present the crucified and risen Lord, thus perpetually reproducing those changes of relationship which the risen Lord had started to produce as a result of his resurrection. What I am trying to say is that outside the group of apostles who were physical witnesses to the resurrected Lord, no one gets to see the physically risen Lord. But, instead, all the really important elements of the resurrection—the irruption into our lives of gratuity as forgiveness, permitting a recasting of all relationships—all of this is made constantly available to us by the Holy Spirit, so that we are able to become witnesses to the resurrection in our own lives. . .Suffice it to say that what the Holy Spirit brings is the whole life and death of the risen Lord, reproducing that life in the lives and deaths of the faithful, so that they become witnesses to that risen life and death."[19]

The *COF*'s final statement in this section is. . .**God's work of reconciliation in Jesus Christ occurred at a particular time and place. Yet its powers extend to the believer in all ages from the beginning of the world. It is communicated by the Holy Spirit and through such instruments as God is pleased to employ** (3.11). We might begin to unwind this statement by considering that God's saving work on behalf of the world began with and in the history of Israel. It began with the call of Abraham, continued in and through the Exodus and giving of the Law at Sinai, the establishment of the nation Israel and eventual exile, and in and through the history and ministry of the prophets. God's saving work, then, can be understood as having been particularized in history—in the history of a particular people.

But in Jesus Christ, things have been changed. Now God's saving work, first in the history of Israel and then in the person, life, death and resurrection of Jesus (Mk. 15:24-37), has been *universalized*. Its saving powers now extend to the believer in all ages and from the beginning of the world. This last statement represents the way in which the person-event of Jesus Christ became decisive for the disciples' (and the writers of the New Testament) understanding of God's saving action. They were certain that the benefits of what had occurred in the life and ministry of Jesus would extend forward into the future. But they also were able to think of it, in some sense, as extending backward in history (Gal. 3:6-8; 1 Cor. 1:1-4).

As already mentioned above, the early Christians knew themselves as now living under the presence and guidance of the Holy Spirit (Jn. 3:5-8, 6:63; Ro. 8:11). This Spirit had made them "ministers of the new covenant" (2 Cor. 3:4-6). Proclaiming the universal message of salvation in and through Christ (Jn. 3:16), and living as a community that signed and signaled this salvation, now animated their lives. The Spirit was communicating the message of God's salvation through them. This included through the use of the many gifts the Spirit had given to the members of the church (1 Cor. 12:4-11). Perhaps this latter truth is part of what is meant when the *COF* says that God communicates the saving message by the Holy Spirit. . .**and through such instruments as God is pleased to employ** (3.11).

Finally, the entire *COF* is guided and informed by John: 3:16, "For God so loved the world, that he gave his only begotten Son, that whoever believes in him should not perish, but have eternal life." In light of this, an interesting observation comes from those modern, and post-modern, philosophers who have carefully studied the ancient philosophical and religious world (and all known peoples and societies were, in fact, religious in some form). Namely, among all the means for the achievement of salvation known and present in the ancient world the Christian claim was utterly original and unique. People might be saved from their fears, mistakes, and so on in any number of ways. But only within the the Hebrew tradition, and more especially with the appearance of the Hebrew named Jesus, was it claimed that human beings are to be, and can be, and finally will be saved *by an unconditional love*.[20]

God Acts Through the Holy Spirit

(4.01—4.29 in the Confession of Faith)

Chapter Eleven

THE CALL AND WORK OF THE HOLY SPIRIT

The county in Alabama in which I live, Jackson, is located in the foothills of the Appalachian Mountains. Its geological make-up is such that it has become a favorite destination for cavers (spelunkers) from throughout the region and across the nation. There are about a thousand known non-commercial caves in the county. At a meeting of the Rotary Club, an experienced caver was our speaker. In part of his talk, he told us of how he once, very foolishly, violated a cardinal rule of caving: namely, never go alone! He attributed his disregard of the rule to the arrogance and ego of youth. He entered a cave and explored it for the better part of a day. Then, he discovered, to his horror, that he had lost his way. He frantically searched for the way out until, after a couple of hours, he sat down in exhaustion, anxiety, and mild despair. There is, of course a happy ending to this story or he wouldn't have been there to tell us about it! He had been obedient to a second cardinal rule of caving: let someone else know where you are going and the time you expect to return home. Thankfully, he had told these things to his wife. When he was a more than an hour late in returning, she called the appropriate people and after some hours of searching they found him and led him to safety. He was convinced that without their quick response, their initiative, his survival would have been uncertain.

The Human Condition

Everything that the *COF* says about God acting in the Holy Spirit is predicated on two biblical presuppositions. The first is that we human beings are, to use one important biblical image, *lost*. We may not believe this about ourselves, we may deny it, ignore it, or reject it outright, but it *is* the biblical account of our human condition. Scripture speaks about this condition with many other images, and to list only a few: we are blind, in exile, in bondage, we have closed hearts, we hunger and thirst (we are starving) and, most graphically, we are dead. We have missed the mark or the goal of our existence; we have deviated from the path of life; we are rebels against a rightful and loving King; and we are traitors to the goodness of God (see Rom. 3:10-18). The fact that we find these descriptions unpalatable, or unduly negative, or antiquated, or merely religious babble, or unacceptable is indicative, in scripture's view, of our truly desperate situation—we are totally unable to help ourselves, extricate ourselves, out from this condition. Unlike the caver in the story above, we are so lost that we may not even know that we are lost. We may consider our situation to be normal, human, simply the way things are, and the way things will continue to be.

Morrow writes, "Unless one takes this radical human predicament seriously, all talk about the call of God the Holy Spirit is pointless."[1] And he writes, "The human predicament is what Scripture calls 'being dead in sin' and without hope in the world (see Eph. 2:1-2; Col. 2:13). A most graphic picture of this human condition is found in the thirty seventh chapter of Ezekiel, the vision of the valley of dry bones. In this graveyard, the dead people say, 'Our bones are dried up, and our hope is lost; we are cut off completely' (Ez. 37:11). Whether or not these dead persons will live again is at God's discretion. Simply put, people who are in bondage to sin and death *can't make the first move* (italics mine)."[2] The situation of human beings is such that we have neither the *desire* nor the *ability* to come to God. It is like the title of an old movie I recently watched on cable television: *No Way Out*. There is literally no way out for human beings—no method of self-salvation, self-improvement, or self-transformation that can overcome our desperate condition. We cannot find our way out of the cave.

The second biblical declaration that undergirds every word in the *COF*'s treatment of God working through the Holy Spirit is this: God, in freedom and love, has chosen to do for human beings what they have neither the desire nor ability to do for them-selves. This, of course, is the story the Bible tells about God from the very beginning and all throughout. God in the history of Israel, the history of Jesus Christ, and the history of the Holy Spirit is the God who takes the *initiative* to be in a movement toward human beings. It is a movement aimed at overcoming our abuse of freedom and consequently our bondage to sin. Israel understood this: "The Lord did not set his love upon you, nor choose you, because you were more in number than any people. . .But because the Lord loved you. . .has the Lord brought you out" (Dt. 7:7-8).

I once heard a sermon on the parable told by Jesus that is recorded in Matthew 20:1-16. It is the parable about the landowner who went in search of laborers for his vineyard. Throughout the parable, the landowner makes repeated trips to town to find more laborers. Shockingly, at the end of the day, the landowner pays the same wages to those who were hired at the end of the day as he does to those who were hired early in the morning. A footnote in my Bible says that the parable represents a challenge to conventional views about what constitutes a just reward. The preacher acknowledged this but also asked us to think of the landowner as a picture of God; a God who makes trip after trip, who is relentless in his search for laborers to work in his vineyard. The God of the Bible is a God who keeps coming toward us. God comes to the Hebrew people who were bond-slaves in Egypt and comes in the entire history of Israel; God comes in Jesus the Christ and in the history of the church; and God comes *still* in the Holy Spirit. In all of these comings, God is at work doing for us what it is impossible for us to do for ourselves.

With this in mind, we are better able to understand what is claimed both about human beings and about God in this section of the *COF*. About God, a key word is "grace:" **"God's grace," "saving grace," "God's grace in Jesus Christ," "covenant of grace,"** and **"means of grace."** What is meant by this word? One writer answers this question by also saying what grace is not: "Grace is both the activity of the Holy Spirit and the effects of that activity (Ro. 5:5). What grace is not, though, is a 'something,' a special kind of stuff or substance, which God confers on people. Christians have ways of talking which seem to suggest this sort of thing: as, for example, when people speak of 'having grace,' or 'being given grace,' or 'praying for grace.' Such language seems to imply that there really is a kind of spiritual medicine called 'grace,' which is not unlike a vitamin, and which God injects into people to brace them up keep them going. To conceive of the matter in this way, however, is simply to be led astray by the ambiguities of words. *Grace is not something other than God which he prescribes to us as a moral tonic. Grace is nothing more or less than God communicating himself to creatures. More specifically, it is God himself dwelling within people as the Holy Spirit and working in them their identity in Christ*" (italics mine).[3] Grace, then, is not a 'thing' but it is God coming to us in Jesus Christ and the Holy

Spirit and, as the *COF* will stress, God dwelling with us and within us as the Holy Spirit. The Holy Spirit continues the ministry of God's coming to us in Jesus Christ.

The Call and Work of the Holy Spirit

In the summers of my early youth in the 1950s, several boys from our neighborhood, including me, would eat breakfast and then head for the nearby pasture that served as our make-shift baseball field. Usually we would stay all day, skipping lunch, and play until nearly sundown. We knew without fail when it was time to go home. We knew because our friend Junior's mother, Mrs. Gothard, would stand on her front porch and yell at the top of her lungs, sounding like a bull horn, "Junior! . . . Junior Gothard! Get your bottom home (only Mrs. Gothard often used a more graphic word for Junior's posterior). It was the daily signal not only for Junior but for all of us. We picked up our bats, balls, and gloves and we headed home. We had heard the all important call!

The *COF* says **God acted redemptively in Jesus Christ because of the sins of the world and continues with the same intent in the Holy Spirit to call every person to repentance and faith** (4.01). The God of Israel is a God who calls. When Adam and Eve were hiding in the garden, hiding from God because of their disobedience, God called to them, "Where are you?" (Gen. 3:9). God called Abraham and Sarah. God called Moses. God called Elijah and Deborah. God called Isaiah,

Jeremiah, Amos and Hosea. God's call came to young Mary. Jesus began his public ministry by calling disciples. The fact of God's calling is such a significant biblical theme for the Apostle Paul that some scholars argue that "calling" is the key to understanding his entire theological program (as opposed, for example, to the idea that "justification by faith" is the theological center of his message). It *is* the most frequent one-word description used by the apostle to describe believers: The believers in Rome (1:6, 7); Corinth (1 Cor. 1:2); Galatia (Gal. 1:6); Ephesus (Eph. 4:1,4); Philippi (Phil. 3:13-14); Colossae (Col. 3:15); and Thessalonica (2 Thess. 1:11) are all designated as "called ones."[4] The God of the Bible is a God who calls. God calls people out of bondage to sin and into covenant life and relationship. God in Christ called people to the same. And God the Spirit, who is the Spirit promised and given by the crucified but risen Christ, still calls people to the same.

The Christian life cannot begin without the Spirit's calling. The *COF* says **the call precedes all desire, purpose, and intention of the sinner to come to Christ. While it is possible for all to be saved with it, none can be saved without it** (4.03). If we are Christians, it is because we have heard the call of God through the ministry of the Holy Spirit. We do not "find God", or come to God, as a result of our own choosing or initiative. An "I can do it myself" psychology finds no place in scripture.

When the *COF* says God the Holy Spirit calls **"every person"** to repentance and faith (the meaning of these words will be discussed in subsequent chapters), we can hear an echo of one way in which Cumberland Presbyterian theology differs from some older Reformed and Presbyterian theologies (particularly elements of Calvinism). Our belief is that God the Spirit's call is universal in scope rather than only particular and limited. We *do not* believe that the Spirit calls only some and fails to call others. We believe that the call of the Holy Spirit is to and for every person. We also can hear an echo of the older theological debates when the *COF* says **persons may resist and reject this call of the Holy Spirit** (4.04). Cumberland Presbyterians do not believe that the call of the Holy Spirit is irresistible (Acts 7:51, and see Isa. 65:12; 66:4; Jer. 7:13, 16; 35:17). This belief is based on the conviction that God's love expressed in the one covenant of grace includes respect for the freedom of the beloved. God will not force persons into relationship for such force does not, and cannot, belong to the essence of love. The tradition teaches us, especially in the life of Jesus, that God gives without dominating. Domination is no part of love.

God is persistent in calling (Rom. 3:23-26). **Whoever will, therefore, may be saved, but not apart from the illuminating influence of the Holy Spirit** (4.03). "God faces a situation in which persons created in the divine image have neither desire, purpose, nor intention to honor God nor to give thanks to God.

The situation calls for what the Confession describes as the 'illuminating influence of the Holy Spirit.' *The call of the Holy Spirit seeks to penetrate human rebellion and self-deception, and to lay bare the true human predicament. This is the initial and necessary stage of God's work of redemption*" (italics mine).[5]

The *COF* says **the call and work of the Holy Spirit is solely of God's grace and is not a response to human merit** (4.03). This statement means that Cumberland Presbyterians do not consider salvation to be a "joint work" between God and persons (as in Arminianism). Salvation, rather, is entirely of God's initiative and God's free grace. It is altogether the gift of God to sinful persons. What about the question of faith? Isn't faith a necessary contribution to salvation made by persons? The Cumberland Presbyterian view is that even faith is a gift from God (Eph. 2:1-10; Titus 3:4-5). Trusting (faith) in God is made possible by the gracious inward work of the Holy Spirit. As the *COF* says, **Faith is a gift made possible through God's love and initiative** (4.09). The *COF* announces a great mystery and an equally great miracle when saying **persons may resist and reject this call of the Holy Spirit, but for all who respond with repentance and trustful acceptance of God's love in Christ, there is salvation and life"** (4.04).

The Confession speaks of the ordinary means, or instruments, through which the Holy Spirit works to call people:

These are: **the scriptures, the sacraments, the corporate worship of the covenant community, the witness of believers in word and deed, and in ways beyond human understanding** (4.02). "It has always been assumed by the church and the theologians of the church seeking to understand the mystery of the continuous reenactment of the event of revelation—that the possibility of this reenactment (of, say, a man or woman of the (present century): 'encountering God in Jesus Christ,' 'being born again,' 'being grasped by the power of the New Being,' or 'coming to faith,'—there are many possible ways of expressing it—depends on the continuing and active presence of God within both the life of the community and the life of the individual. For both the establishment and the presence of a deep relationship to God and of 'faith' require the presence of God and not just the words (however persuasive), the actions (however loving), or even the life (however noble) of another person. Thus, it has from the very beginning been affirmed that the power of the Word, of sacrament, and of a loving life either to establish or preserve the faith of persons in the community lay, not primarily in the abilities of the members of the community, but lay in the *working of the Holy Spirit* (italics mine) in the community and through these media. It is the Holy Spirit resident in the community that continues the original revelation over time, that empowers the believing community to be the preaching, worshiping, and loving 'Church' (whenever it *is* that), and that relates and re-relates each person and each generation of Christians to God."[6]

Morrow adds important words about what the *COF* means when speaking of the fact that God works in "**in ways beyond human understanding**:" "The Confession urges Christians to be sensitive to the mystery of God the Holy Spirit in the world. In particular, Christians should resist the tendency to look no further than ordinary means as instruments of the Holy Spirit. Before Peter ever arrived in Caesarea, God the Holy Spirit has been calling Cornelius *through means never identified*. Cornelius had already begun to respond to the call of God. Through Peter the Holy Spirit put the finishing touches on the call. Every person who seeks to be a witness to the Gospel should remember that before he or she ever speaks to a person, the Holy Spirit has already been calling that person in ways beyond human understanding."[7] Long ago, at the end of long summer days, I responded when Mrs. Gothard called Junior and the rest of us to come home. The work of God the Holy Spirit is to call every person home to a saving knowledge and experience of Jesus Christ; and to obedient life in the one covenant of grace (Rev. 22:17).

Excursus: The Broader Work of the Holy Spirit

Before going on to discuss, in the following several chapters, what the *COF* continues to say about the work of God the Holy Spirit, I consider it important to set the *COF*'s treatment of the Spirit into a larger context. It is, of course, notable that the *COF* of 1984 focuses on two important works of the Spirit: namely the Spirit's work in the salvation of persons (sinners) and, as will be seen in later chapters, in their continuing growth toward maturity in Christ. Both, to say the very least, are important for our theological understanding and life of faith and service. But, as will be discussed below, the Holy Spirit's work, as witnessed in the Bible, is much broader than what is covered in the statements of the *COF*.

The question might be raised: "Why did the authors of the *COF*, and the church's ratification of their work, choose to treat the work of the Holy Spirit in a limited way?" Of course, it is highly improbable that any confession, produced by any church, can cover everything. Confessions, after all, are at best intended as accurate but summary statements. But there is a more substantial answer to the question. It is found, I believe, by considering the history and general pattern of older Presbyterian and Reformed confessions. The pattern was worked out largely by and through the efforts of the 17th and 18th century church theologians known as the Protestant Scholastics. The pattern found expression in the various confessions they helped produce some centuries ago.

The Scholastics were concerned to systematize the teachings of the Bible. Their goal was to order the varied teachings in a logical and coherent way. When considering the work of the Holy Spirit, they focused, laser-like, on the Spirit's activity in the salvation of individual persons. This focus was not only the fruit of their biblical studies. It was also the result of the new appraisal of the importance of the individual that marked their moment in history. In an earlier chapter, I mentioned that the European Enlightenment (17th and 18th centuries) had placed the individual, in an unprecedented way, in the forefront of common intellectual thought. And this thought also became popular thought. Earlier, in the 16th century Protestant Reformation, the reformers had, partially in light of the spirit of the times, had placed the individual in the forefront of theological thought. The Scholastics followed suit and worked out what became known as the "order of salvation" (*ordo salutis*). It explained the work of the Holy Spirit has being directed to the salvation of individual persons. This order became the standard pattern by which Presbyterian and Reformed confessions set forth the doctrine of the Holy Spirit.

What is the order of salvation? It is the Spirit's work in the calling, convicting, converting, saving, justifying, sanctifying, assuring, and preserving of sinners. It broke down the work of the Spirit (a work, by the way, that in real life experience can hardly be compartmentalized in this fashion) into a scheme, progression, or order. One Reformed theologian says, "The order of salvation describes the process in which the work of salvation, wrought in Christ, is subjectively realized in the hearts and lives of sinners. It aims at describing, in their logical order and in their inter-relations, the various movements of the Holy Spirit in the application of the work of redemption."[8] The Cumberland Presbyterian Church began its life, of course, under one of the confessions produced by the Scholastics (Westminster of 1647). And it continued, when developing its own confessions (1813, 1883), to maintain the order or pattern found in the older confessions. The early CP confessions spoke of the work of the Holy Spirit under the heading of "Divine Influence." Joe Ben Irby writes, "By *divine influence* CPs meant that essential universal operation of the Holy Spirit based on the universal atonement whereby fallen humankind is convicted of sin, made aware of the need of salvation, and enabled to respond in such a way as to rescue the sinner."[9]

I have added this excursus on the Holy Spirit for two reasons. 1) To provide a brief look at the historical and theological cont4ext of the CP treatment of the Holy Spirit, including in the *COF* of 1984, and 2) To note, again, that the Bible's treatment of the Holy Spirit is much broader than that of the *COF*. What I am *not doing* is suggesting that the authors of the *COF* of 1984 were "wrong" to follow the historical method and pattern of the older confessions. The Spirit's work in the salvation of individuals is, after all, clearly a true and important biblical theme. Nor am I suggesting that the authors of the *COF* were somehow unaware, and should have been aware, of the broader work of the Spirit as disclosed in the Bible as a whole. Neither was the case. For those interested in studying the broader work of the Spirit, there are ample resources available for such study.

The excursus, rather, is intended to raise a question about possible future revisions of the *COF*. It is my contention that a broader treatment of the work of the Holy Spirit would be instructive and formative for both CP understanding and ministry. A few, of many available, possibilities for expanded work might be raised by the following questions: 1) As CPs join with others in responding to the present ecological crisis (regardless of one's politics in this regard), what might statements about "The Holy Spirit and Nature" contribute to our response? 2) As CPs seek to dialogue and interact with people of other religions (in an increasingly globalized and on a "much smaller" planet, what might statements about "The Holy Spirit as the Source of all Human Culture, Art, Creativity, and Wisdom,"[10] contribute to the dialogue and interaction? And 3) As CPs continue, necessarily, to live in a world dominated by the world-view of modern science, and particularly the dominance of the theory of evolution, what might statements about "The Holy Spirit as the Ongoing Creativity of God in all of Creation" contribute to our understanding?

CPs will continue to preach, teach, and bear witness to God the Holy Spirit's work in the salvation of sinners. The church is under the divine imperative to do so. But the broader work, I believe, should not be ignored or neglected. The Spirit's comprehensive (including cosmic) work should not be entirely limited to individual sinners, or individual Christians, or even to the church. J. Moltmann writes, "The Holy Spirit is not concerned about the church as such. He is concerned with the church, as he is concerned with Israel, for the sake of the Kingdom of God, the rebirth of life, and the new creation of all things."[11] Or, as S. Guthrie writes, "The Holy Spirit does not belong to us Christians and is not trapped in our hearts or in our church. The Holy Spirit is the Spirit of God who is Creator, Preserver, and Defender of the life of *all* God's creation and *all* God's creatures."[12]

Chapter Twelve

REPENTANCE AND CONFESSION

A character in James Michener's novel *The Source* suffers the consequences of her husband's devotion to the wrong god. She grieves the loss of her son who was sacrificed to the god Melak. Now her husband celebrates the harvest by visiting the temple prostitute. Michener describes the woman's mood as she is deeply pained by her husband's behavior in the name of religion. "And while others celebrated, she walked slowly homeward, seeing life in a new and painful clarity: with a different god. . .her husband would have been a different man."[1] The desperate situation of human beings was discussed in the previous chapter (and in the chapter on the abuse of human freedom). One biblical way of speaking about our condition is that we are given to idolatry (John Calvin declared the mind to be "an idol-making factory"). We worship and serve ("go after") the wrong gods (Dt. 6:14). Our need is to forsake these gods in order to return to the God who has the power to make us into "different" people.

The word "repent," like many other words in the Bible, had a quite ordinary meaning in ancient Israel before being pressed into theological service as a way of talking about the relationship between God and his people. The Hebrew word *shub* meant "to return" or "to turn and go in a new direction." The idea was that of leaving something behind; having done with it. When used in the Hebrew Scriptures, it designated the act whereby Israel as a whole, or individual Israelites, returned to covenant life, loyalty, and obedience—in short, returned to God.

Recognition of the need for corporate repentance meant that it was ritualized for the entire nation in the annual Day of Atonement. With respect to individuals, repentance meant sincere contrition, involving acknowledgment of wrongdoing in the sense of both admitting guilt and feeling guilty (Lev. 5:5, 17; 6:4). The guilty one might signal repentance by fasting, weeping, rending garments, and donning sackcloth and ashes (2. Sam. 12: 13-17; Jon. 3:5-10). There was a strong ethical component to repentance. It included resolving to make amends: to do what was right and to make restitution (Isa. 1:17-18, 27; Amos 5:14-15; Lev. 6:5). Since the heart of covenant life was "love for God and neighbor" (Lv. 19:18), a sin against one's neighbor was also considered to be a sin against God. Repentance was the path to renewed life with neighbor and God. It was the returning from "wicked ways in order to experience restored life" (Ez. 18:21-23). It was receiving a "new heart and a new spirit" (Ez. 18:31; see Psalm 51).[2]

In the New Testament, the ministry of Jesus began with a call to repentance: "The time is fulfilled; and the kingdom of

God has come near; repent, and believe in the good news" (Mk. 1:15, NRSV). For Jesus and those who first heard him, this call to repent would not have had precisely the same meaning as in the Hebrew Scriptures. It was not a call aimed at encouraging persons to turn from personal sin (violations of covenant faithfulness). Rather, it was an announcement, a report (good news), of something altogether wonderful. God was acting in a new way. It was the good news, to people who for more than four hundred years had lived under foreign domination (exiles in their own homeland), that God was about to restore his kingdom (meaning the expulsion of foreign oppressors and the restoration of Israel's national sovereignty). Jesus declared that the kingdom was dawning, it was indeed near. Therefore, people could and should repent. The word is *metanoia* and it means "to change one's mind."

Jesus called people to change their minds about their current historical circumstances. God was about the "shake things up." Things were going to change on the national scene. People, therefore, could change their minds, from lack of hope and despair, in order to see the coming, the dawning, of the kingdom. "For Jesus, this change of mind is a joyous thing. . .(for him) it is like accepting an invitation to a party."[3] It is interesting to note how often the parables and other words of Jesus about the kingdom are characterized by the theme of joy. The theme is also present in his actions, as in his many acts of table fellowship with sinners. The coming of the kingdom was an occasion for joy. The over-all point here is that Jesus' original call for repentance was not associated with remorse and guilt. It was more akin to the joy felt by the Hebrew people when they returned to Jerusalem from exile in Babylon four hundred years before Jesus.

The above does not mean that the more traditional Hebrew understanding of repentance is absent in the Gospels or the remainder of the New Testament. Repentance as an individual Hebrew's return to God, including the elements of remorse, guilt, confession of sin, and restitution also is present in the New Testament. The story of the Prodigal Son, at least in part, is a narrative about repentance. It is about coming to the place where one's mind is changed (Lu. 15:11-32; and see verse 17) resulting in a return home to the father. In Luke 19:1-10, we have the story of Zacchaeus, the rich Hebrew tax collector, who declared to Jesus, "Look, half of my possessions, Lord, I will give to the poor, and if I have defrauded anyone of anything, I will pay four times as much" (vs. 8). This was a Hebrew who was serious about making restitution! Many other examples of personal repentance are to be found in the Gospels. Turning to the Apostle Paul, we find that he makes less frequent use of the word "repentance" as meaning a "return to God." The reason is clear. His ministry was primarily to the Gentiles who did not need to return to God for they did not know God in the first place. They were never in a covenant relationship to God. Therefore, Paul called them not to return but "to turn" (*epistrepho)* to God for the first time. With the two afore-going paragraphs as background, we turn now to consider the statements of the *COF*.

In the *COF*, the first use of the word "repentance" is found in the second sentence of statement 4.02: **The Spirit moves on the hearts of sinners, convincing them of their sins and their need for salvation, and inclining them to repentance and faith toward God.** Once again, we come upon the CP theological view that it is God who initiates the process leading to salvation. God makes the first move. God does the convincing and inclining. Repentance, then, is something that God makes possible; it is not an achievement of human beings. Repentance, a repentant attitude, is to be considered as a gift from God. Perhaps we can better understand this CP theological affirmation by reflecting briefly on the history of God's dealings with his people.

In Israel, persons were given the covenant as a standard by which they could determine their need for repentance. Without the prior gift of the covenant of grace (understood not only as law but, moreover, relationship to God), they would not have even known of their need for repentance. They would not know that it was God to whom they were to return. God had chosen them for covenant relationship, and not the reverse. In the New Testament, it was Jesus who was God's gift of himself in the one covenant of grace. It is now Jesus who is the standard for and path of repentance (return) to God. Jesus has fulfilled and renewed God's one covenant of grace (its profound and thoroughgoing renewal in Jesus is the sense in which the New Testament can and does speak of it as the "new covenant"). Jesus is the "way" (Jn. 14:6) into covenant life. Conversely, the life of Jesus stands as a demonstration of what it means to live in rebellion against God.

Finally, it was God in Christ who, following the cross, resurrection and ascension of Jesus, gave the Holy Spirit to his followers. It is now the Holy Spirit (at the same time the Spirit of God and the Spirit of Jesus) who awakens human beings to their need of return, or turn, to God. It is this history of the gracious action of the triune God that is the logic involved in the CP understanding that salvation is entirely of God (the gift of God) and can in no way be credited to the desire or ability or action of human beings. And it is why the *COF* says **persons do not merit salvation because of repentance or any other human exercise** (4.06). It is true that repentance **is necessary to partake of the saving grace and forgiveness of God in Christ** (4.03). But, thanks to God, repentance is a gift God the Spirit is always offering to us. Acceptance of the gift of true repentance brings about *"a fundamental re-orientation of the way we think about the world and life, a revolution in one's thinking that effects a change of direction in one's life.* [4]

Repentance is that attitude toward God wherein sinners firmly resolve to forsake sin, trust in Christ, and live in grateful obedience to God (4.05). Perhaps it will be helpful to ask what the *COF* mean by *that attitude*? What is the attitude? How is it to be recognized or understood? The *COF* does not say. The dictionary defines "attitude" as: "the way you think and feel about someone or something," and "feeling and thinking that affects a person's behavior." Repentance involves the whole person (thinking and feeling, heart and mind). It is neither a matter of thinking alone or a matter of feeling alone, but both. As for thinking, we can remember that in the New Testament the biblical word for repent is *metanoia*: a change, actually a profound change, of mind. It is turning from being captive to a world-shaped mind in order to receive the freedom of the "mind of Christ" (Ro. 12:1-2). But it reasonable, of course, to expect that repentance will also involve the feeling aspect of the mind: the emotions. And, as we saw in both the Hebrew and Christian Scriptures, the emotions are involved in repentance: for example, sorrow, regret, astonishment (including shame) that we have been in rebellion against God's love, contrition, but also joy, as in Jesus' proclamation of the near kingdom as a cause for such joy.

A failure to understand the profound nature of repentance as involving change of mind and heart and life—as a turning from being mired in rebellion against God—led Morrow to lay a severe charge against much 20th century church practice: “One of the glaring deficiencies in the church’s approach to evangelism is the almost total disregard of the work of the Holy Spirit in repentance. The usual approach is simply to ask persons to accept Jesus as personal Savior by coming forward in a service of worship and giving the minister a handshake. This relatively painless process of becoming a Christian ignores both the reality of the sinner’s state of rebellion against God and the resultant bondage to sin and death. It bypasses the radical experience of repentance as a necessary condition for the gift of faith.”[5] He adds, “In its most fundamental sense, repentance is not of the nature of an apology to God for having committed some particular sin. Rather, it is the cry of a desperate person in a hopeless situation.”[6]

However, in my view, neither should the church seek to standardize, or stylize, the act of repentance so that a judgment can be made as to when it has (or has not) occurred. This too can be a danger to the church, and particularly a danger to persons whose experience of repentance does not conform to style. It has been sufficiently demonstrated that we human beings are a diverse lot in terms of psychological make-up. For one thing, we have been created with different leading instincts. For some people, the leading instinct is thinking. For example, some people “get something out of worship” when the Holy Spirit has given them something to think about. For others, the leading instinct is feeling. They “get something out of worship" when the Holy Spirit enables them to feel something. And there are other forms of leading instinct: the drive toward action; the appreciation of beauty; the use of imagination; and so on. It would be a mistake to think the Holy Spirit does not take human individuality into account when inclining us toward an attitude of repentance and actual repentance. In the end, the only real test of whether repentance has occurred is the life that that bears the fruits of that repentance—the fruits of a life in which the Holy Spirit is at work: "But the fruit of the Spirit is love, joy, peace, patience, kindness, goodness, faithfulness, gentleness, and self-control" (Gal. 5:22-23; and see Mt. 3:18).

In response to God's initiative to restore relationships, persons make honest confession of sin against God, their brothers and sisters, and all of creation, and amend the past so far as is in their power (4.07). This statement stresses the ethical component of repentance. It reflects the Hebrew tradition of restitution, or making amends. It is why, as mentioned earlier, Zacchaeus told the Lord that he would give back four-fold to anyone he had defrauded (Lu. 19:1-10). About this statement, Morrow calls our attention to Alcoholics Anonymous: "Alcoholics Anonymous has grasped the essential nature of sin as bondage from which persons cannot free themselves. This organization has also understood the meaning of genuine repentance. Alcoholics who finally in desperation cry 'Help' are guided into a serious demonstration of repentance. This includes confession to persons they have wronged, payments of debts previously avoided, and performance of kindness to other persons in need. The church would do well to think through how it might become the instrument of the Holy Spirit in guiding persons through the rigorous experience of making amends for past sins."[7] I would like add the following observation: The fact that confession of sin and repentance was a corporate, as well as individual, experience in both Israel and the church of the New Testament should remind us that it is not only "persons" who are called to make honest confession of sin "against God, their brothers and sisters, and all of creation, and amend the past so far as in their power." Groups of people, congregations, and denominations may also be prompted by the Holy Spirit to recognize past sins and to engage in the act of repentance with mind, heart, and action. In many CP congregations, repentance is ritualized in worship in a "prayer of confession."

I close this chapter with the following beautifully constructed words serving as a summary: "In the Hebrew Bible, to repent means primarily to return to God. Its metaphorical home is exile. To repent means to return from exile, to re-connect with God, to walk the way in the wilderness from Babylon to God. In the New Testament, repentance continues to have the meaning it has in the Hebrew Bible. The gospel of and about Jesus sees repentance as following the way of Jesus . . . the path of dying and rising, and return. And repentance in the New Testament has an additional meaning. The Greek roots of the word combine to mean 'go beyond the normal mind that you have.' Go beyond the mind that you have been given and have acquired. Go beyond the mind shaped by culture to the mind that you have 'in Christ.' Repentance is the path of salvation. It is the path of re-connection, the path of transformation, the path of being born again, the path of dying and rising, the path of response to the message of the kingdom of God."[8]

Chapter Thirteen

SAVING FAITH

I have read that no one comes out of childhood without at least some damage having been done to their capacity for trust. A child lives, at least for a short time, with near absolute trust, and then is struck by the fact that his or her parents have said one thing and done another. Elementary age children, or perhaps even earlier, quickly learn that another child may be a friend one day and not be a friend the next. The usually stormy years of puberty introduce thoughts and feelings about whether it is possible to trust what is happening in one's own body. Teen-agers struggle with which of their peers can be trusted. Powerful feelings of affection for another may occur in these years only to be suddenly disappointed, even devastated, when there is break-up and rejection. The world is a very complicated place and terrible events occur that serve to shake one's basic sense of trust in life. Few people, if any, reach adulthood without at least some diminishing of the ability to trust. And adults, of course, are not spared by age from the pain, uncertainty, and confusion caused by the breaching of trust. In many ways, the challenge of life is whether one can learn to trust again.

Saving faith is response to God, prompted by the Holy Spirit, wherein persons rely solely upon God's grace in Jesus Christ for salvation (4.08). Saving faith is that movement by and from within the whole person (mind, heart, and will) in which God—who has acted in Jesus Christ for our salvation—is acknowledged as completely trustworthy. It is a human movement made possible by the prompting, influencing work of the Holy Spirit. In the Hebrew Scriptures, such faith as trust is first expressed in the story of Abraham and Sarah. When God called them, they believed and responded trustingly (Gn. 12). In the New Testament, this trust is given the name "faith" (Heb. 11). Throughout the Hebrew Scriptures, the object of faith—the one to whom which faith is directed—is God (and God's promises). In the New Testament, the object of faith is Jesus Christ in whom God has acted in fulfillment of the one covenant of grace.

Faith is a dynamic relationship of personal trust in God; not believing "something" is trustworthy but that "someone" is trustworthy. However, sometimes in the Christian tradition, "faith" has been employed to mean "believing things about God" as well as "believing God;" or "trusting certain things (beliefs, ideas) to be true about God" as well as "trusting God." This is often called the intellectual aspect of faith (*assensus)*. As one writer puts it, "The intellectual element in faith in a person is to believe certain things about this person, her nature, word, and work. One does not need to know everything, nor even know everything that is possible, but it is essential to know at least something. One, for example, cannot trust in Jesus Christ without believing that he is the Messiah, the incarnate Son, the crucified but risen Savior."[1] Nevertheless, first and foremost as set forth in the *COF*, "saving faith" *is* a **response to God** rather than believing things *about* God. "Because faith is a personal response of confidence in and fidelity to the living, gracious God, it is altogether different from blind submission to church teachings or mechanical adherence to a set of religious beliefs and practices."[2]

Such faith includes trust in the truthfulness of God's promises in scripture, sorrow for sin, and determination to serve God and neighbor (4.08). "Sorrow for sin" indicates that repentance and faith are closely related (Acts 2:38-44; 17:30, 34; 26:20). The faith that is prompted in us by the Holy Spirit includes being shown the truth about ourselves; the truth of who we are—sinners in need of forgiveness and salvation. "Repentance is more than the recognition of sin. It is recognizing that sin is under the judgment of God."[3] It is recognizing the depth of our rebellion against and resistance to God. In an interesting perspective on the Holy Spirit's work in producing sorrow for our sin, the Puritan Thomas Watson wrote, "God does prescribe an exact proportion of sorrow and humiliation. . .A knotty piece of timber requires more wedges to be driven into it. Some stomachs are fouler than others, therefore need stronger physic (medicine). But wouldest thou know when thou hast been humbled enough for sin? When thou art willing to let go thy sins. The gold has lain long enough in the furnace when the dross is purged out; so, when the love of sin is purged out, a soul is humbled enough for divine acceptation, though not for divine satisfaction. Now, if thou art humbled enough, what needs more?"[4]

The "determination to serve God and neighbor" points up the ethical dimension of faith. Such faith (faith that saves) includes *obedience* to the God known in Jesus Christ. "Faith is not passive. . .divinely given, involving a total re-orientation of life, it is also supremely active. . .faith is the inward compulsion, not only to trust God but, trusting him, to obey him, to do exploits in his name, to bring forth fruits of righteousness, to find expression in faithfulness. Christians walk in faith (2 Cor. 5:7). They are strong in faith (1. Cor. 16:13). They rejoice in faith (Ro, 15:13). They are the household of faith (Gal. 6:10). They bear the shield of faith (Eph. 6:16). Their faith works by love (Gal. 5: 6). Faith is one of the three things that abide (1 Cor. 13:13). The greatest of these is love; but the love for God, which is the very essence of love, is itself rooted and grounded in faith. It is the trusting response of love to him who first loved us."[5] Faith as faithfulness means the same as what faithfulness is in a committed human relationship: we are faithful (or not) to our spouses, our partners, our friends. It is loyalty, allegiance, the commitment of the self at its deepest level, the commitment of the *heart*. Its opposite is not doubt or disbelief.

Rather, as in human relationships, its opposite is *infidelity*, being unfaithful in our relationship to God. This is why the word *adultery* is so often used in the Bible to describe lack of loyalty and commitment to God.[6]

Persons do not merit salvation because of faith, nor is faith a good work. Faith is a gift made possible through God's love and initiative (4.09). Throughout this section, on the saving work of God the Spirit, we have noted that it is God who has taken the initiative to respond to our abuse of freedom, our estrangement and alienation, our sin, and our damaged capacity to trust. Apart from God's gracious movement toward us, we would and could know nothing about God, including the meaning, need, and possibility of saving faith. Such faith is not a human possibility. Rather, it is a gift of God (Eph. 2:8; 6:23). The gift is made knowable to and receivable by us through the prompting work of the Holy Spirit. It is trust in God that is evoked by God. We must remain clear about this. **Yet God requires the response of faith by all who receive salvation and reconciliation** (4.09). While it is God the Holy Spirit who makes faith possible, God does not have faith for us. "Faith is both a gift of God and a free human response. But it is not a human achievement. It is the gift of the Holy Spirit who works *liberatively* rather than *co-ercively* (italics mine), therefore, it is also an act of human freedom."[7]

How is the gift received by us? Earlier, we read in the *COF* that **the Holy Spirit works through the scriptures, the sacraments, the corporate worship of the covenant community, the witness of believers in word and deed, and in ways beyond human understanding** (4.02). The Apostle Paul said, "So faith comes from what is heard, and what is heard comes through the word about Christ" (Ro. 10:17). One author has suggested that while we cannot give ourselves the gift of faith, we can place ourselves in situations in which the gift can be received. For one thing, we can place ourselves in the church so that "we can hear over and over again the unbelievably good news that God loves, forgives, and accepts us despite everything we have been or done—or not been and done. Trust in God becomes possible as we hear constantly anew how trustworthy God is. That happens in the church as it tells itself over and over again, Sunday after Sunday, the story of God's steadfast love for a sinful world and sinful human beings (each one of us included). . .we also can risk beginning to do what faith requires. Faith in God is possible only when we live by faith. How will we ever learn that God is trustworthy until we give up trusting in ourselves? How can we trust God if we do not willingly and thankfully obey God? How can we believe that we unworthy, undeserving people are forgiven, loved, and accepted until we begin to forgive, love, and accept other unworthy, undeserving people? Faith comes with obedience. Without obedience, there can be no faith."[8] But **when persons**

repent of sin and in faith embrace God's salvation, they receive forgiveness for their sin and experience acceptance as God's children" (4.10).

In the life of faith, believers are tested and suffer many struggles, but the promise of ultimate victory through Christ is assured by God's faithfulness. Both the scriptures and the experiences of the covenant community throughout the centuries witness to this promise (4.11 and see Jn. 16:33; Ro. 3:3-4, 4:19-21, 8:28-39; 1 Cor. 1:4-9; 1 Thess. 5:23-24; 2 Thess. 3:3-5). CP's know themselves as people who have been tested (in classic language: by the world, the flesh, and the devil) and who have experienced many struggles in the life of faith. The struggles are of both an internal and external nature. As Newton has taught us to sing, "Through many dangers, toils, and snares; I have already come"—and we know that we cannot escape such struggles in the present or in the future. CP's also tend to be wary of being overly confident in "our own faith." We are more likely to resonate with the man who said, "Lord, I believe, help my unbelief" (Mk. 9:24).

But CP's are, at the same time, supremely confident in the faithfulness of God. Our faith is never in ourselves (not even "our" Christian faith). Rather, it is in the God who has acted in Jesus Christ and the Holy Spirit for our salvation. Here is an anecdotal story about faith: While I was still an active pastor, a young adult and father came to me stating, with sorrow, that he had lost his faith. We talked about the many reasons he felt this was the case. He was not happy about this fact, but it was simply so. I suggested that he, for the next several weeks, or months, act as if he hadn't lost his faith. He accepted my suggestion. He continued to come to worship with his family. He continued to serve on a ministry team in the church. He continued with his prayers. One Sunday, after a couple of months had passed, he greeted me with a big smile and hug. No significant words were spoken in that moment, but I knew what he meant by the smile and embrace. There was a happy ending to this story. Who can count the number of such stories even from within the CPC alone? The *COF* affirms that scripture and the experiences of the covenant community throughout the centuries witness to the promise of God's faithfulness and to ultimate victory through Jesus Christ.

Excursus: A Footnote on Saving Faith

Several times Paul refers to faith with a grammatical construction that can be interpreted either as "faith in Christ" or "faith of Christ" (Gal. 2:16, 20; 3:22; Ro. 3:22, 26; Phi;. 3:9).[9] In Galatians 2:16, the Apostle Paul says, "Yet we know that a person is justified not by the works of the law but through faith in Jesus Christ.[j] And we have come to believe in Christ Jesus, so that we might be justified by faith in Christ,[k] and not by doing the works of the law, because no one will be justified by the works of the law." As you can see, my version of the Bible

(NRSV) has a little "j" at the end of the phrase "but through faith in Jesus Christ." And it has a little "k" at the end of the phrase "faith in Christ." In the first case the footnotes reads, "or the faith of Jesus Christ" and in the other it reads "or faith of Christ." I mention this because there is a widespread scholarly debate, even as I write, about the proper way to translate these phrases.

Did Paul mean to say, in each instance, "faith in Jesus Christ," or did he mean to say "faith of Jesus Christ." In other words, does Paul here say we are made right with God through faith *in* Christ, or does he say that we are made right with God through the faith *of* Christ? The scholars are debating back and forth, and no one really knows how to properly translate what Paul has written. What is known is that before Martin Luther's translation of the Bible (roughly five hundred years ago) most manuscripts opted in favor of "faith of Christ." But Luther, in his own translation into the German vernacular, chose to render the phrase as "faith in Christ." Subsequently, most English translations of the Bible have followed Luther. But some translations, such as mine, have included footnotes that call attention to the issue of what many of the earliest texts say.

Are we saved by our faith in Christ or the faith of Christ? Perhaps we will simply say both. But if you are like me, you have occasionally wondered if you have the right kind of faith, or the right amount of faith (even of a mustard seed), or authentic faith, or saving faith? But what if the emphasis in salvation is not on *our* faith? What if the really important thing is not our own faith but, rather, Jesus Christ's faith in God? He was the one who was utterly, completely, and totally faithful to God. There is one thing this debate may encourage us to do. We may choose to stop spending so much time wondering if we have "enough faith" or the "right kind of faith;" after all, that can be a form of focusing on the self. And as Paul said in another place, he was dead to all that kind of thing. Maybe we can become dead to it too. It may encourage us, instead, to focus on the greatness of Christ's faith; his absolute trust in and obedience to God.

While working on this book, I came across the following footnote in Joe Ben Irby's book *This They Believed.* He writes, "A novel view of 'saving faith' is that of Rev. J.B. Fly who wrote in opposition to the section on 'Saving Faith' in the Confession of 1883. According to him, 'saving faith' is not an act of the sinner at all, but rather the act of Jesus Christ himself."[10] Reverend Fly's opinion, of course, was rejected by those who produced the *COF* of 1883. But it is interesting that here was a Cumberland Presbyterian who was advancing this idea nearly a hundred years before the present scholarly debate!

Chapter Fourteen

JUSTIFICATION

The *COF* begins its discussion of the topic of justification with the following words: **Justification is God's act of loving acceptance of believers whereby persons are reconciled to him by the life, death, and resurrection of Jesus Christ. When they in repentance and faith trust Christ, who is their righteousness, God gives them peace and restores their relationship with him** (4.12 see Gn. 15:6; Ps. 32:1-2; 103:8-13; Lu. 18:9-14; Rom. 3:19-31, 5:1-2; I Cor. 1:30-31; Ph. 3:7-11). This statement is clear enough. But the history behind it is not. This history involves how Paul's metaphor of justification was interpreted in the older theology of the Reformed tradition, as well as in other theologies. It is a complicated history and requires briefly going over some ground covered in earlier chapters.

Paul took the word "justification" from the world of the law courts. It was a legal term. Imagine a criminal standing before a judge and the judge pronouncing a verdict of "Not guilty." The criminal is thus acquitted, or justified—made to be just or "righteous" in the eyes of the law. But also suppose that this criminal was in fact guilty and this was known to the judge. It would be impossible for a just judge to pronounce a verdict of not guilty. Now, when this metaphor was pressed into use in atonement theory, God became the just judge. The human family has broken the law and is guilty. The law requires just and proper punishment. Suppose now that Christ steps in to take the punishment that was deserved by those who were guilty. Since the punishment has been meted out the just judge can now declare the human family not guilty—that is, acquitted or justified. According to older Reformed theologies, this is precisely the meaning of "justification by faith." Christ took upon himself the punishment that we deserved and therefore we can be declared justified (just-as-if-not guilty) by and before God.

There are, however, several difficulties associated with this interpretation. Shirley Guthrie points out a few of them: "If God is a just judge, how can God forgive or declare righteous those who are in fact guilty? If God accepts us as righteous and treats us "as if" we were what we are not, does not God wink at sin and pretend that a lie is the truth? Traditionally, the answer has been that when God judges us, he looks at Christ's righteousness and accepts us for Christ's sake, on the basis of *his* merit. But the problem still remains. Can righteousness be transferred? Are we not still guilty? Even if God lets us get by, are we not still trapped in our sin?"[1]

This line of questioning involves attempting to comes to grips with the belief that God's saving action in

Christ—especially the cross of Christ—is addressed to the problem of the human family having broken God's law and therefore requiring a just punishment. When understood in this way, the rebellion of the human family is thought of in strictly legal terms and therefore requiring a legal solution—a satisfaction of God's law. But, as in an earlier chapter, is this how God's saving action in Christ—his gracious, justifying work—is to be understood?

The *COF* of 1984 goes to great lengths to say that this is *not* the Cumberland Presbyterian Church's understanding of God's saving, justifying work in Jesus Christ. It does so because it has considered and found wanting the two-covenant theology upon which the legal understanding of the atonement is based. If God's primary covenant with the human family was one of law, as the older two covenant theology insisted, then law-breaking was the primary problem between God and the human family. But the *COF* contends that God's primary, and only, covenant was one of grace. The law was given as a result of the covenant of grace. The covenant was always one of God's grace and not God's law.

The fundamental problem, then, of the human family is not one of breaking God's law but, so to speak, one of breaking God's heart. The human family rebelled against and rejected God's fellowship. Now can this fellowship be restored? CPs believe it is God's altogether free, gracious action to restore fellowship—to reconcile—that is God's saving, justifying work in Jesus Christ. The *COF* rejects the interpretation, common in a two covenant theology, that God required the punishment of his only begotten Son as a way of declaring the human family forgiven. The Christology of the *COF* regards Christ's entire life and death as God's act of reconciling love. Above all, it communicates that the death of Jesus is not a punishment required by God to satisfy God's legal demands, but a willingly offered, self-donating act of sacrificial love aimed at the restoration of relationship.

The meaning of justification is that through the work of the Holy Spirit, applying the saving benefits of Christ's work and life to the life of the sinner, the sinner is no longer under a sentence of condemnation (Rom. 8). The *COF* goes on to point out that this does not mean that the sinner is now sin-free: **Although believers sometimes disrupt their peace with God through sin and experience separation from God, yet they are assured that it is by God's grace that they are accepted and the relationship is sustained. Only by growth in grace can the believer experience the fullness of relationship to God** (4.13). This point underlines something that is true for the life of the believer according to the New Testament. There is an "already but not fully" dimension to the Christian life. We have been saved, and yet we are still being saved. We have repented, but we must continue repenting. We have confessed, but we must continue to confess. We have faith, but we must continue to grow in faith. And we are justified, no longer condemned, but we must still struggle against the continuing remnants of a sinful nature. And so the *COF* says, "**Those who are reconciled to God through Jesus Christ continue to know a sinful nature. They continue to experience within themselves the conflict between their old selves and their new selves, between good and evil, between their wills and God's will, between life and death"** (4.14). Thankfully, the work of the Holy Spirit in the life of believers is both an initial work and a continuing one. The good news is that God the Spirit is faithful to us in the journey. I am here reminded of the title of a book about discipleship by Eugene Peterson. He describes the Christian life as a *Long Obedience in the Same Direction.*

Excursus: A Scholarly Debate about Justification

Despite what has just been about the meaning of justification, a contemporary debate has arisen about what Paul meant by his use of the metaphor of justification. New Testament scholars, such as N.T Wright, agree that justification—understood as having to do with the salvation of persons—was the interpretation of Paul's metaphor by such Reformers as Martin Luther and John Calvin. And he agrees that their understanding has been a part of the Lutheran and Reformed traditions ever since. However, according to Wright and other like-minded scholars, the Reformers were simply wrong to have understood Paul in this way.

Wright argues that justification was used by Paul to answer the question of "who constituted the church" and not the question of "how persons are saved." He maintains that, for Paul, justification was an ecclesial (churchly) word rather than a soteriological (salvation) word. Wright's argument is that "justification is not about 'how I get saved?' but 'how I am declared to be a member of God's people?'" He contends that Paul's word for how one is saved is "call" or "calling." One is saved by responding to the call of God in Jesus Christ as prompted by the Holy Spirit. Justification, on the other hand, denotes the identity of those who have been called, or saved. In other words, it denotes the people of God. As such, Paul used the word justification to describe the new social form of the church—made up of both Jew and Gentile. Justification by grace was Paul's terminology for the joining together of disparate peoples who are now, in Christ, one people. Justification is the word for the description of this new social reality. Wright does say that the meaning that has been given to justification, as applying to the salvation of persons, is in fact a correct meaning. It is just that Paul did not, and never, used the term justification to connote this meaning.

I have commented on this debate because if Wright and his colleagues are proven to be correct it perhaps will mean that future revisions of our *COF* may need to take their work into account. If their view is sustained and finally accepted, justification would better be discussed under the section of the

COF having to do with the church. It will be out of place in the present section having to do with the work of the Holy Spirit in salvation (the "order of salvation). We need not be alarmed if this turns out to be the case. After all, Reformed theology, including Cumberland Presbyterian theology, is called Re-formed precisely because of an open-ness to being revised, or reformulated. When there are new illuminations and insights and understandings provided under the guidance of the Spirit, enabling the church to hear the Word of God in Scripture more faithfully and accurately, reform is the order of the day.

Chapter Fifteen

REGENERATION AND ADOPTION

Perhaps at this point a brief pause is in order to remind ourselves that in the last few chapters we have been discussing what older Reformed confessions of faith called the "order of salvation." The so-called order was developed, by 17th and 18th century theologians, as a way of presenting the saving work of God the Holy Spirit in a person's life. The *COF* of 1984 for the most part followed this order. It is important, however, to stress that the biblical metaphors found in the order and used to describe the work of salvation—calling, repentance, confession, saving faith, justification, regeneration, adoption—and those of the Christian life that follows salvation—sanctification, growth in grace, preservation, and assurance—are not to be understood as steps on a ladder, or points along a well defined continuum. Rather, each biblical metaphor describes the "one event of salvation" but from a different angle or, perhaps better, each metaphor is a different pictorial representation of the "one reality" of God's saving work. A diamond, for example, may be examined as a whole but also according to its individual facets. The images and metaphors the biblical writers employed are intended to help persons (us) grasp the free, gracious, loving, and saving work of God in Jesus Christ and the

Holy Spirit. This chapter is devoted to two more of these important images: regeneration and adoption.

In our Western world the advertising industry is absolutely dependent on one little word: "new." Each year we, the consumers, are greeted with new models of all sorts of things: automobiles, golf clubs, lawn-mowers, *coffee* makers, and the like. Each year, in fact each season, we are treated to the latest in new fashion wear. When visiting the big box stores, we find the shelves stocked with items that are branded "New and Improved" (perhaps even when the changes are so slight as to not merit the word new). The advertisers, and those they represent, are simply giving us what we want and expect—that to which we have grown accustomed (addicted?) Americans are in love with what is new. Perhaps the trinity by which we really live is: "New, Much, and Quick."

The word "new" is, of course, significant to us in other ways. We are grateful for the lives that have been saved, or improved, by new developments in medicine and its application. We are grateful (most of the time) for the amazingly rapid developments in the realm of electronic technology. We are grateful for the march of science and new ways for understanding both ourselves and the universe in which we live. We are grateful for new legislation that contributes to greater fairness and justice for all. We are grateful for new literature, poetry, and art that can stretch our imaginations. But when it comes to "the new" perhaps nothing is more wonderful to most of us than the experience of a new-born child—a new baby! This latter can bring us closer to one of the most important ideas to be found in scripture. The word "new" as in "new birth" and "new creation" is at the heart of the story that scripture tells. These ideas (and realities) are major ones for apprehending God's work in and through the Holy Spirit.

Regeneration is God's renewal of believers and is solely of God's grace. Those who trust in God's grace are recreated, or born again, renewed in spirit, and made new persons in Christ (4.15). As is evident from this statement in the *COF*, the operative word in the concept of regeneration is "new." There is a cluster of biblical images in scripture, three actually, that can help us appreciate more fully what is meant by the regenerating work of God the Holy Spirit in a person's life.

New Birth—The word regeneration literally means "another genesis (beginning)" or also "a second or new birth." The image of new birth is especially common in the Gospel of John and the first letter of John. Its most well known use, of course, is by Jesus in his night-time conversation with Nicodemus recorded in John 3. Jesus speaks to Nicodemus about being "born again" which may also be translated as "born from above." "Do not be astonished that I said to you, 'You must be born from above'" (Jn. 3:7). Unless Nicodemus undergoes this new birth he will not be able "to see the kingdom of God" (Jn. 3:3). The new birth is not a human possibility. It is something that God makes possible. This is the point being made when Jesus speaks of being born "from above"- it is a birthing by the power of God. The same idea is said straightforwardly in the first chapter of John: "But to all who received him, who believed in his name, he gave power to become children of God, who were born not of blood or of the will of the flesh or of the will of man, but of God" (Jn. 1:12-13). Jesus' statement that Nicodemus "must be born from above (again)" should not be interpreted to mean the initiative in new birth belonged to Nicodemus. As Ferguson points out, "'You must be born again' is not good news!. . .new birth is not something we do but something God gives."[1] The new birth imagery is found in other places in the New Testament. In 1 John, Christians are described as those who are born of God (1 Jn. 2:29; 3:9; 4:7; 5:1, 4). 1 Peter says "Blessed be the God and Father of our Lord Jesus Christ! By his great mercy he has given us a new birth into a living hope through the resurrection of Jesus Christ from the dead" (1 Pt. 1:3; see 1:23). James writes, "In fulfillment of his own purpose he gave us birth by the word of truth, so that we would become a kind of first fruits of his creatures" (Jam. 1:18).

2) *New Creation*—In the Hebrew Scriptures, the final goal of history is God's bringing forth of a new creation (see Isa. 65:17; 66:22; and this idea is developed further in the apocalyptic literature). In the New Testament, it is the Apostle Paul

who makes use of the idea of "new creation" to describe God's saving act in Jesus Christ and the Holy Spirit: "So if anyone is in Christ, there is a new creation; everything old has passed away; see, everything has become new" (2 Cor. 5:17). It has been said that this verse and the passage in which it occurs, 2 Corinthians 5:16-21, presents "Paul's theology in a nutshell: God's saving act in Christ effects new creation and issues forth in the life of the believer. The proclamation of 'new creation' stands as the single summary of all that happens in the divine act, process, and life of salvation."[2] And, "it is the message that God now creates a new reality on the earth, beginning among his people, and later in the whole creation. Heaven and earth will be renewed in this new reality" (also see 2 Pt. 3:12-13).[3] It was the power of God in the resurrection of Jesus that began the process of new creation. The Holy Spirit works in the lives of individuals to make them "new persons"—through this act of regeneration, they become participants in and witnesses to the new creation that God is now bringing forth. As the *COF* says, **when empowered by the illuminating influence of the Holy Spirit, believers are able to love and glorify God and to love and serve their neighbors** (4.18). But the new creation involves more than individual persons. God is also working to about a cosmic renewal at the end of the age (Mt. 19:28; Acts 3:21). Paul, in Romans 8:19-23, speaks of the present groaning of the old creation and the birthing process of the new creation (also see Eph. 2:5; Col. 2:13; Gal. 6:5).

3) *Resurrection*—**Regeneration is necessary because all persons who are separated from Christ are spiritually dead and unable of themselves to love and glorify God** (4.16). It makes perfect sense, of course, that the writers of the New Testament would employ the resurrection of Jesus as a metaphor for the Holy Spirit's work in regeneration. "You were dead through the trespasses and sins in which you once lived. . .But God who is rich in mercy, out of the great love with which he loved us, even when we were dead through our trespasses and sins. . .made us alive together with Christ. . .and raised us up with him" (Eph. 2:1-6). "Blessed by the God and Father of our Lord Jesus Christ! By his great mercy he has given us a new birth into a living hope through the resurrection of Jesus Christ from the dead" (1 Pt. 1:3). Paul also employs the metaphor of resurrection in his discussion of baptism (Ro. 6:1-4; Col. 2:12). The regenerating work of the Holy Spirit is to bring us forth from the grave of sin and rebellion against God. **Regeneration is accomplished by the Holy Spirit showing sinners the truth of Christ, enabling them to repent and believe God in the light of that truth and to receive the saving grace and forgiveness given in Jesus Christ** (4.17). "What is being underscored in all these passages is that regeneration, however it is described, is a divine activity in us, in which we are not the actors but the recipients. As well as to tell a lame man to walk, a blind man to see, as to tell a dead man to live, a man without spiritual life to have it, or to say, 'you must be

born again!" There is a paradox in the gospel at this point. For we discover that the one thing most needful is the one thing outside our power to perform."[4]

All persons dying in infancy and all who have never had the ability to respond to Christ are regenerated and saved by God's grace (4.19). The background of this curious statement is a particular interpretation of the doctrine of original sin. In the fourth century, Augustine argued that the sin of the first parents (Adam and Eve) was passed on to subsequent generations through biology: through the sexual act. We mentioned in an earlier chapter that CPs do not accept this Augustinian formulation. It did, however, become the official teaching of the Roman Catholic Church and that of the several of the Reformers including John Calvin (with whom the Presbyterian tradition originated). Basically, it means that all persons are born with a "sinful nature" that they acquire through biology! This raised the question, in an earlier time, as to the eternal destiny of infant who succumb to death (as well as "all who have never had the ability to respond to Christ"). The early Presbyterian confession formulated at Westminster (1647) theorized that some infants must be among the elect (those chosen for salvation), while others must not be. But all were born with a sinful nature. This was the result of pushing the belief in biological inheritance to its logical end. CP's have an alternate view of original sin—the fact that all of us sin in rebellion against God. We believe that—without seeking a full or complete (or logical) explanation—sin simply is what we all do. We "pick it up" as we grow and participate in this sinful world. We see no reason to claim that infants (and others) who are deprived of the knowledge and experience of regeneration are not destined to eternal life by God's grace. In fact, we find many scriptural evidences to suggest the contrary (Lu. 18:15-16; Jn. 3:3; Acts 2:38-39).

Adoption is the action of God to include in the covenant family all who are regenerated and made new persons in Christ. This action assures community with God and with one's brothers and sisters in Christ both now and in the full redemption of the family of God (4.20). Adoption is not a metaphor for regeneration, per se, but describes the *new status* of those who are regenerated—those who have come to faith in Jesus Christ. Paul is the writer who made use of the idea in the New Testament. The Hebrew people did not have the custom of adoption. However, they, as a result of God's covenant of grace, were frequently referred to as sons and daughters of God. So this may be in the background of Paul's thought. Roman law, in the time of Jesus and Paul, did include the practice of adoption. It is likely that Paul picked up on the idea as a metaphor for explaining the truth and significance of the Gospel to his Gentile audiences. Jesus was *uniquely* the Son of God. Those who are regenerated by the work of God the Spirit—who come to faith in Christ—become sons and daughters of God by adoption. We, who are not sons and daughters of God by nature, are given a share in the divine nature of God in Christ by the regenerating work of the Holy Spirit (see Ro. 8:14-17; Gal. 4:3-7; Eph. 1:5-6).

Chapter Sixteen

SANCTIFICATION AND GROWTH IN GRACE

The *COF* says **sanctification is God's setting apart of believers as servants in the world** (4.21). Sanctification is an act of God. We can grasp the meaning of the word by recalling that when priests set aside something for special use in the Temple that thing was said to "be sanctified, or made holy." The item, whatever it was, was now intended only for sacred or holy use. The first statement in the *COF* employs this idea, as does scripture, and applies it to God's action of setting apart the covenant family for his purposes in the world (Ro. 6:6-14, 20-22; 1 Cor. 6:9-11; 2 Cor. 6:14-18; 7:1; Eph. 4:17-24; 5:25-27; 1 Thess. 5:23-24; 2 Thess. 2:13-14; He. 9:13-14; 1 P. 1:1-2).

About growth in grace, the *COF* says **as believers continue to partake of God's covenant of grace, to live in covenant community, and to serve God in the world, they are able to grow in grace and knowledge of Jesus Christ as Lord. Believers never achieve sinless perfection in this life, but through the ministry of the Holy Spirit they can be progressively conformed to the image of Jesus Christ, thereby growing in faith, hope, love, and other gifts of the Spirit** (4.22; see 2 Cor. 3;18, 9:10-11; Eph. 3:14-21; Ph. 2:12-16; Col. 3:5-17; 1 Thess. 3:12-13; 2 Tim. 2:20-21; 1 Pt. 2:2-3; 2 Pt. 1:3-11).

In recent years, I have attempted to stress the importance of both sanctification and growth in grace and the realities of the Christian experience to which they point. I have done so because I believe a great deal of the American Church, perhaps including our Cumberland Presbyterian Church (?), has for a long time been somewhat stuck at the level of "conversion theology." There is an understanding of the Gospel that focuses almost entirely on "getting persons saved." This is hardly unimportant because evangelism is a command given to the church by the Lord. And the fields are always "white unto harvest" (and, sadly, in the past half century or so most growth in congregations has resulted not from evangelizing the lost but from the re-cycling of members from one congregation, and denomination, to another). Nevertheless, there *is* something that comes after conversion. It is sanctification and growth in grace. It is the recovery of the latter that has the potential to awaken the church to its evangelistic calling.

Another way of addressing sanctification and growth in grace is to speak about "Christian discipleship." Sanctification is responding to the summons of Jesus Christ to follow him. It is living as his disciples and witnesses of God's love for the whole world. If sanctification and growth in grace mean that believers are enabled by the Holy Spirit "to grow in knowledge of Jesus Christ as Lord," why is it, how is it, that deep knowledge of the Christian faith, and our Cumberland Presbyterian theology, are at such a low ebb today? In my opinion, and only that, there has been an effective, rather deadly effective, substitute for authentic Christian discipleship (sanctification and growth in grace) at work in much of American Christianity over the past century.

I have sometimes spoken of this substitute, only half-jokingly, as being the anti-Christ. It is what is known to us and practiced by us as "church membership." This is a strong statement that perhaps some will find objectionable. But it seems to me that persons have been able to become members of the church, and I might add pastors in pulpits, without also being committed to grow in an authentic understanding and practice of Christian discipleship. Nearly every congregation in America has as much as half of its membership on an "inactive roll." We might imagine someone approaching Jesus and saying, "Lord, I would like to follow you, but please place me on the inactive roll?" Well, something like this actually did happen during Jesus' ministry (Luke 9:57-62) and Jesus was not amused or sympathetic! The practice of church membership as we have known it may have been, perhaps unwittingly, an effective way to inoculate persons from authentic discipleship (I consider it to be something of a weakness that the *COF* uses the word "disciples" only twice—3.09 and 5.04—and neither as a reference to what it means for Cumberland Presbyterians to be followers of Jesus). The substitute for discipleship is religion (basically formal outward observance). That religion can be a substitute for authentic discipleship led Karl Barth to say,

“Church is the place where many people go to make their last stand against God.”

In our American setting, individualism also militates against authentic discipleship. Persons, even when they have answered the formal covenant questions in the affirmative, may participate and otherwise be invested in the congregation and its ministry only on the basis of their personal choices or preferences. Membership ordinarily has not meant that personal choice in these matters has been trumped by what is clearly meant in the scripture by the word discipleship. So, for these and many other reasons, I have called the practice of 20th century church membership the anti-Christ. I have come to think that a great deal of membership is “Christian life on our terms” (a definition of idolatry) whereas discipleship is “Christian life on Jesus’ terms.” Perhaps few of us, if any, will be particularly good at discipleship. But we need no longer confuse it with church membership.

After this somewhat negative detour, let’s return to the positive meanings of sanctification and growth in grace. It was said above that sanctification is an act of God, a setting apart of believers as servants of God in the world. It is also a process guided and empowered by the Holy Spirit. Sanctification and growth in grace involve the journey that persons and congregations make in, with, and toward the Triune God. Conversion to Christ may happen in a moment. Sanctification and growth in grace is the work of the Spirit in persons and in the church over the course of a lifetime.

Karl Barth said, "Saints (those being sanctified) are those who now share in the holiness of Jesus Christ, the 'Holy One,' through being related to him. Christians are aware that they are not yet fully redeemed. However, even as sinners, they are enabled through the power of the Holy Spirit to serve him obediently in the world."[1] About this the *COF* says **the struggle with sin continues, for believers are still imperfect in knowledge and the power to do God's will. Their freedom to trust, love, and serve God and neighbors is compromised sometimes by distrust, hate, and selfishness. This inner struggle drives them again and again to rely on God's power to conform them to the image of the new person in Jesus Christ** (4.23 see Ro. 7:7-25; Gal. 5: 16-17; 1 Jn. 2:9-11).

As Cumberland Presbyterians, we do not believe that full, complete sanctification is possible in this lifetime. As Waldo Beach has written, "Just as sin is a process and not a state, so, too, salvation is a process and not a state. As against a kind of 'flap-jack' view. . .which believes that God, like a cook over the great stove of history, flips the sinner like a pancake once and for all from a complete state of sin to a complete state of salvation, the normative Protestant view has stayed by Luther's belief that the Christian is at once and the same time sinner and saint. He is one who is always turning away in rebellion and also always being turned back to God and neighbor by God's mysterious, patient, and unfailing mercy."[2] Full and complete sanctification will come only with the resurrection of the body at the end of the age. But if sanctification and growth in grace are neglected, that is if authentic discipleship is neglected, we will have foreclosed on how far, perhaps how very far, God the Spirit may take us toward being the new persons and the new congregations who are being conformed more and more to the image of Jesus Christ, and in this very lifetime.

Chapter Seventeen

PRESERVATION OF BELIEVERS

The *COF* next considers the work of the Holy Spirit in the doctrine known as "The Preservation of Believers." **The transformation of believers begun in regeneration and justification will be brought to completion. Although believers sin and thereby displease God, the covenant relationship is maintained by God, who will preserve them in eternal life. The preservation of believers depends upon the nature of the covenant of grace, the unchangeable love and power of God, the merits, advocacy, and intercession of Jesus Christ, and the presence and ministry of the Holy Spirit who renews God's image in believers. As a consequence of temptation and the neglect of the means of grace, believers sin, incur God's displeasure, and deprive themselves of some of the graces and comforts promised to them. But believers will never rest satisfied until they confess their sin and are renewed in their consecration to God** (4.24-4.26; see Ps. 37:27-28; Lam. 3:22-24; Jn. 5:24; Rom. 8:38-39; Cor. 4:13-18; Ph. 1:6; 2 Tim 1:11-12).

In older Reformed confessions, and in the Cumberland Presbyterian Confession of 1813, this teaching was called "The Perseverance of Saints." The doctrine was given its present designation in the 1883 Confession. It seems there was a desire among Cumberland Presbyterians to emphasize the power and faithfulness of God in preserving believers rather than the potential misinterpretation that believers somehow persevere in and of themselves. The importance of the doctrine is that those whom God saves God will also preserve in the faith. It stresses the Cumberland Presbyterian belief that salvation is not a joint-work, or effort, between God and persons but is entirely the gracious work of God alone. Persons neither save themselves nor do they preserve themselves in salvation. If salvation were a joint work, then persons would always be plagued by the question of whether they might forfeit, or have forfeited, the salvation God has made possible them in and through Jesus Christ.

The earliest leaders of the Cumberland Presbyterian Church spoke of this doctrine as "comforting, but dangerous if mishandled."[1] They knew about the temptation to misinterpret its meaning. It could, for example, be used in support of a "once saved, always saved" belief. Irresponsible persons might take this to mean they were now "off the hook" when it came to obedience and responsibility to Christ. But such a misguided interpretation was considered to be a sign that a person likely had not experienced regeneration and justification in the first place. To invoke God's grace as an excuse for sinning is satanic rather than regenerate (Ro. 6:1).

The *COF* makes it clear that regenerate believers "**sin and thereby displease God**" and behave in ways that "**incur God's displeasure**." But Cumberland Presbyterians also believe that persons who have experienced authentic regeneration will, because of the internal ministry of the Holy Spirit, "**never rest satisfied"** until they are "**renewed in their consecration to God**." Properly understood, this is a comforting doctrine to Cumberland Presbyterians. It tells us that God is a gracious and faithful God. And that to this God belong all the glory for both salvation and preservation. It is, for Cumberland Presbyterians, more a doctrine in praise of the Word and work of the Triune God than a doctrine about persons and whether or not they in and of themselves can or will persevere (Isa. 59:1-2).

Dr. Thomas H. Campbell did admirable work when comparing the Cumberland Presbyterian view of this teaching with that of the Westminster Confession. He writes, "Calvinism, as set forth in the Westminster Confession, reasons that because the unchangeable decree of election fixed the saint's destiny from before the foundation of the world, the saved person *cannot* fall away from a saved state and be lost. Cumberland Presbyterians do not say the regenerated person *cannot* fall, but that the person *will not* fall. This conviction is based, not on a decree of election made before the world was, nor on a view which says that God has you and is going to keep you regardless of whether you want to be kept or not, but on the belief that the regenerated individual is a new creation with new desires and purposes. 'If anyone is in Christ, he is a new creature; old things have passed away; behold, all things are become new' (2 Cor. 5:17). Consequently, there are some things the regenerated person will not do. This implies no violation of the freedom of the will, but is the result of a will transformed by the power of God when the individual came trusting in Christ for salvation."[2]

Chapter Eighteen

CHRISTIAN ASSURANCE

The *COF* concludes its section on God working through the Holy Spirit with the doctrine of "Christian Assurance." About this doctrine, the *COF* says **believers who seek to know and to do the will of God, and who live in him as he lives in them, may in this life be assured of salvation and thus rejoice in the hope of fully sharing the glory of God. This comforting assurance is founded upon the divine promises, the consciousness of peace with God through Christ, and the witness of the Holy Spirit with the believer's spirit that they truly are God's children. Assurance is the promise of the believer's full inheritance** (4.27—4.28).

The assurance of the believer was one of the most comforting doctrines to come out of the 16th century Protestant Reformation. The Roman Catholic Church opposed this teaching and rejected the idea that a believer could have the present assurance of salvation. Philip Hughes explains the Roman Catholic position: 1) The RCC taught that the blood of Jesus availed only for the purging of sins committed before baptism; hence the need for penitential deeds, and after this life, purgatorial fire to deal with post baptismal sin; 2) It distinguished between venial and mortal sins, according to which the committing of mortal sin resulted in the loss of salvation; and 3) It held that a person's justification depended not only on the work of Christ but also on one's own good works performed before and after justification as meritoriously contributing to and also increasing one's own justification.[1] Hughes says, "From this teaching no one could be sure that the grace possessed today might not be lost tomorrow or that one would not die in a graceless state of mortal sin. Because of the finite fallibility and fallenness of the human creature, for salvation to depend on the merit of one's own good works and not wholly on the merit of Christ's work of redemption left everything in uncertainty."[2]

The utter angst (*anfechtung)* of 16th century German reformer Martin Luther often serves as an example of the lack of assurance. As a Roman Catholic, he lived in constant and tormented uncertainty about his security in Christ. He found peace only when he came to believe in, through his reading of Romans and Galatians, justification by faith alone with nothing else required or added to the saving work of God in Jesus Christ. When Luther, Calvin, and other Reformers read the scriptures anew (no longer under the aegis of the Roman Catholic Church), they came to the solid conviction that salvation is solely the work of the Triune God and not, in any fashion, a joint work between God and persons. They extolled the faithfulness of God in the salvation and preservation of believers. They also came to believe that scripture taught that believers can have assurance of salvation in this life. We, as Cumberland Presbyterians, are grateful heirs of this Reformed teaching.

As the *COF* states assurance **may not immediately accompany initial trust in Christ** (4.29), but "it will increase" as the believer participates in the life of the church. This is true because God will **confirm to believers the promise never to leave or forsake them** (4.29). The *COF* bases its commitment to this teaching on the following scriptures: Ro. 5:1-5; 2 Ti. 1:11-12; 1 Jn. 2:3-6, 5:13; Mt. 28:19-20; Ro. 8:15-17; Eph. 1:13-14; He. 6: 17-10, 13:5; 2 Pet. 1:3-4, 10-11; 1 Jn. 3:2-3, 14-15, 19-24, 4:13; Ro. 15:13; He. 6:11-12; 2 Pet. 1:10-11. No single text concerning assurance has been more important to Cumberland Presbyterians than the great words of Paul found in Romans 8:31-39. And perhaps especially those words with which he concluded: "For I am convinced that neither death, nor life, nor angels, nor rulers, nor things present, nor things to come, nor powers, nor height, nor depth, nor anything else in all creation, will be able to separate us from the love of God in Jesus Christ our Lord" (vs. 37-39).

I once asked a friend, Reverend Ken McCoy, about his Christological views. Without hesitation, he replied: "It's expressed in a hymn: 'O Love That Will Not Let Me Go.'" Here are the words of this hymn: "O Love that will not let me go, I rest my weary soul in thee; I give thee back the life I owe, that in thine ocean depths its flow may richer, fuller be. O Light that followest all my way, I yield my flickering torch to thee; my heart restores its borrowed ray, that in thy sunshine's blaze its day may brighter, fairer be. O joy that seekest me through pain, I cannot close my heart to thee; I trace the rainbow through the rain, and feel the promise is not vain that morn shall tearless be. O Cross that liftest up my head, I dare not ask to fly from thee; I lay in dust life's glory dead, and from the ground there blossoms red life that shall endless be."[3] That the Holy Spirit has awakened us to an experience of a "love that will not let us go" is the foundation of Christian assurance. Cumberland Presbyterians believe in the Christ who promised, "My sheep hear my voice. I know them, and they follow me. I give them eternal life, and they will never perish. No one will snatch them out of my hand" (Jn. 10:27-28).

Chapter Nineteen

THE CHURCH (1)

When I was an older teen-ager in the late 1960s, there was a popular show on television called *Happening*. It was aimed at my particular age group. It was televised by ABC and produced and directed by Dick Clark. The show was devoted to rock and roll music and was populated by young people who danced to the music and appeared to be having a ferociously and amazingly good time. The show was a massive hit among young people. How could it not have been? One feature of many teen-age lives, then and now, is the feeling that if something great is happening, it must be happening somewhere else! But once a week, at least vicariously, millions of us could join in on the party. We could, in spite of our often seemingly ordinary and mundane lives, participate in this dramatic happening.

"Happening" is a good word to describe what the New Testament means by church. The church is a people who are undergoing a dynamic event. They are participating in a mode of being, including a frequent gathering, which is utterly extraordinary. The Greek word for church, *ecclesia*, means "called out and assembled." In the ancient world, the representative of the king, the herald, would ride into town and call the people together to hear a royal proclamation of the king; or sometimes even an appearance by the king. People would scurry from their homes to hear this important message. Their lives might be and sometimes were changed by the news they heard. Their gathering was called an *ecclesia*. They are subjects of the king who have been called out for a specific purpose. Similarly, a military officer might ride into town and call for all the young men to gather in an *ecclesia* to find out who would be newly enlisted or conscripted into service. The church in the New Testament is a gathered community which has heard an announcement. This announcement is one that has changed their lives. It is an event that has set their lives forward in a new motion. There is nothing static in the New Testament meaning of church. And nothing that is institutional. The church is a dynamic happening, we might say like a dance, between a word being heard and a response being given.

In the New Testament, the Holy Spirit is the herald who calls the church into being and motion (Acts 2). Karl Barth elaborates on this: "The essence of the church is the event which is called in the New Testament, 'the fellowship of the Holy Spirit.' The fellowship of the Holy Spirit is nothing other than the actually operative might and power of the work of the Lord Jesus Christ, which has become a Word addressed to particular people and has awakened their answer. The fellowship of the Holy Spirit creates the living community. There is no passage in the New Testament on the basis of which the church might be seen or understood in and of itself, so to speak, or in any other way than as the fellowship of the Holy Spirit. Again, there is no passage of the New Testament which would allow or incline us to understand the fellowship of the Holy Spirit as anything other than the event which takes place between the living Lord Jesus Christ and certain people, in which his life and suffering, his death and resurrection becomes a divine Word to them which they may, must, wish to and can give their human answer."[1]

In the New Testament, the church is not a *voluntary association* created or brought into being simply at the initiative of persons. Rather, it is brought into being by God at work in Jesus Christ and the power of the Holy Spirit. It is God's workmanship (Eph. 2:10). The church is brought forth at God's initiative and summons. It is created according to God's eternal purposes in Christ (Eph. 1:4ff) so that he might show the exceeding riches of his grace (Eph. 2:7). It is for this reason the present section in the *COF* begins with the words, "God Creates the Church." The church is no mere human organization. In the New Testament, one cannot even "join" the church, as if the matter were one of human choice, decision, and agency. One and all, rather, are in the fellowship of the Holy Spirit, or covenant community, as a result of the gracious calling and gift of God. The ancient secular *ecclesia* did not gather of its own accord or decision and then hope that a herald with a message might somehow show up! No, the *ecclesia* was summoned together by the call of the already present herald. The church is God's by God's own design and purposes, and ours by God's grace alone.

The church in the New Testament is not a one-time summons after which the church has an existence all its own and a capacity to operate under its own power. The church never becomes a merely human thing—a building, a place to go to worship, an organization or an institution. Neither was it once summoned into being but now existing with that summons being a memory from some point in the past. The church exists, always and everywhere in the New Testament, as an ongoing and continuous meeting between the God of summons and the people of response. If there is no awareness of and hearing of the summons (the Word of the living God) and no active and obedient response (praise and obedient discipleship) there is no church.

It is this ongoing, never-ending hearing and response that constitutes the church. And where it is happening, there the church is a people in motion. They are being alternately gathered by the Spirit to praise God and then sent forth into the world to serve. The church is that people called to worship by the Holy Spirit in order to celebrate the message and the messenger (The Triune God). Then the Holy Spirit sends the church forth to be, in a variety of ways, the "burning love of the Creator for his creation" in and for the world. As Barth puts it elegantly, and in emphasizing the dynamic nature of the church, "It (The church) speaks of the Lord Jesus Christ risen from the dead and of His congregation hurrying from there toward His future self-revelation."[2] There is no more extraordinary *happening,* indeed miracle, than truly to be the church.

Marks of the Church

The *COF* of 1984 uses four words to talk about the nature of the church. In doing so, it follows in the footsteps of previous Reformed and Cumberland Presbyterian confessions, and before them the creeds of the early churches, and before them as these ideas are found within the Bible. These words, and the realities to which they point, have historically been called the *marks of the church.* **There is one, holy, universal, apostolic church. She is the body of Christ, who is her Head and Lord** (5.01). The first word, then, is *one*. The *COF* elaborates on this word: **The church is one because her Head and Lord is one, Jesus Christ. Her oneness under her Lord is manifested in the one ministry of word and sacrament, not in any uniformity of covenantal expression, organization, or system of doctrine.**(5.02). In the New Testament, there is a definite unity, or oneness, in diversity to the event or happening that is called church.

The church is not called into being by a multiplicity of lords or persons. There is only one Lord who so calls. It is the Lord who prayed for his followers that they "may be one, as we are one, I in them and you in me, that they may become completely one" (Jn. 17:22-23). Paul wrote of the church as being the "body of Christ" (1 Cor. 12:12ff). While there are clearly different parts to the body, each with its own gift and function, the body is a singularity. Christians everywhere were a part of this same body and no congregation anywhere could claim to be "*the* body" in a way that denied that all other congregations were also the body. As the *COF* indicates, in the beginning this unity was not based on a developed system of organization or a clearly defined system of theological doctrine, but on the worship in word and sacrament of the one Lord who is Jesus Christ. The church is one because he is one. The spiritual unity of the church, under her one Lord, included a visible and practical intention toward unity among the churches in the New Testament. For example, there clearly are close relations among the churches (Acts 11:22; 15:2). A conference is held in Jerusalem that involves the church being gathered from throughout the known world (Acts 15). And Paul, in his collection for the church in Jerusalem, is concerned to forge a close bond among the churches (2 Cor. 8ff).

The second word is *holy*. The **church is holy because she is founded on the finished and continuing work of Christ in setting her apart for God's glory and witness in the world. Her holiness thus rests on God's sanctifying her for her redemptive mission, not upon any personal holiness of her members** (5.03). The word "holy" (or sanctify) meant to set something apart for special use. Thus, as indicated in an earlier chapter, a priest from the temple might venture into the public market in order to buy something as mundane as an ordinary cooking pot. Back at the temple, this ordinary pot would be set aside with prayer and consecrated for special use in the temple. The pot was now said to be "holy." It has been set aside for sacred use. It can never be returned to use as an ordinary pot. This concept, of course, was applied to Israel as the holy people of God as chosen and set apart for God's service in the world. And it is carried forward in the New Testament and applied to the renewed Israel which is God's church. The holiness of the church is always the holiness of Christ rather than the personal holiness of the members. Christ is holiness incarnate, fully and completely. He is the one whose life is totally obedient and dedicated to the service of God. His is the life that is fully set apart to God.

The members of the church always remain in the process of "being made holy." We are holy, we have been set apart in baptism, but our holiness is not yet that of Christ's. This full holiness awaits the final consummation. This is why the *COF* says of the church:**Her holiness thus rests on God's sanctifying her for her redemptive mission, not upon any personal holiness of her members.** The *COF* certainly does not intend to imply that the members of the church can be indifferent to the matter of "their" holiness. Nothing could be further from the truth. We cannot be lazy, indifferent, or cavalier about the fact that we have been made holy (bought with a price and set apart for service) and that we are called to lives of holiness (being yielded to God in such a way that our behavior, our ethics, disclose that we are being obedient to the purpose and mission for which we have been set apart). The church in the New Testament is a holy nation (1 Pt. 2:9). It is a fellowship of the saints, those who are being sanctified (1 Cor. 1:2). The church lives under the call to be holy (2 Cor. 7:1; 1 Thess. 4:3). The church is to be wholly yielded up to God (Rom. 12:1; 1 Cor. 6:19f). Perhaps, above all, Jesus prays for the sanctification, the holiness, of the church:"Father. . .sanctify them in the truth" (Jn. 17:11, 17).

The third word is *universal* or *catholic*. The *COF* says: **The church is universal because God's act of salvation in Jesus Christ is universal and cannot be limited to any place or time. Her universal nature rests upon the universal activity of God's Holy Spirit to make Christ's atonement effective for all peoples. It is expressed in the church's commission to make disciples of all nations** (5.04). This word certainly does not mean that the church is expressed in a single worldwide organization. Rather, it means that Jesus Christ died for all classes without distinction, so that in his church there are no external qualifications of age, sex, generation, descent, or status. In him, these distinctions have no reality. They still exist and legitimately, or illegitimately, they are reflected in the life of the church. But the church is not to be ordered by them. It is catholic in its true reality. For, in Christ, "there is neither Greek nor Jew, circumcision or un-circumcision, Barbarian, Scythian, bond nor free (Col. 3:11) male nor female (Gal. 3:28)". The church is not to be identified with any human grouping, nation, culture, or structure. Its boundaries cannot be drawn in terms of any human differentiations. Despite the need for external manifestations of unity, it is not identified with any one ecclesiastical construct. Its catholicity is rooted in the representative action of Jesus Christ, the one for the many in whom the many are one.[3]

The final word is *apostolic*. The *COF* says: **The church is apostolic because God calls her into being through the proclamation of the gospel first entrusted to the apostles. The church thus is built on the apostolic message which is faithfully proclaimed by messengers who follow in the footsteps of the apostles** (5.05)**.** The church is apostolic. This implies more than genealogical descent of organization or ministry from the apostles. It means that the apostles, with the prophets, are the foundation of the church (Eph. 2:20). They are the first and authentic witnesses of Jesus Christ (Acts 1:8). It is through them that the record and message of the gospel has come. They are raised up for this purpose. Thus they are the criterion for true proclamation and teaching. The true church may be recognized by its fidelity to apostolic testimony and doctrine. It believes and proclaims what it has received (1 Cor. 12:23; 15:1ff; 2 Thess. 2:15; 2 Tim. 1:13; 2:2). This apostolic tradition does not lie in the sphere of fallible human memory. By the Holy Spirit, it has been committed to writing in order that the apostolicity of the church might be safeguarded (Lk. 1:1f; Jn. 20:21; 21:24). To the prophetic testimony of the Old Testament there has been added the apostolic testimony of the New Testament (1 Cor. 15:2). In other words, apostolicity includes the preservation and honoring of Holy Scripture. Where scripture is read and preached as the basis of evangelism and edification and the supreme rule of faith and practice, there is the apostolic church (1 Tim. 3:15ff).[4]

Chapter Twenty

THE CHURCH (2)

The *COF* has four additional statements under its treatment of the church. The first says: **The church, as the covenant community of believers who are redeemed, includes all people in all ages, past, present, and future, who respond in faith to God's covenant of grace, and all who are unable to respond, for reasons known to God, but who are saved by his grace** (5.06). One way to get at the meaning of this statement is to ask, "When did the church begin?" It might seem a strange question except Cumberland Presbyterians have a different viewpoint than that of many other contemporary Christian churches.

The more commonly held view seems to be that the church proper began at Pentecost (Acts 2). It is not unusual to hear Pentecost called "the birthday of the church." But the Cumberland Presbyterian Church maintains that the church should be understood as continuous with the people of God in the Old Testament. According to its understanding of covenant, Cumberland Presbyterians believe the New Testament affirms that what God has done, and is doing, in Jesus Christ *is continuous* with what God was doing before in the life and history of Israel. There has always been "one covenant of grace." This view means that Cumberland Presbyterians can and do speak of the church as beginning with the call of God to Abraham and Sarah (Gen. 12). It was then that God began, in history, to create a people that would know and serve him on behalf of and for the sake of the world. It was in this call and covenant that God promised that this people, God's called out people, would be one through which "all the families of the earth shall be blessed" (Gen. 12: 3).[1]

An additional support for this view comes from contemporary biblical studies. These studies have contributed greatly to our understanding that both Jesus and Paul were utterly faithful Jews. It seems impossible either of them could have imagined, or even entertained the idea, they were "creating" a movement that was not continuous with Israel. Their projects were not to do away with Israel as the people of God but to renew this people. The difference that Paul had with certain Jews was not that they were Jews, but that they were not recognizing that the Messiah had come! And his message was not that the Jews could be saved by their God, but that, amazingly, Gentiles can now be included in God's act of salvation! There is, of course, a great deal that could be said about this subject. But the point here is the church, in the view of both Jesus and Paul, was not something altogether different from Israel. And, therefore, we can affirm that the church (God's called-out covenantal people) began with Israel and continues in the life and ministry and saving call of Jesus Christ.

In my judgment, this entire discussion is at the root of the *COF*'s statement that the church includes all people in all ages, including the past, who have responded to God's covenant of grace. And that it is truly a covenant of grace is underlined in the *COF*'s claim that the church includes those who have been, or are, unable to respond for reasons known only to God.

The second statement about the church is: **The church in the world consists of all who respond in faith to God's saving grace and who enter into formal covenant with God and each other. The children of believers are included in this covenant community and are under the special care and instruction of the church and their parents or guardians** (5.07). This is a question about, "Who belongs to the church?" There is a complex, but important, background to this statement that must be considered if we are to fully appreciate its meaning. The background has to do with the historical discussion and debate, among the Reformers and later early Cumberland Presbyterians, concerning in what sense the church is "invisible" and in what sense it is "visible." The 16th century Reformers and later Cumberland Presbyterians, and our *COF*s prior to 1984, maintained that we can speak both of an "invisible church" and a "visible church."

The simplest answer, as to why, is that in the countries (Reformation era Germany, Switzerland, England, etc.) in which everyone was considered to be a Christian by birth and baptism (usually as an infant) it became clear that not everyone who was baptized turned out really to be a Christian. So the question arose: How do you know who is really a Christian? How do you know who is truly a Christian whether they were baptized as infants or adults? How do you judge the fruits of a life in a way that you can know this for certain? Who truly knows this, or can know it? Who is truly regenerate in Christ and who is not? Well, God can and does know! This led to the assertion that there is an "invisible church." God alone truly knows who is in this church, who is really Christian, and who is not. This assertion was carried forward in most Reformed confessions and in our own Confessions up to 1984.

On the other hand, the "visible church" is the church that can be seen on earth. It is the church, the congregation, to which you and I belong. It is the people with whom you sit in the pews, sing in the choir, with whom you go on mission trips, commune with around the fellowship table and so on. In the older thinking to which we have been referring, it remained that you could be in this church without being truly regenerate. We all know that it is rather easy "to join" a church. Authentic following of Jesus, true discipleship, is another matter. But there is a visible church for all to see. The distinction between the church as invisible and visible seems logical, a matter of common observation, and even biblical: "Not everyone who says to me, 'Lord, Lord', will enter the kingdom of heaven, but only the one who does the will of my Father in heaven" (Mt. 7:21).

But there are problems with this distinction. These problems are likely the reason the present *COF* does not refer to it. The first problem, and argument, is that the distinction between the invisible and invisible church was, in reality, a historical and theological *concession* to the fact that the church, after the conversion of the Roman Emperor Constantine in 312 AD and up to and through the time of the 16th century Reformation, found it relatively easy "not to be the church." At least not the church as it was known in the Bible and in its pre-Constantinian form. Here is one description of what happened:

"(After Constantine and the church officially became the church of the empire) a new understanding of the church arises. Previously the church was assumed to consist only of those who believed in the God revealed in Jesus Christ. This faith often cost Christians dearly, sometimes even their lives. As a result, only those who were serious about faithfulness to Christ claimed membership in the church. After Constantine, there is social pressure to be a part of the church. On occasion, people are actively coerced to become members; dissenters and heretics are persecuted. In fact, after the reign of Constantine it is difficult not to be a member of the church. Consequently, the church is re-defined. It is no longer clear which members in the church truly 'believe' (referring to the New Testament meaning of faith/belief/trust). It becomes possible that many of those who are members of the church (which now is effectively everyone in the empire) are not 'true' Christians. The concept of the invisibility of the church emerges. This was a fundamental shift in the meaning of the church as presented in the New Testament."[2]

It has been said that before Constantine you could clearly tell clearly who was a pagan and who was a Christian. After Constantine, there were few pagans but you couldn't any longer tell who was a Christian. When everyone is considered to be a Christian, because it is the religion of the empire, country, or culture, what does it mean then to be a Christian? What does it cost? This latter question points to the fact that after Constantine the Christian faith began to be "spiritualized." It was no longer a people, a community, living a radically different life in the world, but people having an interior, private, spiritual relationship to Christ. The point here, though, is that the idea of the invisible church arose because there was a time when nearly everybody was considered to be a Christian simply by virtue of where they were born.

Perhaps our *COF* does not mention the invisible and visible church concept because it wants to encourage the church never to be, or become, invisible in the world. It is not that the *COF* fails to recognize that God alone knows who is truly regenerate. Rather, it is a reminder that the church in the New Testament was a truly visible community. It was a community that attempted to live in faithful obedience to the way of Jesus Christ and the reign of God. And this visible community offered a truly alternate way of life to all who entered into it. This community stood out and often over- against the surrounding world and its values and practices. It did so in a way that often got the church into trouble, as it had their Lord.

The invisible/visible dichotomy has led to centuries in which the church has been pretty much able to assume that the surrounding culture, the government, or the nation shares its values. The church, then, can make sense of the invisible/invisible concept. In other words, for a long time lots of people have been Christians and only God knows who they are. But the *COF* likely rejects the invisible/visible concept not as a matter of who is truly saved and who truly belongs to the church. Rather, because the people whom God called in Israel and in Jesus Christ were to be visible in every sense of the word. They were to visibly represent the presence and cause of God in the world. Jesus came into the world and was visible in his life and message. He was visible in his suffering death. He clearly called his disciples to be visible in the world (salt and light, e.g.). In fact, understood in this way, the idea of the invisibility of the church makes no sense at all. I remember reading the words of Dietrich Bonhoeffer who said, at the time of Hitler in Germany, (and I here paraphrase from memory),

"The church of Jesus Christ must now be truly visible; the invisible church is of no use to the kingdom of God." This was a call for Christians to visibly take up the cross as a form of resistance to the powers of evil.

A word needs to be said about the last sentence in 5.07: **The children of believers are included in this covenant community and are under the special care and instruction of the church and their parents or guardians.** The question of in what sense children belong to the covenant community, and especially whether infants should receive baptism, was a lively one at the time of the 16th century Reformation. Some Reformers, a minority at the time, argued that persons should belong to the church only by their volition. This was the "believer's baptism" wing of the Reformation. They rejected the baptism of infants outright. It smacked to them of what was wrong with the invisible church idea. They said only those can belong to the church who, in and of themselves and under the regenerative power of the Holy Spirit, commit themselves to the way of Christ and therefore his church. It was possible to be a Christian only by personal decision.

The majority of the Reformers, however, held to a view they believed to be consistent with the tradition of Israel and the early church. God, they said, chose people rather than people choosing God. There are remarkably few volunteers in the Bible. Even Jesus said, "You have not chosen me, but I have chosen you." So the Reformers emphasized the prevenient grace of God more than individual choice or decision. They also considered the nature of the church to be that of a family. In a family, the persons who are members of it are so not by choice but by birth. In a family, the children receive all the signs of belonging long before they are old enough to express gratitude for family membership. Hebrew children were clearly members of the covenant people, the covenant family. These Reformers observed while the baptism of children is not explicitly mentioned in the Bible there are several texts that speak of the baptism of entire households. Additionally, these Reformers may have been aware that in the Hebraic thought-world solidarity of family was prized above individualism. At any rate, they continued the practice of baptizing children as members of the covenant community.

There are still church traditions in which children are viewed as "outsiders" (this is certainly not to say that children are not valued and nurtured in these traditions) until they make a personal choice for Christ and church. Our *COF*, however, reflects the corporate, covenant view of the nature of the church. Cumberland Presbyterians believe that children are never outsiders to Christ or the church. They belong to the covenant community as much as anyone else. I would add that Cumberland Presbyterians have had, and perhaps do have, different views on this matter. Some have argued, for example, that children are indeed members of the covenant community (never outsiders) but they should not be considered members of a local congregation except by personal decision. But no Cumberland Presbyterians, to my knowledge, believe that children, whether they have been baptized or not, and when reaching the appropriate age should fail to respond personally—in a commitment to discipleship—to God's regenerative work in their lives.

The Threat to the Church

The *COF* makes a statement that raises the issue of what might be called the threat to the church: **Because the church in the world consists of persons who are imperfect in knowledge and in the power to do God's will, she waits with eager longing for the full redemption of the family of God** (5.08). Why does the *COF* make this statement? Quite simply, the history of Israel, God's people, is a history of faithfulness and unfaithfulness, of obedience and disobedience, of loyalty and disloyalty. It has been pointed out that the very name Israel means "one who strives against God." And, in the New Testament, we see this same pattern. Perhaps its clearest expression is found in the letters to the seven churches in John's Revelation. For example, "You have the name of being alive, and you are dead" (Rev. 3:1).

Karl Barth (1887-1968) offers a powerful and penetrating analysis of the danger to the church and I will draw from him extensively in the following paragraphs (choosing to offer a single footnote at the end). Barth begins by observing, "With respect to its Head, the church is divine in nature and manner. As the body of that Head, it is without doubt and unequivocally *human*. In and of itself, it is an element of creaturely and therefore threatened reality. Its existence is an existence secured, unthreatened, and incontestable only from above, only from God, not from below, not from the side of its human members." He goes on to say about the church, "It is God's faithfulness which promises and guarantees the continuance of the church. That and that alone, for from the side of its human members, there is no such guarantee available. Their faith, although awakened by God's Word and Spirit, is not their own inalienable possession which cannot be lost, and that applies also to their knowledge, their obedience, their love, their hope, and their prayer. The possibility of unbelief, false belief, superstition, of indifference, ignorance, hate, and doubt, even of the powerlessness of their prayer—all lie close at hand and will continue so to lie as long as time lasts, as long as the final revelation of the victory of Christ has not yet dispersed these shadows, insofar, the existence of the church is a threatened existence." He continues by pointing out some of the threats (or temptations) that face the church:

1) He says the church may succumb to sleep. "It can be that the light of the divine word which has placed men in the light and also enlightened them, places them still in the light, and yet no longer enlightens them because their eyes have

become heavy with sleep. We know what the Gospel says about the watchful servants. Over against them stand the servants who suddenly can only blink, whose open eyes are still sleeping inwardly and who therefore cannot in fact see. They know the Bible, the ancient creeds, the confessions of faith, and their catechism. They acknowledge their authority. They nod their heads in earnest faithfulness and say obediently, Yes! Yes! But they have already missed the point, that the old words, yes, the witness of God, are an address directed to them, an address to which they themselves must answer here and now with their own words, with their own lives, in dialogue with the needs and tasks of the present world, as if they had heard them for the first time." While the Master speaks, the disciples are asleep.

2) The church may become "squint-eyed." "We know what the Gospel says (Matt. 6:22) about the healthy eye and another sort of eye in contrast to this, that the latter is false, and as a result the whole body becomes full of darkness. The light of God's word shines on Christians and they see it too. But they also look elsewhere. They have no idea of denying God or being disobedient to him. Perhaps they want to serve him with great zeal. But they seek also that which pleases themselves and other men as well as that which pleases God, and they will not entertain the thought that these are two very different things. Somewhere along the way they have fallen in love and become involved with themselves: perhaps in the interests and

corresponding morality of their surrounding society, perhaps in just the natural and usual human way in this country or that, perhaps out of dominant optimism or even pessimism—or, what is yet worse and more dangerous they may have fallen in love with themselves in the form of their own form of Christendom which has been handed down to them, in the particular honorable forms of faith and worship, in some special form of Christian experience and life, in particular arrangements of the relationship between church and state, between Christian and political existence. They speak of the 'Word of God,' and never notice that they actually mean one of these forms or arrangements. They say 'Christian faith' and mean faith in the eternity of this arrangement. They say 'Christian faithfulness' and mean faithfulness to such an arrangement. On it they now set out to build the church, and they even suppose they may and must also offer this to the world as 'Christianity.'"

3) "The worst form of temptation for the church is that which is described in the Gospel with the picture of 'the blind leading the blind' (Matt. 15:14). The eyes of Christians can become blind. They are flooded by the light of the divine word, but what good does it do them? It no longer reaches them because they are somewhere else: in a self-made world of their own religious dreams. In effect, they have only a memory left of the fact that Jesus Christ was, is, and will be the Lord. The Bible has become for them a source of verbal material for their own thoughts. And their own thoughts proceed from the

premise that the religious man is his own Lord: God's law is the ideal which he lays down for himself, the Gospel is the aid with which he comforts himself, sanctification is the discipline which he imposes on himself, the kingdom of God is the 'brave new world' which he can and will build for himself. The church has become, then, the world, in a certain sense the prophet of the world, its proclamation is of a man who has become God, of flesh that has become the Word. And still they have not noticed that they have thereby become nothing and completely meaningless for those around them."[3]

I have included these observations from Barth because the *COF* reminds us we remain imperfect as the church. This fact, however, should not keep us from being alert to the threats to the church by which we "may become nothing and completely meaningless" to those who are around us. The world needs the church to be the church and therefore we need to beware lest we become heavy with sleep, squint-eyed, or as the blind who are leading the blind. The pattern of Israel and the church, as revealed in the New Testament, was one of obedience and disobedience, loyalty and disloyalty, leaving and return. While the church acknowledges, in ongoing repentance, our failures, we also live with gratefulness for the patience and faithfulness of the living God. So, the *COF* concludes its statement about the imperfection of the church with these words about waiting for the full redemption of the church: **Until that time God wills that all believers worship and**

witness through the church in the world and promises to guide her life and growth through the Holy Spirit (5.8). There is, and never will be, a threat to the church *from above*.

The Purpose of the Church

The *COF* closes its section on the church by saying: **The church in the world never exists for herself alone, but to glorify God and work for reconciliation through Christ. Christ claims the church and gives her the word and sacraments in order to bring God's judgment and grace to persons** (5.09). There are many ways, scriptural and otherwise, to speak about the purpose of the church. In all of them, one thing should be clear. The church does not exist for herself alone. As Rowan Williams has written, "The church exists for sake of the kingdom of God; it is 'engaged' in the same business as its Lord; that of opening the world to its horizon, to its destiny as God's kingdom."[4] We follow the one who was emptied of all self-concern (Ph. 2:5-11). We serve the God who so loves the world that he gave the Son (Jn. 3:16). It is also right to say that the church exists for the sake of the world. Not the world as we might hope it to be, or even surely pray that it will become, but the world as it is now. It was into this world that Jesus Christ became incarnate. It is in, to, and for this world that Christ's body, the church, seeks to glorify God and work for reconciliation. It is in, to, and for this world that we, as the church, remember and are nourished by the Word and sacraments, so that we might bring the word we have heard to the world: the word of both God's judgment and grace.

N.T. Wright speaks of the purpose of the church: "According to the early Christians, the church doesn't exist in order to provide a place where people can pursue their own private spiritual agendas and develop their own spiritual potential. Nor does it exist in order to provide a safe haven in which people can hide from the wicked world and ensure that they themselves arrive safely at an otherworldly destination. Private spiritual growth and ultimate salvation come rather as by-products of the main, central, over-arching purpose for which God has called and is calling us. This purpose is clearly stated in various places in the New Testament: that through the church God will announce to the wider world that he is indeed its wise, loving, and just creator; that through Jesus he has defeated the powers that corrupt and enslave it; and that by his Spirit he is at work to heal and renew it."[5]

Chapter Twenty-One

CHRISTIAN COMMUNION

When the *COF* speaks about the church as a "Christian Communion," it begins with a simple statement: **All who are united to Christ by faith are also united to one another in love** (5.10). The Christian faith, following Jesus, is a "together thing." In the New Testament, following Jesus always meant putting you into a group, a community, a congregation. In God's design, Jesus and other people are a package deal. You cannot buy separately. As biblical scholar Gerhard Lohfink writes, "The question whether the demands of Jesus can be fulfilled is not one which can ultimately be answered by an individual, especially and individual sitting at a desk. Jesus' ethic is not directed to isolated individuals, but to the circle of disciples, the new family of God, the people of God which is to be gathered. It has an eminently social dimension. Whether or not this ethic can be fulfilled is something is something that can only be determined by groups of people which consciously place themselves under the reign of God and wish to be real communities of brothers and sisters—communities which form a living arena for faith, in which everyone draws strength from each other."[1]

In recent years, there has been a growing trend in which

people say they admire Jesus, want to know about Jesus, but they don't want anything to do with the church. They want some kind of "spirituality" that may include Jesus. But they do not want to be involved with organized religion—meaning a congregation. They want a private, solo relationship to God. Some of us who are in the church may sometimes desire the same thing. After all, dealing with other people, even in the church (and maybe especially in the church), can be aggravating, messy, draining, demanding, disappointing, hurtful, or all of the above and more. It would seem to be much easier to practice some kind of private faith. After all, people have different opinions about almost everything, including the meaning of faith. It would be easier to avoid disagreements and confusion and go solo with God. People, all of us, have all kinds of problems from mild to severe. Why get involved with that? It would be easier to keep life simpler and less stressful. After all, I have enough issues to deal with all on my own.

However, in the New Testament, there is not a scintilla of evidence that anyone can have their own, private, individualized relationship to God. Following Christ, to repeat, is always a together thing, a group thing, a community thing. Christian communion, then, is not optional fare in the Christian life. It is a requirement. Whatever Jesus came to do in this world, he did not intend to do it by himself. So, he called people and put them together. He was with them and they were with him. That the Christian experience is a social reality is a cardinal rule of our faith.

The *COF* lays out the meaning of Christian communion (*koinonia*) in three simple phrases. First, being the church means Christians are "**to share the grace of Christ with one another**" (5.10). Grace is one of the most important words in the Bible. Scott Peck tells the story of a man from a northern state who made a trip through the southern states. One morning he went into a small café. He ordered breakfast—eggs, bacon, and toast. When the server brought his plate, he saw the eggs, the bacon, and the toast, but there was something else. There was a "white blob" on the plate. Calling the server, he asked, "What is this?" She replied, "Those are grits." He said, "Well, I didn't order grits." She said, "Sir, you don't order grits, they just come." Grace is not an abstraction in the Bible and the Christian faith. Grace is God coming to us, relentlessly coming. Grace is God coming to us in Jesus Christ. Grace is God coming to us in Holy Spirit. Grace is God coming to us in word and sacrament, in worship, and in the goodly fellowship (communion) of the church. Grace is not that which we order. Grace is God coming to us freely and of God's own judging and saving initiative.

In Christian communion, we encourage one another to pay attention to the coming of grace, the coming of God, into our lives. I recently heard a sad, but metaphorically significant, true story. A man in New York got on a subway and began to brandish a gun. He waved it first this way and then that way. But he became utterly frustrated because no one was paying attention to him. They were all on their cell phones! Perhaps this is an instance of their cell phones saving lives. But I was struck, of course, by what the story says about the power of distraction. Christian communion involves helping one another with the issue of distraction. And we do so that we may not fail to recognize the coming, the appearing, of the God of grace into our midst, into our lives, and into our world.

Secondly, the *COF* says Christian communion means that we are "**to bear one another's burdens**" (5.10). This is a clear Christian imperative (Gal. 6:2). A few months ago, I had the privilege of being in the presence, during a single day, of a 99 year old member of the congregation I was serving, a 93 year old, a 98 year old, a 92 year old, and an 85 year old. That comes to 457 years of lived experience! None of them are still able to attend worship. But, uniformly if not in the same exact words, they told me that the burdens of older age were made lighter by, 1) memories of life in the congregation, and 2) the continuing concern shown to them by members of the congregation. The highlight of the day, for me, was when the 85 year old man talked about the visitors he received from the congregation. He told me of one man who comes by once a month for the express purpose of cutting his toe-nails. That image remained in my mind all afternoon. It reminded me of Jesus, in the Gospel of John, with a towel in hand and stooping to wash the feet of his disciples. I also thought of many of the ways that Christians bear the burdens of others in love. Like the firemen on 9/11, and other first responders, Christians rush toward their brothers and sisters in Christ when the burdens are heavy, and not away from them.

One writer puts it like this: "The church exists. . . .to encourage one another, to build one another up in faith, to pray with and for one another, to learn from one another and teach one another, and set one another examples to follow, challenges to take up, and urgent tasks to perform. This is all part of what is known loosely as *fellowship*. This doesn't just mean serving one another cups of tea and *COF*fee. It's all about living within that sense of joint enterprise, a family business, in which everyone has a proper share and proper place."[2] It is interesting, and enlightening, to take a Bible concordance in hand and look up the number of times the New Testament uses some form of the words "one another." The time I did it I counted over thirty. "One anothering" is a good biblical expression for what the Bible means by Christian communion. As a matter of fact, a few years back several Cumberland Presbyterian congregations used a curriculum entitled *One Anothering* as a means for aiding in the deepening, and or renewal, of the congregation's life together.

Finally, the Confession says Christian communion compels us "**to reach out to all other persons**" (5.10). Christian communion gathers us with Christ and one another. But Christian communion is never just about or for us—it is for everyone. The church, in one sense, truly exists for those who are not here yet. Christian communion is not only centripetal, but also centrifugal. The Holy Spirit pushes us outward toward other persons in order to share with them, in word and deed, the good news of God's action in Jesus Christ. The Christian message is that "what constitutes our belonging together, morally and spiritually, is our corporate relation to God. That is to say that what unites us with other human beings is not common culture or common aims, but something *external* to human community itself, the regard of God upon us."[3]

One way of thinking about reaching out to other persons involves the difference between "*transactions with others*" and "*encounters with others*." The Holy Spirit, through the church—the covenant community, trains and forms us in and for the experience of encounter. It trains us to understand and experience that the Christian life is not just thinking about God, or religious ideas, nor simply having feelings about God, but actually encountering God! The heart of our faith is that God gives God to us in Christ and the power of the Holy Spirit. It is a real meeting with God.

Transactions are the casual meetings we have, some-times with many people, throughout the course of a day. We come into contact with persons primarily for some kind of transaction with them. So, we buy a cup of *COF*fee from the person behind the counter at McDonalds. We do business with the bank teller. We buy milk and pay the clerk in the convenience store. Most of the time, these meetings involve saying "Hello. How are you? My, the weather is bad today! What did you think about the big game?" These are merely transactional meetings. They are important as social lubrication, of course, but seldom does very much that is of human depth happen in them.

Encounters are different. These occur when there is time, and developing trust, so that meaningful listening and sharing takes place. The best examples of encounter are found in the stories of Jesus. When he met people —the woman at the well, Zacchaeus, Thomas—he engaged in meaningful encounters with them. He met them from the deep place in him that touched the deep place in them. And so their lives were changed! Reaching out to others may begin with our praying for, being open to, and seeking opportunities for real encounter with other human beings. Who knows what doors the Holy Spirit might open if this were to become a priority for us as a response to the meaning of Christian communion, and the Lord of Christian communion.

Linda and I were on vacation and I went alone to a *coffee* shop. It was crowded. A man came in, purchased *coffee*, and asked if he could join me at the table? He sat down and immediately began to talk to me about his recently acquired recreational vehicle. He talked about the good price he had wrangled out of the salesman, a real bargain. He talked about the good gas mileage. He talked about the interior and how efficient everything inside was. The bed was soft and comfortable. He even took a picture of the vehicle out of his wallet and proudly showed it to me. And he went on and on. I admit that I was growing weary. This all seemed quite over the top. Then, thankfully, he fell silent for a few seconds as we both drank our coffee. Then he spoke again. "Yeah, me and my wife saved for years to buy this thing. We got it right after I retired. But then she suddenly got sick on me and died. She never even set foot in the damn thing." At that point, everything changed. It went from being a transaction with a stranger to an encounter. I realized he really wasn't all that interested in his RV. It was a way to make conversation. He had set me up. He wanted to say to someone, even a complete stranger, "I am sad and hurting." You simply never know. Sometimes, maybe often, the Holy Spirit will bring to us opportunities for meaningful encounter with others, even when we are not looking for them.

Chapter Twenty-Two

CHRISTIAN WORSHIP

As I write, the latest fanciful and popular television commercials for the Geico Insurance Company involve characters who are said to be known to us primarily as a result of "what they do." For example, Peter Pan is shown returning to his high school reunion. Peter, of course, is characterized by his perpetual youth. His supposed classmates, however, are all forty years older. The tag line is this: "If you are Peter Pan, you stay young forever. It's just what you do." Cumberland Presbyterians gather weekly on the Lord's Day to worship the living triune God. It is just what we do. It is the most characteristic thing that we do. It is "central," rather than peripheral, to our self-understanding, identity, and activity in the world.

Christian worship is the affirmation of God's living presence and the celebration of God's mighty acts (5.12). The *COF* begins by reminding us that worship is a meeting with another; it is a personal encounter of the most profound kind. It is an affirmation of God's personal and *living presence* with his people. At Sinai, Moses and the Hebrew people encountered God as a living presence. They responded in worship. During the sojourn in the wilderness, "the community named the tent which housed the ark of the covenant the tent of meeting because this is where God met with the covenant community. After giving Moses the instructions about the tent of meeting, God said, 'I will meet with the Israelites there. . .I will dwell among the Israelites, and I will be their God'" (Ex. 29: 43, 45).[1] The Gospels indicate that some of the persons who met Jesus understood themselves to be, somehow, in the presence of the living God. This presence evoked their gratitude and worship (Lk.17:1-9). And, after Easter, those to whom the crucified but resurrected Christ appeared responded in worship ("My Lord and my God!"–Jn. 20:28; and see, in fact, the witness of the entire New Testament). After the giving of the Spirit (Acts 2), Christians at worship understood themselves as being in the presence of the triune God through the person, presence, power, and work of the Holy Spirit. Christian worship, then, is not an activity taking place within, so to speak, a museum; and therefore dedicated only to the memory of the distant past. Christians at worship certainly remember the past, and also anticipate the future, but do both through the prism of their present encounter with the living God.

Worship is a celebration of God's mighty acts. It is an acknowledgment of *who* God is and *what* God does. God's mighty acts are his saving actions in the history of Israel, the history of Jesus Christ, and the history of the Holy Spirit. The Hebrew Scriptures exist as a recording of God's saving activity on behalf and in the midst of the people of Israel, especially the exodus from Egypt. "The content and focus of worship in the

New Testament are God's actions, especially God's redemptive actions in and through Jesus. As a key illustration of this, the NT passages that have been identified by scholars as hymns/odes and confessional formulas concentrate heavily on celebrating the actions of God and/or Jesus. For example, Phil. 2:6-11 declares Jesus' self-humbling, sacrificial obedience, and consequent exaltation to unique glory and Col. 1:5-20 heralds his divine status and unique agency in creation and redemption. Likewise, in Romans 10:9-13 where we apparently have a reference to a practice of corporate confession of faith, the focus is on Jesus' resurrection and its redemptive consequence for believers. Another passage widely regarded as preserving an early confessional form (Ro. 4: 24-25) recounts Jesus' redemptive death and resurrection, and declares them as also acts of God. As yet a further illustration, the content of the heavenly worship portrayed in Rev. 4-5 consists in praising God as almighty (4:8) and creator of all (4:11), and in praise to Jesus for his self-sacrifice and its marvelous redemptive consequences (5:9-12). It is certain that for the author this scene of heavenly worship is to inform and shape worship in the earthly churches to which he directs his text. . .It is clear that the New Testament presents worship as fundamentally a proper response to God's creative and redemptive actions. That is, in this view worship is a grateful reaction to God's prior acts, the declaration and celebration of them the core content and aim in worship."[2] Because of the truths of God's living presence and

God's mighty acts, the *COF* says worship **is central to the life of the church and is the appropriate response of all believers to the lordship and sovereignty of God** (5.12).

In worship God claims persons in Christ and offers assurance of love, forgiveness, guidance, and redemption. Believers respond to God with praise, confession, thanksgiving, love, and commitment to service (5.13). This statement speaks first of what God does in worship. And what God does is to demonstrate, again and again, God's covenant loyalty and faithfulness. It is God's one covenant of grace that is the theological heart of CP worship. The covenant is based upon God's love for his people. The response of the people in worship is also one of love. It has been particularly true of the Reformed tradition to regard worship in terms of the exchange of covenant love. "As Calvin said, the first tablet of the law was summed up by Jesus as the first and greatest commandment, the commandment to love God. Worship is, therefore, in terms of the love relationship between God and the people of God. Paul treats several liturgical questions in First Corinthians 10-14 in terms of this covenant love. For this reason, many early Reformed preachers, such as New England's Thomas Shepard, Scotland's John Willison, and New Jersey's Gilbert Tennent, often preached on the wedding feast of the Lamb at communion. They understood worship in terms of covenant love."[3] So do Cumberland Presbyterians.

Christian worship includes proclaiming the gospel of Jesus Christ, celebrating the sacraments, reading and hearing the scriptures, praying, singing, and committing life and resources to God. This common worship of the church validates and sustains such other worship as the church finds meaningful for celebrating the living presence of God (5.14).This statement focuses on the content, or ordering, of worship. The CPC and CPCA have adopted no single and set form of worship (no officially approved liturgy). New Testament scholars are agreed that it is impossible to discern such a set form in the scriptures. "Unquestionably, the NT texts give us evidence about earliest Christian worship; but we must also respect the limits of that evidence and its circumstantial nature. For example, except for 1 Cor. 10-14, we have hardly any extended description of or teaching about corporate worship, and were it not for the apparent problems with corporate worship in the Corinthian church, we would likely not have this particularly valuable but very limited body of material. . .In any case, we cannot find any clear ordering of worship actions in any of the NT texts."[4]

We do know, of course, that most of the earliest Christians were Jews and they continued for some time to worship in the synagogues, as Jesus had done. And, given that the Christian faith arose within Judaism, we can expect, and have evidence that, earliest Christian worship included elements from the practice within the synagogues—such as reading of scripture, sermons, praying, singing, giving alms, and the committing of life to the service of God. The earliest description of Christian worship dates from the second century and is contained in Justin Martyr's *First Apology*. He describes Christians "as gathering from town and country on the 'first day of the week,' the day of Christ's resurrection and so the beginning of a new creation. They would listen to 'the writings of the prophets,' and the 'memoirs of the apostles.' The president of the assembly interpreted these scriptures (the sermon). Prayers were said for the church and world. Bread and a cup of mixed wine were brought to the president, who gave thanks to God over them for creation and redemption. The bread and the wine, signs of the body and blood of Christ, were distributed and consumed. Deacons took them to the absent. In light of this description, it may be possible to see already the reflections of a service of word and sacrament."[5] While many of the actions of worship were carried over from the synagogue, we can say the distinctive dimension of Christian worship was the addition of the Lord's Supper. It, above all, was the action that made Christian worship 'Christian.'

Although having no officially adopted liturgy, CPs and CPCAs do have a *Directory of Worship* that is contained in the *COF*. It provides several suggested outlines for worship and much helpful information about the elements and actions of worship. Additionally, CPs joined with several other Reformed churches to produce the *Book of Common Worship*. It provides insight into much that has been learned about the order and content of the earliest Christian worship. Both of these resources are invaluable to congregations which desire to enrich their understanding and practice of Christian worship.

About worship, and given that CPs have no official set form or order, it should also be said that CPs believe there is a profound relationship in worship between *form* and *freedom*. In a nutshell, freedom follows from form. For example, a basketball player must learn and master the fundamentals (forms) of the game before he or she can transcend the forms in acts of creativity (freedom). Without the forms (dribbling, passing, shooting, etc.), there could be no game. Without the freedom (an incredible dribble, pass, or shot), there could hardly be any enthusiasm for the game. A musician must learn and master the musical scale (form) before transcending the scale in acts of unique creativity (freedom). Philosophically speaking, there can be no freedom without form. CP's have inherited certain forms of worship from scripture, the earliest Christians, and from the Reformed tradition. These forms are important to us. We also pray that the Holy Spirit (like a good coach or musical mentor) will enable us to express our unique creativity (freedom) in worship. God, after all, wants *us* for relationship and not our forms; even though it is these forms that can and do enable us to give ourselves to God.

Any discussion of the content and order of Christian worship should not fail to take into account its Christological pattern. The *Directory of Worship* provides an excellent introductory statement about this pattern: "Christian worship is in the name of Jesus Christ, in the power of Jesus Christ, and in the freedom of Jesus Christ. Jesus, through his birth, life, death, and resurrection offered up perfect worship to God, and, as Christians, we are free to participate in that perfect expression of praise. Therefore, the life and ministry of Jesus Christ is central to Christian worship, and all Christian worship seeks to reflect and be shaped by that life and ministry. Jesus Christ is the living Word whose presence and spirit alone make valid all of Christian worship. [6] The meaning of this statement may become clearer, if need be, when reflecting on the New Testament witness that Jesus Christ is both son of man and Son of God. As Son of God, he brings God to us. And this is the first movement of Christian worship. It is God moving toward us in Jesus Christ and the power of the Holy Spirit. In worship, God reveals not just things about himself but God's very self to us. Equally true is that Jesus, as son of man,—as a human being in solidarity with humanity—offered up perfect service, obedience and worship to God. This is the second movement in Christian worship.

So Jesus, in his humanity and solidarity with us, brings us to God. All Christian worship, therefore, finds its foundation in the revelation Jesus Christ has made to us and in the response to God that Jesus makes for us. Does this mean that in Christian worship we merely seek to emulate the response of Jesus? Decidedly not! Christian worship *is participation* (through the ministry of the Holy Spirit uniting us to Christ) in the perfect worship of Jesus. The church, then, does not invent worship. Rather, through God's grace, the church joins in the unceasing worship being offered by her Lord. To worship in Jesus' name is to join that worship being offered by the church's high priest (Heb. 4:11-16) and the whole host of heaven (Rev. 5:11-14). This is the Christological pattern of Christian worship.

God is to be worshiped both corporately and privately. Corporate worship is practiced in the gathered congregation, in small groups within the church, and in larger gatherings of believers. Private worship, through meditation, prayer, and study of the scriptures, is practiced in various settings, especially in the home by individuals and the family (5.15). These statements are clear enough in their meaning. Both corporate worship and private worship are important, even necessary, activities for Christians. I take note of the use of the word "practice" with respect to worship. And it evokes a memory. When I was pastor of the Milan, Tennessee congregation, I heard a story about a football running back at the University of Tennessee. His name was Travis Stephens. He never played a down in a game for the first three years he was there. But he practiced as if everything might depend on him. He was beat up day after day, year after year, in the grueling practice sessions. He was a player who always thought about the good of the team rather than himself. Finally, though, his senior season arrived and he was given the opportunity to play. He proceeded to break all the single season rushing records in the history of the football program. There is a sense in which Christian worship is practice. We gather weekly to practice our faith. Sometimes, admittedly, reciting the same creeds, singing the same hymns, listening to (and giving) the same sermons, etc. may occasionally seem like drudgery to us. But slowly we are being formed, shaped into disciples. And we never know when, after weeks or years in worship, we may find ourselves "in the game." This is to say that in our daily lives in the world we may be brought into that moment, or situation, in which we are the very ones needed, and who have the opportunity, to bear significant witness in the world to the good news of God's action in Jesus Christ. And without all the "practice" it is possible, perhaps probable, that when such moments came, we would miss them!

From a Sermon on Christian Worship

I would like to make use of a portion of a text, Ephesians 5:6-20, to make a single point about the significance and meaning of worship to and for Cumberland Presbyterians. I encourage persons to read the entire passage but Ephesians 5:15-20 is included here: "Be careful then how you live, not as unwise people but as wise, making the most of the time, because the days are evil. So do not be foolish, but understand what the will of the Lord is. Do not get drunk with wine, for that is debauchery; but be filled with the Spirit, as you sing psalms and hymns and spiritual songs among yourselves, singing and making melody to the Lord in your hearts, giving thanks to God the Father at all times and for everything in the name of our Lord Jesus Christ."

It is a cardinal rule of reading scripture that it is important to consider the context in which a given text appears. The over-all context of the letter to the Ephesians, and especially the text above, is that the Christians to whom it was addressed lived in the city of Ephesus. This fact calls forth a pastoral memory. When I was a very young pastor, my wife and I visited in the home of members who had just returned from a vacation. I remember being slightly startled when the man said, "We just got back from Las Vegas." At that point in my pastoral and personal journey, I was unaware that Christians went to places like Las Vegas. Why would they? I thought Christians, at least in my part of the world, went to places like Gatlinburg, Tennessee, or Bellingrath Gardens in Mobile, or the Ave Maria Grotto in Cullman, Alabama. If they were "back-slidden" and wanted to live on the edge, they might go to Panama City, Florida. But Las Vegas?—This was quite a revelation to me.

I tell you this story because the ancient city of Ephesus was a lot like Las Vegas, with Bourbon Street in New Orleans thrown in for good measure. At the center of the city stood the great temple of Diana, or Artemis—the goddess of fertility and therefore sex. Ephesus was a place that was dedicated to the pleasing and pleasuring of the self (perhaps this is why Paul wrote, in Eph. 5:10, "Try to find out what is pleasing to the Lord"). It was a seaport town. This meant lots of sailors—no offense to sailors. But it was a city in which the pleasing of the self and its desires was the main priority for commerce, entertainment, and even religion. You could cruise into Ephesus, so to speak, get off the boat, and be greeted by a Chamber of Commerce sign reading, "What happens in Ephesus stays in Ephesus."

Paul's concern when writing to the relatively tiny congregation in Ephesus can be expressed in this question: "How can you and do you remain Christian, followers of Jesus, when you live 24 hours a day, 7 days a week, in a dominant culture in which almost nothing, if anything, will support you in following Christ?" How do you remain Christian in a place that tells you that life is all about you and what you want, what you can get, and what you can pay for?

Paul proceeds to talk about the kind of weird way that Christians will be able to remain Christians even though they live in Ephesus. He might have told them to attempt to elect the right Christian politicians who would clean the place up. But this he did not do. He might have told them to become a kind of inwardly focused sect entirely closed off from the surrounding world. This he does not do. He might have told them to hate their culture and to spend all their time in reaction to it and denouncement of it. But this he does not do. What he does do is deceptively simple, but powerfully important. He tells them to gather together and worship!

It is in and through worship that these Christians will be able to remain followers of Jesus even though they live in a culture that appears to know nothing of or about Jesus. Paul knew that Ephesus would feed every dark impulse of the human mind and spirit, but in and through worship Christians would be fed with bread and wine—they would feed on Jesus. Paul knew that the powers ruling Ephesus were engaged in a massive deception about the purpose and meaning of life. But in worship Christians would hear the truth-orienting word of God. Ephesus would offer to fill your body and brain with every stimulant then known to humankind. But in worship Christians would be filled with the Holy Spirit. So Paul says the people should get together and worship. And it was to be no somber and sad affair. They were to sing joyously and joyfully about the goodness of their Lord. Perhaps Paul meant they were to put themselves into worship the same way they many citizens of Ephesus put themselves into the gladiatorial games and circuses over at the stadium.

One of the most profound things I have read about

worship came from the pen of C.S. Lewis. He said, “You are not really dancing if you must count the steps.” The steps are important of course. They are the fundamentals. But you are really dancing when you transcend the steps and find yourself in the swing of things. Many Cumberland Presbyterian congregations use bulletins or programs of worship. The programs contain the steps of worship, and they are important, very important. Examples of the classic steps may be found in the Directory of Worship in the *COF* and in the Book of Common Worship (authorized and produced by Cumberland Presbyterians and other Reformed churches). The steps are there so we may worship the Lord properly and in continuity with our Reformed and early Christian heritage. But what we hunger for, and what is possible by the power of the Holy Spirit, is a great and joyous dance with the Triune God. It is this dance of worship that enables us to remain Christians with joy, peace, courage, and empowerment.

Chapter Twenty-Three

BAPTISM

Before considering baptism in particular, the *COF* addresses statements concerning the significance and meaning of both of the Christian sacraments (baptism and the Lord's Supper). **Sacraments are signs and testimonies of God's covenant of grace. Circumcision and passover are the sacraments of the Old Testament; baptism and the Lord's Supper are the sacraments of the New Testament. They are given by God and through his presence, word, and will are made effective** (5.16). Sacraments are ritual enactments of who we are as God's people, and testimonies (enacted words) of who God is and what God has done for us. As such, sacraments are not *merely* symbols of our faith, but *fully* symbols of our faith. Wedding rings, in general, are merely symbols of marriage. But there is nothing merely symbolic about my *own* wedding ring. It is fully symbolic of a lifetime of shared commitment, life, and love. It is the latter that *invests* my particular ring with powerful significance in and for my life. Sacraments are signs of God's investment in us—God's utter grace, faithfulness, and love toward us expressed in the one covenant of grace.

Sacraments are actions in which God and we acknowledge covenant love and faithfulness. Just as marriage brings us into a new state of being and existence in the world, the Christian sacraments point out that we have been brought into the same. The sacramental actions are signs and testimonies of a change that we have undergone, and are undergoing. We are no longer who we once were. Our identity has undergone, and is undergoing, a profound transformation. Rowan Williams writes, "The sacramental action traces a transition from one sort of reality to another: first, it describes a pre-sacramental state, a secular or profane condition now imagined, for ritual purposes, in the light of and in terms of the transformation that is to be enacted; it tells us that where we habitually are is not, after all, a neutral place but a place of loss or need. It then requires us to set aside this damaged or needy condition, this flawed identity, so that in dispossessing ourselves of it we are able to become possessed of a different identity. . .not constructed by negotiation and co-operation like other forms of social identity. The rite requires us *not* to belong any more to the categories we thought we belonged in, so that a distinctive kind of new belonging can be realized."[1] The New Testament consistently bears witness to the new belonging, the new identity, that is enacted in, and made visible by, the performance of the sacraments. To select only one example, the sacraments visually proclaim the following truth: "Once you were not a people, but now you are God's people; Once you had not received mercy, but now you have received mercy" (1 Pt. 2:10).

The Cumberland Presbyterian *Directory of Worship* includes the following theological reflection on the sacraments: "Baptism and the Lord's Supper, the two sacraments instituted by Christ, are part of the full expression of corporate worship. They are understood to be signs of Christ's presence with us and thereby belong to the regular worship of Christians. The primary importance in both sacraments is what God does and the reality of God's self-giving in and through water, bread and wine. Like all aspects of worship they are corporate acts in the deepest sense, and they always point to the saving grace of Christ and Christ's benefits offered to us. Especially do the sacraments re-enact the redemptive acts of God by which we are united to Jesus Christ and made one in Christ. The power and meaning of the sacraments depend upon the presence of Jesus Christ, the incarnate Word. They are also linked to the proclaimed word, and are inseparably connected to the Word, incarnate and proclaimed. They are in a true sense a visible Word. The Word and the sacraments together give the fundamental shape to all Christian worship."[2]

Jesus Christ ordained the sacraments of baptism and the Lord's Supper for the church (5.17, and see Mt. 28:19-20; Mk. 14: 22-25; 1 Cor. 10:16-17, 11:23-26). **They are administered by and through the church as part of her common worship, being entrusted to properly ordained ministers under the authority of a judicatory of the church** (5.17). This second sentence has a history going back to the Reformation, especially the fact that the sacraments are entrusted to properly ordained ministers. Roman Catholic theology held that priests alone could preside over the sacrament. It was argued that in their ordinations priests had undergone an "ontological" change; that is a change in their being which qualified them to consecrate and serve the sacraments. The priest had received "something spiritually special" in his very being that the layperson had not, and could never, receive. The Reformers rejected this view. In ordination, the minister receives nothing from God that is not also given to all God's people. People, of course, do have different gifts for ministry and are therefore assigned different functions. But still, according to Reformed theology, the minister receives nothing in his or her "being" that is with-held by God from all other Christians.

There is nothing "spiritually special or especially spiritual" about the minister. The purpose of the sacraments being entrusted to the minister, under the authority of a presbytery, is simply a matter of safe-guarding the sacraments. That is, to help insure they are properly understood and performed. The minister is assigned this responsibility not because he or she is somehow possessed by a "mystical" (or magical?) spiritual power, but because he or she has been trained and authorized by the church to perform this function on behalf of the church. As the *COF* says of the sacraments, **they are administered by and through the church as a part of her common worship**. It has been an encouragement for many congregations that, in recent years, elders have been trained and authorized by presbytery's to administer the sacrament of the Lord's Supper in situations where an ordained minister is not available. Christ gave the sacraments to the church and not to priests and ministers.

Following its statements about the sacraments in general, the *COF* next speaks in particular about baptism. **Baptism symbolizes the baptism of the Holy Spirit and is the external sign of the covenant which marks membership in the community of faith. In this sacrament the church witnesses to God's initiative to claim persons in Christ, forgive their sins, grant them grace, shape and order their lives through the work of the Holy Spirit, and set them apart for service** (5.18). Baptism is the rite of Christian initiation; it is the doorway into the life of Christ and the church, marking persons as members of the body of Christ and incorporating them into the one covenant of grace. Since the time of the 16th century Reformation, the churches of the Reformed tradition, eventually including Cumberland Presbyterians, have understood water baptism as representing the baptism of the Holy Spirit (that inward work of the Spirit described in earlier chapters which awakens sinners to their need of Christ and brings them to saving faith). The *Directory of Worship* speaks of baptism: "Baptism is the sign of God's love for us and of Christ's grace extended to us. In baptism, God claims persons as his own and marks them as particularly his, heirs of the covenant of grace.

Baptism signifies and represents the forgiveness of sin, the engrafting into Christ, the coming of the Holy Spirit into our lives, and the death and resurrection to new life. It is both proclamation and affirmation. It proclaims that God's grace and love reach out to people before they are able to respond, and it affirms our new identity as members of the body of Christ. It sets people apart from the rest of the world, and claims them as participants in the ministry of Jesus Christ."[3]

It might be noticed that the *Directory of Worship* expands the meaning of baptism that is found in the *COF*. In addition to symbolizing the work of the Holy Spirit as the *COF* says, the *Directory* states that baptism also signifies, "forgiveness of sins, the engrafting into Christ, and the death and resurrection to new life." This expansion is very significant. Since the time of the Reformation, an often bitter dispute over the meaning of baptism, and the mode of performing it, has marked American Protestant church relationships. What baptism *actually* symbolizes and how it is to be *performed,* and what can be discerned from scripture about these questions, severely divided congregations from different traditions (and still does). It is worth noting that the majority of Cumberland Presbyterian congregations are located in the southern United States. Thus they are located where a different and single meaning of baptism is prevalent in the surrounding Christian culture. This prevailing view, based on passages from Paul (Rom. 6: 3-5; Col. 2:12), insists that baptism is to be understood as symbolic of the believer's immersion into "the death, burial, and resurrection of Christ." This is a fervently held belief. To those who hold it, it is of such importance that any other possible meaning, or meanings, of baptism, and any other way of practicing baptism, (except by bodily immersion in water) is rejected outright. These Christians are convinced that scripture (meaning the Apostle Paul) is patently clear on the subject.

One way to think about the obvious conflict over what baptism means and how it is to be performed is to consider something scholars report about the writings of the Apostle Paul. It is a striking fact that he seems to have known very little about the earthly life of Jesus and the details of his ministry (remember that Paul wrote before the Gospels were written). If Paul knew of such details, he never speaks of them. What Paul does know about, and glories in, is the cross and resurrection of Jesus. It is these realities that dominate his theology and writings. The cross and resurrection of Jesus seems even to have impacted his style of thinking and writing. In much of what he writes, it is possible to detect an "up and down" pattern. The pattern appears in his logic and in the witness he bears about Jesus. Therefore, it is not unusual, or surprising, that Paul assigns this meaning (death, burial, and resurrection) to baptism in his letters to the Romans and Colossians. It simply fits his way of thinking and doing theology. It reflects the power of the cross and resurrection upon his life and thought.

But there are other voices in the New Testament which speak about baptism. The synoptic Gospels (Matthew, Mark, and Luke) report the baptism of Jesus, and the Gospel of John alludes to it. Rather than the up and down pattern found in Paul, the Gospel writers employed the image of *descent* when reporting the baptism of Jesus. It was at his baptism that the Holy Spirit descended upon Jesus like a dove and the voice spoke from heaven (understood as downward) declaring him to be God's well-favored Son. It was the work of the Spirit in the life of Jesus, and in his baptism, that captured the imagination of the leaders of the Reformed tradition and subsequently the Cumberland Presbyterian Church. The granting of the Holy Spirit was interpreted as the fundamental meaning of baptism for Christians, as it apparently had been for Jesus. The descent of the Holy Spirit, for them, was fittingly symbolized by the sprinkling or pouring of water upon the head of the candidate for baptism. Cumberland Presbyterians do not deny that for Paul, and some other early Christians, baptism symbolized the death, burial, and resurrection of Jesus. It does stand there in scripture (in Romans and Colossians). It is just that Cumberland Presbyterians do not believe this is all that scripture says about baptism or indicates that baptism may symbolize or mean.

Along with multiple scriptural voices about baptism in scripture, we also now have access to many more of the documents, theologies, and practices from the very earliest centuries of the Christian church. This fortunate circumstance is due to the efforts of modern biblical scholarship and especially, with respect to worship, the modern liturgical renewal movement. This movement, going on for the last one hundred and fifty years, was a scholarly retrieval of this early material. As a result, we have been able to come to a surprising certainty. Namely, early Christians were quite diverse in their understanding of the meaning of baptism and the mode by which to perform it. As to mode, some early Christians baptized by immersion and some by sprinkling or pouring water. As to meaning, early Christians employed a truly wide array of biblical images to describe what God was doing in baptism. I will include some of them at the end of this chapter.

If we fast-forward to the 16th century and the Protestant Reformation in Europe, we discover that different groups of Christians latched on to single meanings of baptism and single modes for its conduct. It is very important to remember that these Reformers had access to the Bible (and they were now reading the Bible anew; no longer under the aegis of the Roman Catholic Church) but not to the records of the early church as have been recovered over the past two centuries. Perhaps the Reformation Christians, who broke up into different parties and for whom the first centuries of the church existed only in the shadows, determined that giving baptism one meaning, and insisting on performing it rightly only in one way, had apologetic value. It enabled them to say, "This is how we are distinguished from you. And this is why we are right and you are wrong!" This form of apologetic, as we mentioned earlier, survives today. But we now know that the early church, as a whole, was simply not reductionist regarding the meaning of the sacrament of baptism. Rather, the evidence shows they were quite expansive in their use of imagery related to how to understand the meaning of baptism. The event was so singular and profound that they searched the scriptures, and human analogies, for multiple ways to speak about it.

There is something here of profound import for Cumberland Presbyterians. The work of the liturgical renewal movement, and of other scholars of the early church, enabled our *COF* and our *Directory of Worship* to express fidelity to both the classical Reformed understanding of baptism's meaning and, at the same time, to benefit from what has been learned from early Christianity. The statement in the *COF*—that baptism symbolizes the baptism of the Holy Spirit—is faithful to the classic Reformed theology of baptism. The statements in the *Directory of Worship*—that baptism also symbolizes forgiveness of sin, engrafting into Christ, and, especially, death and resurrection to new life—reflect awareness of the modern liturgical renewal movement. Are they in contradiction? Absolutely not! What they together represent is both a fidelity to tradition and also openness to reform in light of new understandings. This is an example of what it means to be a church in the Reformed tradition (namely, such a church is capable of change, reform). Perhaps, more importantly,

Cumberland Presbyterians are now freed from the age old disputes about the meaning and method of baptism (although most CP and CPCA congregation still exist in settings where Paul's way is the only way). As to meaning, we are freed to be expansive as was the early church, and without apology. As to method or mode, the *COF* states plainly in 5.21: **In administering the sacrament the pouring or sprinkling of water on the person by the minister fittingly symbolizes the baptism of the Holy Spirit** (the classic Reformed position); **however, the validity of the sacrament is not dependent upon its mode of administration** (the earliest Christians employed diverse modes).

What about the baptism of infants? Our *COF* endorses this practice when saying: **The sacrament of baptism is administered to infants, one or both of whose parents or guardians affirm faith in Jesus Christ and assume the responsibilities of the covenant"** (5.19). The practice of baptizing infants has also been a matter of dispute among Christians for centuries. Whether scripture supports or does not support this practice has been at the center of the dispute. What we now know for certain (again as a result of the work of the liturgical renewal movement) is that some early Christian congregations definitely engaged in this practice and some other congregations did not. The point I want to make is we can no longer, if ever we did, appeal to the practice of the early church to settle the question. Already, as far back as we can reach, Christians embraced different views about the matter. Neither can we settle the matter based on a direct appeal to scripture. While the practice is not explicitly set forth in scripture, the accounts of "whole households" receiving baptism have been considered an argument in its favor. Persons can and will demand that scripture settles the question against the baptism of infants, but thoughtful people will demur from this demand.

A special argument against the baptism of infants arose at the time of the Reformation (it had been the practice of the Roman Catholic Church for over a thousand years). Namely, it was customary for every child to receive baptism simply by virtue of their having been born in a particular "Christian country." The state and the church were fundamentally one. This appeared to some of the Reformers, particularly those belonging to the left-wing of the Reformation (Anabaptists, Hutterites, Baptists, etc.), to be a practice that had severely weakened the church. It was obvious to them that baptism meant very little to many people who had been baptized as infants. And, in their view, it was not only "unscriptural" but had become more a "state and culturally approved function" than an explicitly Christian one. But, despite this argument at the time of the Reformation, it is simply an historical fact that there were some, probably many, early Christian congregations that practiced the baptism of infants long before the church was supported culturally and endorsed and approved by the state.

In the end, in my view, the best, and perhaps only, reason to support the practice of the baptism of infants is because a strong, clear, and consistent theological case can be made for it (as opposed to an explicitly scriptural one). The *COF* suggests that just such a case can be made. There is not space here to discuss a fully orbed theology of baptism, whether of infants or adults. But this much can be said. First, the meanings of baptism are the same for the infant and the adult. Second, the practice of the baptism of infants is founded on a particular view of the nature of the church (and ecclesiological theology). The CPC, according to the one covenant of grace, views the church as a "family." One does not choose membership in a family. One is simply born to be in it. An infant, it is hoped all infants, will receive the love, compassion, nurture, and support of the family long before he or she comes to understand what this means. The infant, and then small child, is given all the signs of belonging to the family—a name, a place at the table, a bed to sleep in, etc. And just as circumcision signed the belonging of the children of Israelites to the covenant community (based on God's prevenient love of and grace toward them), so the baptism of infants functions in this way for Cumberland Presbyterians. Thirdly, in families, it is hoped, and expected, that a child will reach the point of gratitude for having received the love, nurture, and support of his or her family. Just so, Cumberland Presbyterians hope, and expect, that children who have been baptized will reach a point of affirming the meaning of their baptism and therefore make a personal affirmation of their faith in and love for Jesus Christ (some CP congregations have encouraged this through the practice of confirmation). This is made more predictable when it can be said of a child that **one or both of whose parents or guardians affirm faith in Jesus Christ and assume the responsibilities of the covenant** (5.19). I would like to add, given the continuing demise of Christendom in American culture, that in the years to come the baptism of infants, as well as adults, might once again take on the powerful significance that it had among the earliest Christians who lived in cultures that did not recognize Jesus as Lord.

An alternative to the Cumberland Presbyterian view of the church (and the view we believe is found in scripture), arose at the time of the Reformation. The CPC view is founded upon, as we have been discussing, the Hebraic concept of corporate-ness, of covenant community, of solidarity of family. The new view was grounded in the elevation of the individual. As has been discussed in an earlier chapter, the Reformation was roughly contemporaneous with the European Enlightenment. The centerpiece of Enlightenment thought was its placing of the individual in a newly exalted status (he or she could now make up his own mind, not influenced by hierarchies like church, king, or state, etc.). Some of the Reformation leaders were influenced by this development. They made one's relationship to God primarily an individual matter. It was the individual who had to decide, or choose, to have a relationship to God/Christ. This was a very complex development but it resulted in the rejection of the baptism of infants (so rejecting the corporate, familial concept of the church) in favor of a "believers only baptism." Thus there also arose an individualistic ecclesiology. No one is or can be a member of the church, belong to the community of Christ, except by personal volition. The point here is that what you believe about baptism depends on what you believe about the nature of the church. Personally, I am extremely grateful for the CPC corporate understanding of the church. I am especially grateful for it in light of the modern, post-modern, secular elevation of the individual to being an autonomous, free-standing, all-important self. No wonder there is such widespread isolation, loneliness, and desperation among a people who have been trained to think life is all about the individual.

While I have preached, taught, and administered baptism according to the statements of the *COF*, I have also shared with congregations the fruits of the research done in and by the liturgical renewal movement. I have done so for reasons of sacramental, congregational, and personal enrichment for those who have been baptized in water and Spirit as disciples of Jesus Christ. Here are some of the meanings assigned to baptism by the earliest Christians (those of the first three centuries):

- Baptism as Social Sign. It seems the case that the principal meaning of baptism for some early Christians was that it was a sign that Christian Jews and Gentiles have now been brought together and united in the one body of Jesus Christ. Thus baptism was a sign of an altogether new social reality in the world.

- Baptism as Doorway. The Gospel of John records that Jesus said, "I am the door" (Jn. 10:9). Early on, this image was applied to baptism. It is easy to understand why. Baptism was the rite of entry into the church and incorporation into the life of Christ and his people. Baptism was the door which opened upon covenant life in the kingdom of God. The memory of this image may still be seen in many European church buildings, and those in other countries, in which the baptismal font stands just inside the door of the sanctuary.

- Baptism as Union with Christ. Baptism was being united to Christ in both his dying and rising. In some early baptismal rites, candidates would disrobe, enter the baptismal waters, receive baptism, and then be given a symbolic white robe. The robe represented their having "put on Christ" (Rom. 13:12-14; Eph. 4:22-24; Col. 3:10). Following baptism, new Christians were no longer united to the world they had left behind (many early Christians did, in fact, leave behind family, religions, and stations in life in order to follow Jesus) but united to Christ and his people. The Christian experience, represented in baptism, was one of being "in Christ" (2 Cor. 5:17; Col. 4:7; Phil 4:1; Rom. 16:3). This was understood to be a real and substantial union, and not just a symbolic one,

- Baptism as New Birth. New birth was one of the most frequent images applied to baptism. The image was taken from Jesus' encounter with Nicodemus (Jn. 3). Natural birth is leaving the mother's womb and entering into a wide new world. It is learning to walk, talk, embrace, learn, grow, be socialized, receive, give, love, and serve and so much more. When a person passed through the baptismal waters in the early church, that person now had a new life. He or she would be taught to walk, talk, and live as a disciple of Jesus Christ. This new life, far from being a solo journey, required the assistance of others. The "infant Christian" required nurturing in order to grow toward maturity in Christ.

- Baptism as Spirit Experience. Early Christians recognized that the Gospels presented Jesus as a Spirit person. The Spirit of God was involved in his conception. The Spirit descended upon him at his baptism. His ministry was one of confronting evil spirits in the power of God the Spirit. He promised the disciples that the Spirit—the Holy Spirit—would be given to them when he had taken leave of this world. In John's Gospel, the resurrected Christ appeared and breathed the Holy Spirit upon the disciples. In Acts 2, the Spirit is given to the church on the day of Pentecost. The early church regarded baptism as the experience in which new believers were given a share in the Spirit. As the Spirit had descended upon Jesus at his baptism, so the Spirit descended into the lives of those who passed through the waters of baptism. Down they went into the waters, and up they came as newly in-Spirited people.

- Baptism as Forgiveness of Sins. The early church also associated baptism with forgiveness of sins (Lk. 3:3; Acts 2:38). The phrase "forgiveness of sins" seems to have had a quite specific meaning for Jews and early Christians. This meaning drew upon the memory of that time when the people of God were living in bitter exile among the Babylonians. Israel's prophets had interpreted this exile as God's punishment for Israel's sins. But the prophets also promised that God would forgive the sins of the people and deliver them from exile. Thus the announcement of "the forgiveness of sins" and "the end of exile" went hand in hand. Forgiveness of sins was a way of saying the exile was now over! The people were freed to return home and resume their covenant relationship to God. Early Christian preaching and teaching understood Jesus to have proclaimed, in his own life and ministry, the end of exile. People need no longer remain captive to the powers of the world. When a person was baptized, he or she was no longer in bondage to this present evil age. Instead, he or she now enjoyed the freedom of new life in and under God's reign. Forgiveness of sins meant that the baptized person was now a free citizen in the kingdom of God that was announced by and made present in Jesus Christ.

Chapter Twenty-Four

THE LORD'S SUPPER

About the Lord's Supper, the *COF* says: **The Lord's Supper was instituted by Jesus Christ on the night of his betrayal. It is a means by which the church remembers and shows forth Christ's passion and death on the cross. The sacrament is also a perpetual means given to the church to celebrate and experience the continuing presence of the risen Lord and her expectation of the Lord's return** (5.23). It is generally recognized that table fellowship with sinners was at the very heart of the ministry of Jesus. Israel's ancient prophets had promised that the coming of God's kingdom on earth would be a time of celebration characterized by festive eating and drinking. Jesus' own table fellowship with sinners—what some scholars call open commensality—was an enacted proclamation by him that the long awaited kingdom was arriving and in his very own person and ministry. It is understandable that such table fellowship would continue to be at the heart of the early church's life (Acts 2:46).

The Lord's Supper—also called Holy Communion and the Eucharist—harkens back to Jesus' practice of proclaiming the presence of the kingdom of God through these acts of table fellowship. According to the Synoptic Gospels (Mt. 26:26-29;

Mk. 14:12-26; Lu. 22:7-39), it was at and during the special Jewish moment of table celebration known as the Passover that Jesus transformed the meal into what would become the Lord's Supper. John's Gospel, seemingly for his own theological purposes, has the meal precede the Passover celebration by at least twenty-four hours. It is thought that his theme of Jesus as the Lamb of God sacrificed for the sins of the world (Jn. 1:29; 19:36) led him to locate the meal at precisely the time animals were being ritually slaughtered in the Temple. But that the meal itself was vitally important to the churches influenced by John is pointed to in John's great "bread of life" discussion recorded in John 6.

As for the significance of the Supper, Morrow writes, "The Passover celebrated God's mighty act of the salvation of the people of Israel from bondage in Egypt and their creation as the covenant community.. . .It is no accident that Jesus instituted the Lord's Supper in the context of the celebration of the Passover. Anticipating the events that were to occur, Jesus transformed the Passover into the Lord's Supper as a dramatic portrayal and embodiment of the mighty act of God's salvation of the whole world."[1] The words of Jesus were at the heart of this transformation: of the bread, he said, "Take, eat; this is my body." And of the cup, he said, "Drink from it, all of you; for this is my blood of the (new) covenant, which is poured out for many for the forgiveness of sins" (Mt. 26:26-27). Luke remembers that he said, "Do this in remembrance of me" (Lu. 22:19).

The Lord's Supper is an event in and through which, as the *COF* indicates, the church looks backward. It does so in remembrance of Jesus' saving death (and his whole life; "body" represents the whole life of Jesus; so does "blood;" in the Hebraic thought world blood is synonymous with life). But Morrow points out something truly important: "Though the Lord's Supper is a remembrance of the death of Jesus, it is not a celebration of his death. It is a celebration of the new life made possible through the resurrection. It is not the dead Christ who is present in the Lord's Supper but the resurrected, living Christ. The Good News of the resurrection makes the Lord's Supper a celebration."[2] The *Directory of Worship* adds: "This sacrament is more than a memorial to, or a reminder of, Christ's sacrificial death and resurrection. It is a means, instituted by Christ for his disciples, through which the risen Lord is truly present with his people as a continuing power and reality. While the meaning of Christ's sacrificial death is at the heart of this sacrament, it is a resurrected, living Christ whom we encounter through the bread and wine."[3]

The church also looks forward in its celebration of the Lord's Supper. As the *COF* says, the church lives in **expectation of the Lord's return** (5.23). This return represents the consummation of history and the full realization of the kingdom of God. As mentioned above, Israel's ancient prophets spoke of the time of the kingdom as one of festive and joyous eating and drinking. This theme is carried forward in the Book of Revelation where it is imaged as the great wedding banquet that is the "marriage supper of the Lamb" (Rev. 19:9). The Lord's Supper is a celebration of what has been but also a celebration of what will be. It looks forward to that time when "The kingdom of the world has become the kingdom of our Lord and his Messiah, and he will reign forever and ever" (Rev. 11:15). But the church which looks backward in grateful remembrance and forward in faith, hope, and love, also, in and through the Lord's Supper, celebrates that the living Lord, is present now to and with the church. The Lord is the true host of the meal. When he breaks bread for us, and lifts the cup for us, we celebrate his presence with us. The Lord's Supper is a dynamic living event in the living church made possible by the living Lord.

As a practical concern, the Confession says: **Each congregation should celebrate this sacrament regularly. Every Christian should receive it frequently** (5.27). It should be noted that this statement is a concession to centuries of Reformed and Presbyterian history. It is an established fact that the breaking of bread and sharing of cup was at the heart of early Christian worship. In fact, it has been argued convincingly that it was the distinctive element in Christian worship. The early church shared with the Judaism of its day the reading of scripture, the singing of hymns, the giving of alms, the preaching from texts, and more. The altogether new element in Christian worship was the sharing of the meal in memory and celebration of Jesus. If the church had gathered for worship without this meal, it would hardly be "Christian" worship. Thus it appears the early church celebrated the Lord's Supper on each occasion that the church gathered.

So, what happened? As history evolved under Roman Catholic theology, the Lord's Supper was transformed into the weekly mass. The 16th century Reformers rejected the mass on the basis of various theological accretions and practices that had developed around it. They sought to return the Lord's Supper to what they considered to be a more biblically informed and practiced sacrament (some Reformers even rejected the word "sacrament" favoring the word "ordinance"). Unfortunately, the fact that the mass was weekly influenced some of the Reformers to opt for a less frequent celebration (the Scottish wing of the Reformed church opted for once a year). John Calvin, the progenitor of the Reformed and Presbyterian tradition, did not share this opinion. He clearly understood the Lord's Supper should be a weekly celebration. However, despite his efforts, he was unable to establish a weekly celebration in the congregations of Geneva. This fact, along with other factors too numerous to be discussed here, resulted in the practice of infrequent communion in the Presbyterian, and subsequently Cumberland Presbyterian, tradition. In the Cumberland Presbyterian congregation in which I grew up, the Lord's Supper was celebrated only four times a year. This seems to have been a common schedule in the middle of the 20th century. In the intervening years, and with growing knowledge about the meaning, significance, and practice of the meal in the early church, many Cumberland Presbyterian congregations have more frequent celebrations. In many congregations, it is not uncommon for the Lord's Supper to be celebrated at least monthly. This is an encouraging development. As the *COF* says, **each congregation should celebrate this sacrament regularly. Every Christian should receive it frequently** (5.27).

The elements used in this sacrament are bread and the fruit of the vine, which represent the body and blood of Christ. The elements themselves are never to be worshiped, for they are never anything other than bread and the fruit of the vine (5.24). As with many of the statements in the *COF,* this one has an important theological background. At the time of the Reformation, the question arose, with ferocity, as to in what sense Christ was present in the Lord's Supper, or, as it was called in the Roman Church, the mass or Eucharist. The Catholic position was called *transubstantiation*. In some mysterious way, the ordinary bread and wine were transformed, at the time of the priest's prayer of consecration, into the *actual* body and blood of Christ. Christ, then, was present in the host, or elements. This led, among some Catholics, to the practice of the veneration of the host. As to be expected, the Reformers rejected *transubstantiation*. Martin Luther opted for what he called *con-substantiation*. He said the host remains bread and wine but Christ's body and blood were joined to them. Ulrich Zwingli led a wing of the Reformation that opted to consider the elements as simply that—elements. Rather than emphasizing the question of the presence of Christ, Zwingli and his followers considered the Lord's Supper as a memorial of Christ's death. The elements were merely *symbols* of Christ's body and blood. John Calvin argued that Christ was spiritually present in the celebration of the Supper. His view eventually led to an understanding that is common among many Protestants today and, surprisingly, advocated by a few Roman Catholic liturgical theologians. Namely the focus on the nature of the elements that began in earnest in the 9th century and became a source of conflict in the 16th century was wrongheaded. The place that Christ is present in the meal is where Christ is always present—with his people. He is present with them, and in them, as the body of Christ when they break, take, give, and receive bread and the fruit of the vine. He is present in these actions—which were the actions of his very own self-donating life. He is present in the life together and thankful praises of his people!

This re-direction of focus from elements to people should not, however, lessen an appreciation for the elements themselves. As said elsewhere about symbols, the elements of bread and fruit of the vine are not *merely* symbols but *fully* symbols for Cumberland Presbyterians. For one thing, they are elements from nature. This, in itself, can remind us that God in

Christ is at work redeeming all of creation. And that nature is God's gift to us. Nature sustains us. We move in a wrong direction if we de-value nature, the material world. This material, physical world is God's gift to us. We should not think that God is concerned only for, or works only through, "spiritual means." Secondly, scripture indicates that God himself has a high regard for the symbolic. It is God who placed a rainbow in the sky and with symbolic meaning. It is God who instructed the people to build the tent of meeting and to endow it with powerful symbolic meaning. Jesus gave us bread and wine partly because we are a symbol-making, symbol needing people. We, for example, could simply say "Happy Birthday" to a child. But we realize words cannot quite do it all. So we have a cake and candles and sing a song. With ritual and symbol, we are saying something more than can be said with words. It is not insignificant that the world is moved along by the symbolic. My six year old granddaughter just learned at school, in first grade, that there is something called a North Face jacket. And she wants one! The secular world is a highly symbolic world. And many, if not most, of its symbols carry a meaning that confirms humanity in its rebellion against God. How important it is, then, that Cumberland Presbyterians appreciate the symbolic world and reality of God's salvation that we encounter in the Lord's Supper. The symbols are God's/Christ's enacted word. They speak not only to our ears, our heads, but also to our innermost depths. Symbols and symbolic actions have that kind of power. Once again, bread and wine are for us not *merely* symbols but *fully* symbols. So, the *COF* says **because the sacrament represents the Savior's passion and death, it should not be received without due self-examination, reverence, humility, and grateful awareness of Christ's presence** (5.24).

The *Directory of Worship* says: "The sacrament of the Lord's Supper is not to be thought of as an addition to corporate worship; it is rather to be understood as central to Christian worship. It gives distinctive shape to the worship of Christians, and it should be celebrated frequently enough that it is clear to everyone that the Lord's Supper is a central part of corporate worship. In the Lord's Supper God acts to give those who come to the table in faith the spiritual nourishment necessary to sustain them in their Christian lives. The quality and growth of one's life as a Christian are tied inseparably to this sacrament."[4]

As with baptism, the liturgical renewal movement has uncovered many of the ways that early Christians viewed the meaning of the Lord's Supper. Here are some of those meanings:

- Festive Thanksgiving—The word *eucharist* literally means "thanks" or "thanksgiving." The meal was a time when the church expressed joyous gratitude to God for all of God's gifts, and supremely the gift of Jesus Christ.

This meaning of the meal continues to be preserved in the scriptural words most commonly used at the beginning of the celebration: "Friends, this is the joyful feast of the people of God. They will come from east and west and from north and south, and sit at table in the kingdom of God" (Lk. 13:29). Early communions were not devour and somber events for the participants. They were festive occasions grounded in joyous gratitude for the goodness of God.

- Inclusive Fellowship—The word "communion" is a rendering of the biblical word *koinoina*, which also may be translated as "fellowship." These words point to the profoundly social, communal, and relational life among early Christians. But this was no ordinary fellowship in the ancient world. It was an altogether new kind of community. People who had been divided on the basis of class, religion, race, and so on were brought together at the table of the Lord. This new fellowship was unlike anything that previously had existed. It had a different center and circumference. The table fellowship of early Christians witnessed to the new community that God was creating in Christ. This community demolished all barriers that had kept people at a distance from one another.

- Remembrance—Early Christian communions were

occasions to remember Jesus. This emphasis is taken from his very own words, "Do this in remembrance of me" (Lk. 22:19). But what did the church understand Jesus to mean when asking to be remembered? There is a significant difference between our modern concept of remembering and that among the ancient Hebrews. When we speak of remembering, we ordinarily mean that we have thought about or recalled something or someone from the past. Such memories may be "lively" but the thing or person remains, of course, in the past. But remembering was quite different for the Hebrews. When the Hebrew people remembered the Exodus at their Passover celebrations, for example, they believed that God, who is not bound by the constraints of time, brought the saving realities of the Exodus forward into the present. God had been fully present at the Exodus, but God was also fully present in the Passover celebration of the Exodus. The God who is being remembered is also the God who is with us now in the present. Thus, for early Christians, remembering Jesus was more than recalling that he once lived in the past, say as we might remember that Abraham Lincoln once lived in the past. Remembering was the belief that Jesus was fully present to them in the here and now of their lives. This was one meaning of the Holy Spirit. Remembering Jesus was being open to his presence in the present of their lives.

- Sacrifice—When biblical writers spoke of Jesus' death on the cross, they frequently employed the imagery of sacrifice (Eph. 5:2; Heb. 7:26-27). His death was said to be a sacrifice for the sins of the world. What did they mean when using this imagery? This requires taking a brief look at Israel's sacrificial system. In Israel, and also among her world neighbors who practiced sacrifice to their gods, there was a higher and lower motive with respect to the making of sacrifices. The lower motive was that a particular god (or goddess) might need to be appeased or placated. The gods could be whimsical, capricious, volatile, double-minded, mercurial, and even vicious (like, we might say, human beings). It was necessary, to say the least, to stay on their good side. Offering to them sacrifices of various kinds was a way of going about doing this. The higher motive of sacrifice was practiced in Israel (although there were occasions when Israel succumbed to the lower motive). The higher motive was the practice of making a gift to God as an expression of gratitude for God's beneficence. Sacrifice was a way of expressing gratitude for God's magnanimity and grace. The deepest idea was that a sacrifice represented the giving of oneself to God. Animal and agrarian products were offered to express gratitude that God was the source and guarantor of every blessing in Israel's life. Even sin offerings were an expression of gratitude for God's forgiveness. The main point is that Israel had a very different conception of sacrifice than that of her neighbors. Sacrifices were not extractions by God from the people. They were gifts of the people to God. And behind the gifts was the ideal that worshippers could and would, in fact, make a true gift of themselves (that is wholly give their hearts, minds, and loyalty) to God. But was anyone in Israel every able to make a perfect gift of self to God, a perfect sacrifice? The biblical writers answered resoundingly, "Yes!" They regarded Jesus as the one who made a complete, total, and perfect gift of himself to God. He offered up to God what no one else had offered to God. Jesus' offering was so perfect and complete that the ancient Jewish system of sacrifice was now transcended! Early communions were occasions when the church gave thanks for the perfect sacrifice of Christ. The sacrament of the body and blood of Jesus was an enactment of his perfect sacrifice for the sins of the world (the fact that we cannot and do not give ourselves perfectly to God). Now, no other sacrifices are required. Except, as the New Testament says, "the sacrifices (gifts) of thanksgiving and praise" (Heb. 13:15).

- Real Presence—As already indicated above, under remembrance, the early Christians maintained that Jesus was really present to and with them at the Lord's Supper. They were not magical in their thinking, primitive, nor did they believe Jesus was some kind of ghostly presence. But they did regard him as present. The concept of "real presence" has been a source of thorny conflict, dispute, and division between Christians for centuries. How is Jesus really present? For Roman Catholics, the bread and wine actually become the body and blood of Jesus. For Lutherans, the body and blood are conjoined with the bread and wine. For Reformed Christians, the bread and cup remain bread and cup but Christ is regarded as spiritually present in and at the meal. Other reformers regard the bread and the cup as merely symbolic. These remarks amount to a vast oversimplification of ancient teachings each of which has dignity, power, and beauty. The differences they represent have been with us for a long time, and likely will be with us for a long time to come. We can say, however and with certainty, that these different views have one thing in common. When dealing with the question of how Jesus is present in the Lord's Supper, each begins with the elements of bread and wine. It is now known that this became a pre-occupation of the church only about the time of the 9th century A.D. A good deal of recent scholarship (including by some Roman Catholic scholars) has suggested that early Christians did not focus on the elements in this way. They seem to have emphasized that Jesus is really present in his people, his body, in the worshipping congregation, at the time of the meal. For these Christians, Jesus presence was located in his people when bread and wine were consumed. If this view is correct, it is quite astounding. It means that the issue that has vexed Christians for centuries—how to regard the presence of Jesus in the meal—has, in principle, been overcome. All surely can agree that Christ is present in the life of his people, the life of the church. The differences that have been bequeathed to us from centuries past, however, cannot be untangled and un-complicated overnight. Such deeply cherished beliefs do not dissolve quickly, nor should they. But there is, at least, some reason to hope for the future unity of the church in this regard.

- Banquet of the Coming Kingdom—The early Christian meals with Jesus were occasions when the church looked forward to the coming of the kingdom of God in its fullness. The kingdom was regarded as present now (for Jesus had inaugurated it), but its fullness awaited God's consummation of history. This view is expressed in the words, "The kingdom of the world shall become the kingdom of our Lord and his Messiah, and he shall reign forever and ever" (Rev. 11:15). Early Christians believed that their participation in the meal with Jesus was a foretaste, an anticipation, of the great banquet feast that they would enjoy in the coming kingdom of

God. In these meals, they believed they were "tasting the powers of the age to come" (Heb. 5:6).

- It may seem strange, after the above, to speak now of the theme of the "absence of Jesus" with respect to the Lord's Supper. But some contemporary scholars (especially Dr. Robert Brawley, formerly professor of New Testament at Memphis Theological Seminary) think they have found this theme layered into the New Testament. It is based upon the simple observation that the earliest Christians had to contend with the reality that the physical Jesus was no longer present with them. These Christians remembered that Jesus had said, "Truly I tell you, I will never again drink of the fruit of the vine until that day when I drink it anew in the kingdom of God" (Mk. 14:25). Therefore, they had to learn to live with the experience of "until-ness." According to Brawley and others, the meanings given to the sacrament by the early church probably included the recognition of the temporary physical absence of Jesus. What I am certain about is that the theme of absence can be a powerful one in the lives of many people. Here I remember Fred and Louise who lost their beloved son Mike to the disease of AIDS. Shortly following his death, this faithful couple was at worship, as they always were, on the day for celebrating the Lord's Supper. They were struggling faithfully and valiantly with their profound grief and loss. On that day, abandonment and absence (Ps. 22:1; Mk. 15:34) were probably much more powerful emotional realities for them than intimacy and presence. But they came to express their faith and receive grace in a most difficult time. The early church's struggle with the physical absence of Jesus was not an abstraction to them.

Chapter Twenty-Five

THE CHURCH IN MISSION

While working on this book, the city of Detroit, Michigan declared bankruptcy. During television coverage of this story, one newscast focused a camera on one of the main streets in the heart of the city. What caught my eye was a long row of very large, stone, mostly Gothic looking church edifices. They were of the type built in the early and middle part of the 20th century. That era has been called "the golden age of Protestant church building." But, and this was the really striking thing, all of the buildings were now either boarded up or apparently being used for some other purpose. The churches (the people) that once had a mission based from these sites, and to this part of their city, were now gone. This is not to say, of course, there is no longer a Christian people and presence there. A view of the other side of the boulevard revealed a series of battered strip-malls and a variety of buildings seeming to house various small businesses. It is probable, although I cannot say for sure, that several "store-front" congregations of one type or another are housed in many of the buildings. Such is typical of many of our large inner-cities.

But what happened to the people who once worshiped and served in these large, impressive, if now sad looking buildings? And who did so at the very height (in humanly observable terms) of mainline Protestant church life in America. One can guess that certain social changes (racially) led some of the congregations to abandon these particular sites, in spite of how grand they were. Some congregations may still exist in some other location, likely in some of Detroit's suburbs. Perhaps some of the congregations continued as long as possible until an ageing and dwindling membership could no longer financially support such behemoth structures. But maybe, and this is just a guess, some of the congregations simply, at some point, forgot, misinterpreted, or abandoned, for whatever reasons, the mission from God that originally had given them life and purpose. They were no longer, if ever, as the term has it today, "missional congregations." My purpose in remembering and reporting this story is, of course, metaphorical. Whenever a congregation is no longer in the mission to which God has called it, the end result is bankruptcy. As one theologian has put it, "The church exists by mission as a fire exists by burning."[1]

Here is a more positive story, although reported in the wake of an unspeakable tragedy. In February, 2015, twenty-one Egyptian men who were Christians were summarily executed in Libya by Islamic terrorists. A couple of weeks later, the internet service of the magazine *Christianity Today* included a story with the title, "How Libya's Martyr's Are Witnessing in Egypt."[2] The article reported that the Bible Society of Egypt produced a tract only thirty-six hours after the tragedy and distributed it to 1.6 million Egyptians. The tract included biblical quotes about the promise of blessing amidst suffering and a poem titled *"Two Rows by the Sea."* The poem included the words: *"Who fears the other? The row in orange watching paradise open? Or the row in black, with minds evil and broken?"* The director of the Bible Society, an Egyptian Christian, said the design and content of the tract was intended to offer comfort to all Egyptians. The Isaaf Evangelical Church, located on one of the busiest streets in the heart of Cairo, placed a poster on its outer wall at eye-level for pedestrians. It read, "We learn from the Messiah 'Love your enemies, and do good to those who hate you.'" The background of the message was an Egyptian flag. Pastor Francis Fahim said, "The poster is meant to express comfort to all Egyptians, Muslims and Christians." Recalling this story here is simply intended as a reminder that there are Christians all around the world whose hearts burn with the mission to which God has called them.

The genesis of the church's mission, as recorded in the New Testament, is found in Jesus' calling and sending of the apostles (apostle means "one who is sent"). Jesus said, "As the Father has sent me, so send I you" (Jn. 20:21 see also Mt. 28:19-20). Saying that the church is *apostolic* means more than that the church is founded on the original witness of the apostles. It also means that, like them, Jesus sends us into the world. Mission originates in hearing and responding to the call of Jesus. It is, perhaps above all, a fundamental faith in *who* Jesus is and *where* Jesus is.

Matthew's gospel, in the account of the resurrection, provides an image of who Jesus is and where Jesus is in relation to the mission to which he calls and sends us. The angel makes the following announcement: "He has been raised from the dead, and indeed he is going ahead of you to Galilee. There you will see him" (Mt. 28:7). Jesus is the risen Lord who goes before us. One writer artfully says, "There is no place we can go where Christ is not already at work before us—no nation, no home, no place of work or entertainment, no hospital, no place where the homeless, unemployed, and untended are huddled together. We do not have to go into the hostile or callously indifferent world anxiously, defensively, or belligerently. We can go thankfully, confidently, and joyfully because we go not to *take* Jesus but to *meet* him. Long before we ever thought of going into the world, he entered into it and identified himself with it.. . .We do not have to shoulder the impossibly heavy burden of doing his work for him. We are simply invited to participate with him in the work he has done, is doing, and will do."[3]

I am reminded that it has become popular these days to say that "God has a mission to the world" rather than "The church has a mission to the world."And it is in vogue to ask not whether God has a mission but whether God has a church? I think this is something more than simply word shuffling. It is a reminder that the mission to and for the world *really is* God's mission, and that we are called to participate in God's mission (or not). The congregation, in other words, does not have to invent a mission. It only has to look for where and in what ways God/Jesus/Spirit is at work in the world (in our local communities) and to join the triune God in that work. Jesus really does go before us.

The *COF* has four statements about "The Mission of the Church" (in 1984 we still spoke in this way). All four involve, in some way, what might be called God's *evangelical mission* for the church. **The church, being nurtured and sustained by worship, by proclamation and study of the word, and by celebration of the sacraments, is commissioned to witness to all persons who have not received Christ as Lord and Savior** (5.28). The church is gospel-created, gospel sustained and gospel-proclaiming. Cumberland Presbyterians have a holistic understanding of God's evangelistic mission. ***The Cumberland Presbyterian Handbook*** says the following: "Evangelism comes from the Greek word *evangel,* which means 'good news.' The 'good news' is the gospel of Jesus Christ, which the angels proclaimed when Jesus was born. Cumberland Presbyterians recognize that Christians are called to share the good news of Jesus Christ. We share Christ with people in many ways. Often we use words, talking, writing, preaching, or teaching. Just as often, we use actions. Since Jesus cared for the whole human person, the church shares God's love in Christ through many activities. Among these are: education, feeding the hungry, healing ministries, pastoral care, peacemaking, caring for the poor, and working for justice."[4]

The *COF*'s second statement says: **Growth is natural to the church's life. The church is called into being and exists to reach out to those who have not experienced God's grace in Christ, and to nourish them with all the means of grace** (5.29). This statement calls to mind that the purpose of the church (the congregation) is never maintenance but mission. The church never exists for merely what is now and those who are here now, but always with an eye to that which is not yet and those who are not here yet. The church will never reach a place when and where the evangelical gift and task can be shelved, even temporarily. The world is the world and the church must be the church. This means that the church will never be relieved of the mandate to reach out into the world and share with persons the good news of Jesus Christ. There will never be a time when the church is not called to be "sowers of seed" with the expectation that at least some of them, by the activity of the Holy Spirit, will fall on good ground and produce growth (Mt. 13:1-23; Mk. 4:3-9; Lu. 8:1-15).

What about People of Other Faiths or No Faith?

The world was rapidly changing when the CPC and CPCA adopted the *COF* in 1984. In the three decades since, the pace of change has only accelerated. My family enjoys spending time boating on Lake Guntersville in Scottsboro, Alabama. The huge lake, however, can be a fearful and dangerous place. It depends on the weather. If things are calm, you can enjoy the gradual changes brought on by winds and waves. But if there is a storm, and they can come up quickly on this lake, the threat is no longer one of gradual change. The storms on the lake, with their ferocious winds, lightning, and truly strong and turbulent waves, can threaten you with rapid structural change. Unless you leave the lake in time, your boat might be thrown against the shore or even sunk! Most of the world now knows the feeling of living with the fears that can be brought on by the threat of rapid structural change (for many of us it is a good time to reflect of Mark 4:35-41).

The above in no way is meant to suggest that all the changes the world has been undergoing have a negative value. That is by no means the case. It is only to suggest that the pace of change has been dizzying. One of the major changes, of course, is that the world is now much smaller. And, to narrow the point, people of different religions used to live, ordinarily, at quite a distance from one another. That is no longer the case given modern communications, globalization, and the migration of peoples. William Placher writes, "The experience of having a Moslem mosque down the street, a Hindu doctor, or a Buddhist son-in-law, common enough for Christians even in American small towns and suburbs these days, is unparalleled in most of Christian history. Many European Christians live in the midst of even greater diversity, and Christians in Asia and parts of Africa find themselves in a minority in the midst of adherents of other religions. As a result our attitude to non-Christians is on our theological agenda in new ways. It is harder to write non-Christians off as destined to hell or to think of them purely as objects of distant missionary work if they live next door and we have known them all our lives."[5]

The church, in 1984, was exceedingly wise, surely led by the Holy Spirit, to include the following two statements in the Confession: **In carrying out the apostolic commission, the covenant community has encountered and continues to encounter people who belong to religions which do not acknowledge Jesus Christ as Lord. While respecting persons who adhere to other religions, Christians are responsible to share with them the good news of salvation through Jesus Christ** (5:30), and **The covenant community is responsible to give witness to the mighty acts of God in the life, death, and resurrection of Jesus Christ. Where and when this witness is lacking, God is not without a witness. Therefore, it does not belong to the covenant community to judge where and in what manner God acts savingly through Jesus Christ** (5.31).

The balance in these statements, which I like to call Christological balance, seems truly inspired. Cumberland Presbyterians *are* responsible to share with all persons the good news of salvation through Jesus Christ. This is strongly and properly affirmed in the *COF*. But equally affirmed is the idea that we are to do this *as* "people who are, indeed, Christians!" The *COF* reminds us that there are consequences of being a follower of Jesus. One of the consequences is our attitude toward all persons (respect). "As Christians we (should) have reasons inherent in our confession as to why we respect all others who do not share our faith. Jesus calls us to love our neighbors as ourselves, even to love our enemies. Thus we relate to all others, including those of other religions, in ways that are consistent with our confession that Jesus is Lord: love of the adversary, the dignity of the lowly, repentance, servant-hood, and renunciation of co-ersion."[6]

When the *COF* speaks about God as **not without a witness** and with respect to people who do not know Jesus Christ **it does not belong to the covenant community to judge where and in what manner God acts savingly through Jesus Christ**, it is drawing upon a long-standing theological *attitude* in the history of the Cumberland Presbyterian Church. In his important and thorough study of the works of Cumberland Presbyterian theologians (*This They Believed),* Joe Ben Irby says that every well-known Cumberland Presbyterian theologian (by well-known is meant they left considerable writing) believed that God could and would save those (called "the heathen" in most of their writing) who had never had the opportunity to hear and respond to the gospel of Jesus Christ. Additionally, and perhaps more importantly, Irby points out that each of the Cumberland Presbyterian *COF*s endorses this perspective.

I will here let Dr. Irby speak to this issue in his own words: "The writer concurs in the view of the possibility of the salvation of the so-called "heathen" based on the universal atonement made by Christ and the universal operation of the Holy Spirit based on the atonement. 'No person goes to hell that did not have a chance to go to heaven.' While indeed there is no salvation apart from Christ and the regenerating power of the Holy Spirit, it is not necessary that one should know of the historical Christ, the gospel, and the scriptures, when the lack of such knowledge is not fault of his or her own. 'When such persons respond to whatever revelation God may give on the basis of the universal atonement and the universal work of the Holy Spirit, salvation results.' The church's responsibility for missions is not lessened, however, because of the possibility of universal salvation. This is the case, for one thing, because 'many persons may respond to God's supreme and climactic revelation given in the gospel and recorded in the scriptures who would not respond to a lesser revelation.'"[7] The Cumberland Presbyterian Church has been reluctant, and rightly so, to place any boundaries against the grace of God whom we know through Jesus Christ and the power of the Spirit.

As for joining in God's mission in our now more diverse world (but still the world God loves—John 3:16), I find the following words of Rowan Williams, former Archbishop of Canterbury, to be insightful: "The Christian does not ask how he or she knows that the Christian religion is exclusively and universally true; he or she simply works on the basis of the 'christic' vision for the human good, engaging with adherents of other traditions without anxiety, defensiveness or proselytism, claiming neither an 'exclusivist' perspective invalidating others nor an 'inclusivist' absorption of other perspectives into his or her own, nor yet a 'pluralist' meta-theory, locating all traditions on a single map and relativizing their concrete life. . .being Christian now is going to be more of a matter of living out a distinctive witness to the possibility of human community than of 'preoccupation with self-identity' at the public and corporate level."[8]

Chapter Twenty-Six

CHURCH GOVERNMENT AND JUDICATORIES

The *COF* has four statements devoted to "Church Government" and "Church Judicatories." **Jesus Christ as Lord and Head of the church has entrusted the government of the church to officers who make those decisions that will guide the life and ministry of the covenant community. These officers have the responsibility to serve the church, to examine and receive members into the communion of the church, to care for and nurture them in faith, and to discipline with love and justice those who offend the gospel and the laws of the church. The Cumberland Presbyterian Church and the Cumberland Presbyterian Church in America are governed by certain representative bodies: session, presbytery, synod, and General Assembly. Each of these church bodies in its special area of responsibility has legislative, judicial, and executive authority, yet all are to be conducted in recognition of their interdependence and Christian mission. It is the responsibility of these representative bodies, consistent with the church's constitution, to determine matters of faith, practice, and government, propose forms of worship and witness, exercise discipline, and resolve appeals properly brought before them** (5.32—5. 35).

The Cumberland Presbyterian form of church government was inherited. It was bequeathed to us by the events of the 16th century Reformation in Europe. The Reformers, as a result of finally separating from the Roman Catholic Church, searched the scriptures for guidance about how to structure the life of their new congregations. In Geneva, John Calvin was impressed with the fact that "elders" were central to the governing structure of Hebrew communities according to the Old Testament. He also noted that the "office" of elder was carried forward into the life of the New Testament churches. It was this kind of mining of scripture that led Calvin and the Geneva Christians to make the elder (presbyter) the basic leadership position in their congregations. This decision was appropriated by most of the churches in the Reformed and Presbyterian tradition including, of course, the Cumberland Presbyterian Churches. It should be noted that Calvin and his churches also resurrected the office of deacon (diakonos) as they found it in the New Testament.

For subsequent church history, the fundamental innovation of Calvin and Geneva was the decision that church structure should be representative and bottom-up. This was in direct contrast to the heir-archical, top-down structure of the Roman Catholic Church. Over time, the representative system developed into four levels of organic connectivity in service to the Lord's mission. The levels were the local church *session* (elders elected by the congregation), the *presbytery* made up of representatives from the various congregations in a given geographical area, the *synod* made up of representatives from various presbyteries in a given area, and *General Assembly* made up of representatives from the entire church. This has been and remains the basic form of church government in the Cumberland Presbyterian Churches.

Persons interested in a more detailed study of the church's government will be helped by consulting the church's Constitution which is published in the same book as the *COF*. When I have taught about church government in the local church, I have relied heavily upon Morrow's excellent treatment of the subject in *The Covenant of Grace.* I list a few of his main points below with page numbers indicated:

- Morrow's main point is that church government, at all levels, should be understood and used as "an instrument of service" in fulfilling the Lord's ministry and mission (p. 122).

- Persons who constitute these judicatories and their agencies should always focus on serving the church so that it may better serve the world. A legalistic preoccupation with the documents of church government and a bureaucratic preoccupation with its organizational structures serve only the divert attention, energies, and resources away from the performance of mission (p. 122).

- The first and most vital connectional link for the congregation is with the presbytery (p. 123).The connectional ties that bind congregations together in a presbytery are extended through its representatives to the synod and General Assembly (p. 123)

- To the degree that the connectional tie of a congregation to the General Assembly is real and meaningful, the congregation will begin to catch a glimpse of the "one, holy, universal apostolic church of Christ, who is her Head and Lord" (5.01) (pp. 123-124).

Perhaps the single best remark I have ever heard about church government was spoken a few years ago during a meeting of the West Tennessee Presbytery. Reverend William Warren reminded all of us that, "Presbytery is not just a meeting to which we come once or twice a year. Rather, it is a web of continuing relationships through which we together seek and intend to be faithful to the ministry and mission to which Jesus Christ has called us." I very much doubt that John Calvin, Finis Ewing, or anyone else could have said it any better.

Christians Live and Witness in the World

(6.01—6.32 in the Confession of Faith)

Chapter Twenty Seven

CHRISTIAN FREEDOM

One of our responsibilities as Cumberland Presbyterians who have confessed Jesus Christ is Lord is to the world (the world that is as near as the front doors of our church buildings and the global world). We have a particular responsibility toward the world because it is the world that God loves (Jn. 3:16). If we try to express this responsibility with brevity, and in accordance with the New Testament, we can say, "The church is to bear the message of Jesus to the world by *being* that message."[1] We are to *be* this message as truly as we are to believe it. The New Testament countenances no distinction between believing in Jesus and following Jesus; between knowing him as Savior and serving him as Lord; between doctrine and behavior, or ethics; between salvation and discipleship; between what is professed and what is lived. "Faith is not obedience, but as obedience is not obedience without faith, faith is not faith without obedience. They belong together, as do thunder and lightning in a thunderstorm."[2]

Scholars point out that the word "world" has at least three meanings in the Bible. 1) It is used to mean the physical world, the cosmos, our habitat, or what the Bible means when speaking of "the heavens and the earth." It is the created world that God called "good" (Gn. 1-3). 2) It means people—the world is the world of people in all of their similarities and differences: "red and yellow, black and white, they are precious in his sight." And, 3) the world, as especially true in the John literature, is the world as it is in rebellion against God. It is the world as it is in structured unbelief. Jesus said he was not of *this* world (Jn. 17:14; 18:36) and that he opposed its ruler (Jn. 12:31).

Love for the world in the third sense is utterly incompatible with love for God (1 Jn. 2:15-17). It is this world to which the Apostle Paul says we are not to be conformed (Rom. 12:1-2). This world works overtime to maintain a secret. "The world's secret is the non-existence of its gods. At a price of floods of tears and blood, the world keeps denying its secret and seeks to populate nature and history with its idols. The deep reason of its unrest is that it refuses to confess its profane character. The church is aware of this secret of the world. It must not permit itself to be befuddled by reproaches and accusations. Just so it is truly loyal to the world."[3] It is this third meaning of world that gave rise to the well known saying, "The church is *in* the world and *for* the world but not *of* the world." The church, rather, is *of* Christ; it is *of* the kingdom of God.

The sixth section of the *COF* stresses that the fundamental relationship CPs have to this world is one of *bearing witness*. This includes but is not limited to the matter of one Christian person telling the Jesus story to someone else who is not a Christian. Although that is of great importance, it also is the entire church, or congregation, or denomination that is to bear witness to the Lordship of Christ by dent of being a particular kind of community; namely, the kind of community which makes no sense unless Jesus Christ is, in fact, being *acknowledged* and *obeyed* as Lord of life and the world.

The profound responsibility the church has toward the world is expressed well, and according to the pattern of the New Testament, in the following words: "The will of God for human socialness as a whole is prefigured by the shape to which the Body of Christ is called—Church and world are not two compartments under separate legislation or two institutions with contradictory assignments, but two levels of the pertinence of the same Lordship. The people of God are called to be today what the world is called to be ultimately."[4] This is a profound truth. Taken seriously, it means that the church not only *has* a mission to the world but the church also *is* a mission to the world.

A deep truth of the Christian faith is that the world cannot know that it is the world except as the world comes to understand that the message entrusted to the church is the message God intends for the world. The world does not know that it was created by God and is being redeemed by God, or that Christ is the Lord of the world, unless and until it recognizes that the church bears a message to and for it. In the New Testament, it is the existence of the church that "explains" what it is for the world to be the world. It does not matter that the world does not know this. But, of course, it does matter that the church knows this. The church, by the grace of God, has received a revelatory message (the Gospel) and bears this message to the world for the sake of the world. It does this not only with words but by incarnating the message in and through particular practices and the quality of its existence as communities of Christ's disciples.

Christian Freedom

The *COF* begins section six by stressing that Cumberland Presbyterians bear witness to the world about *freedom*. The world is a place of bondage to sin. To the extent that people are *of* this world, they are slaves to sin and death. It matters little, as was discussed in chapter eight, if persons consider themselves to be free, and are free, in any number of ways that the world may define. It remains that persons who do not know the God revealed in Jesus Christ and the power of the Spirit are not free in the way that matters the most. They are not free to know who they really are. They are not free to know their true destiny. They are not free to be properly related to

God or to one another. They are not free from the rulers/s of this world. They are not free from the dominion of the principalities and powers. They are not free from the many possible hells of this world. Neither are they are free from themselves and the way in which they are inclined toward sin "**in all aspects of their being**" (2.03).

One writer speaks of the meaning of freedom in our post-modern culture: "Our culture gives us all sorts of options, a breadth of freedom never before achieved in human history, but it gives us no help at all in knowing what or how to choose. We have, in fact, defined freedom in a solely negative fashion. As the philosopher Isaiah Berlin writes, 'By being free. . .I mean not being interfered with by others. The wider is the area of non-interference the wider my freedom.' Freedom, in other words, is being left alone. Post-moderns can quickly point to all kinds of things we are free *from*, but we have little to say about what we are free *for*. We have an abundance of freedom, but what are we supposed to do with it?"[5] If this is an accurate observation, perhaps we can better understand why there is such pervasive loneliness in our culture. And if we *alone* must make the judgments about what freedom is about and for, we can discern something of the depth of our enslavement to ourselves and to our culture.

The *COF* declares the good news of the Gospel that is for this un-free world: **Through Jesus Christ, God frees persons**

from the shackles, oppression, and shame of sin and sinful forces, from the guilt and penal consequences of sin, and enables them to have free access to God. This freedom, rooted in love, not fear, enables persons to become who God intends them to be, to bear witness to their Lord, and to serve God and neighbors in the vocations of their common life (6.01). Cumberland Presbyterians, then, bear witness to the world about the freedom made possible through and under the Lordship of Christ (Jn. 8:31-36). They bear witness to the world by bearing witness to their Lord: "For we do not proclaim ourselves; we proclaim Jesus Christ as Lord and ourselves as slaves for Jesus' sake" (2.Cor. 4:5).

Jesus was the freest person who ever lived. He was tempted, but without sin; that is to say, without the corruption of his freedom. He was *the* person who was truly in the image of God. His life and being were and are the revelation of what it means to be truly and freely human. Jesus was so free that he could live his life rooted in love (for God and neighbor) rather than in anxiety, estrangement and fear. Yet Jesus lived fully in this world and for this world. He was no navel-gazer. He did not have a "private relationship to God" which did not involve living in the nitty-gritty world and relationships of first century Palestine. His purpose was to offer the world the salvation of God. He brought God into the world in a new way. Everywhere he went he brought his own freedom to those who could and would receive it. He brought freedom from disease and illness.

He brought freedom from demon possession. He brought freedom from social ostracism. He brought freedom from religious legalism. He brought freedom from religious hypocrisy. He brought freedom from fear and anxiety. He brought freedom from the worship of Mammon. He brought freedom from idolatries and addictions. Jesus also firmly and joyfully proclaimed and enacted the nearness of God's kingdom. And he proclaimed the promise of its final full coming in which freedom, justice, and *shalom* would prevail for all.

It is important to stress that the freedom of Jesus was the freedom to be fully obedient to God, even to death on a cross (Ph. 2:8). It was freedom to love and serve God and neighbor; and even enemies! The freedom of Jesus given to those who believe is not simply a ticket to heaven after one dies. It is not a religious way to have a "private spirituality" unaffected by the turmoil and suffering of the world. It is not a freedom to retreat into the sanctuary and "have good services" and safely worship God. No, the freedom of Jesus was and is the freedom to resist evil, to challenge religious, political, and social injustice, to befriend the poor, to set the captives frees, and it was the freedom to die a sinner's death in the world, and at the hands of the world. It is this kind of freedom, the freedom of Jesus, that Cumberland Presbyterians are called to bear witness to, in, and for this world. They are called to declare this freedom by *being* representatives of this freedom.

There is a qualification to be considered. The New Testament witness indicates that while Christians have the freedom of Jesus *now*, they also must wait for the *fullness* of this freedom at the final redemption. This is one of the paradoxes of the Christian faith attested in the scriptures. Just as the kingdom of God is both already but not yet fully present, just as we have been saved but also are being saved, just as we have been sanctified but also are being sanctified, just so we are free in Christ but the fullness of this freedom still lies before us. This is to say what the *COF* says about the reality of the Christian life: **The struggle with sin continues, for believers are still imperfect in knowledge and the power to do God's will. Their freedom to trust, love, and serve God and neighbors is compromised sometimes by distrust, hate, and selfishness. This inner struggle drives them again and again to rely on God's power to conform them to the image of the new person in Christ** (4.23).

Therefore, our proclamation to the world, in word and deed, is about the freedom of Christ rather than our own freedom. That we "sin against the world" by misunderstanding, or even abusing, the freedom that we have in Christ is pointed to in the *COF*'s admonition that: **Believers who, under the pretext of Christian freedom practice sin, thereby violate the nature and purpose of Christian freedom. Believers are free to love and serve the Lord rather than evil** (6.03). Because Christians still struggle with sin, and because so much is at stake for the world, the *COF* twice mentions that believers may have need of **the instruction and discipline of the church** (6.02 and 6.04). This discipline, of course, is reconciliatory rather than punitive and is aimed at assisting believers **"to rely on God's power to conform them to the image of the new person in Christ"** (4.23). This is so they (we) may bear authentic witness to the world about the freedom of Jesus Christ.

The world (again as it is in rebellion against God) is fundamentally opposed to the good news of the freedom that God has made possible in and through faith in Jesus Christ. This is the sub-story about the world that the New Testament tells. It remains, of course, the story of the world as we know it today. Therefore the *COF* points to an additional way in which the Christian message, which is for the world, may be compromised. **Christians owe ultimate allegiance to Jesus Christ as Lord, and must never yield that ultimate allegiance to any government or nation, and should in Christian conscience oppose any form of injustice** (6.05 - presumably any form of injustice sponsored or authorized by any government or nation). "We must obey God rather than men" (Acts 5:29).

The world, even when it opposes the church, or oppresses or persecutes it, or legitimizes injustices that betray God's love for all persons, nevertheless needs the church to tell the world who it is, what it is doing, and, above all, what God intends for it. The church, for the sake of the world and not the sake of the church, will sometimes be *for* the world precisely by opposing it, standing firm against it, including its possible demand for ultimate allegiance. History is replete with examples, ancient and modern, of Christians and churches suffering at the hands of the world by being for the world in the name and power of Christ. Sadly, history also includes far too many stories, both ancient and modern, which reveal that the church has often failed to be *for* the world by accommodating itself *to* the world. In the latter case, the world has been deprived of a witness to the freedom of Jesus Christ.

Chapter Twenty-Eight

GOOD WORKS

Cumberland Presbyterians also bear witness to the world through a ministry of good works: **Believers are saved by grace through faith which produces the desire to do the good works for which God creates persons in Jesus Christ** (6.06). During the Reformation, a dispute arose over the Roman Catholic Church's teaching and practice about good works. Here is one description of the dispute: "Close to the center of the [Reformation} struggle was Luther's disgust with the practices of his day in the Roman Church, among them indulgences, devices of selling insurance policies on the soul (at high premiums, since eternity was at stake) which proved to be a great source of revenue in its building campaigns. The point to note is the legalism behind these practices: the assumption that the doing of these specific outer things added credit up to salvation. Just as life under Jewish law in Palestine, medieval life was covered, to every nook and corner, by regulations governing the little things one was to *do* in order to become a Christian, in the process forgetting the larger matters of 'justice and mercy and faith.'"[1]

Martin Luther's response to this situation was to say, "The goodness of a good man is in him by the free grace of

God's forgiving love, and by no scrupulous piling up of moral credits by *doing* some things and avoiding others."[2] The alternative to this apparent "salvation by works" theology was crystallized in the Reformation doctrine of "salvation by faith alone." When the Roman theology of works was rejected, it became necessary for the Protestants to explain the relationship between "faith and works." It is clear from the various Protestant confessional statements that the Reformers did not reject the importance of good works. They simply insisted that such works are the result of rather than the cause of salvation. Eventually there arose a popular statement to express the Reformed perspective, "We are not saved *by* good works, but we are saved *for* good works." Our *COF* puts it simply: **Good works are the result of and not the means of salvation** (6.08). And: **Good works are done in thankful response to the gift of God's grace. God graciously accepts the works of believers despite their many weaknesses and imperfect motives** (6.07).

In my opinion, the authors of the *COF* acted appropriately when placing the statements about good works in the section on Christians living and bearing witness in the world rather than in the section on salvation. This reflects the belief that good works are not a matter best understood in relation to salvation. Rather, they are best understood in relation to the new life of discipleship, of obedience, of witness. Good works are not something optional following salvation. They are not something that we might or might not do. Rather, they follow from our organic relationship to Christ (Jn. 15:1-11). They are as natural to the Christian life as are apples forming on an apple tree.

Jesus came into the world and did the works of God. He was fully obedient to his Father in demonstrating the Father's love for the world. He proclaimed that "God desires mercy and not sacrifice" (Mt. 9:13). His love for God included love for neighbor. As followers of Jesus, we are called to live as obedient disciples. Cumberland Presbyterians do good works simply because Jesus did them and has told us to do them. We do them because Jesus promised and gave the Holy Spirit who empowers us to do them. We do them because they are the natural outcome of the new life in Christ. And we do them because the meaning of being church is being in the world and doing what Jesus said that we are to do. In this way, the church offers a sign to the world, and for the sake of the world, that the kingdom of God has already appeared in the world and is the true destiny of the world.

Jesus' command concerning love for God and love for neighbor is at the heart of what it means to do good works. R.E.O White offers the following perspective: "The parable of the Good Samaritan defines both *love* and *neighbor.* It vividly portrays spontaneous care and kindness towards any stricken, suffering, helpless individual we happen upon in life's journeying. Christ's illustrations are all equally concrete—the cup of water where water was not always plentiful; visiting the sick, clothing the naked, feeding the under-nourished, befriending the ill-deserving; forgiving the offender, doing good, lending without expectation of return, returning good for evil, prayers for cursing, gentleness for all ill-treatment. The ministry of Jesus is the enduring object-lesson in Christian love—his time, his sympathy, his un-wearying service, ever at the command of the outcast, the helpless, the repulsive, the unvalued, the sinful, the blind, the lame, the leprous; his friendship towards sinners; his unfailing courtesy, his adaptation of his teaching to the comprehension of his hearers, his patience with the disciples; his readiness to devote all attention to 'unimportant people,' his resolute refusal to meet his enemies with their own weapons; his un-embittered, undefeated good will in severest rejection and extreme torture; his ability to love to the uttermost and to the end. And we are to love one another as *he has loved us."*[3]

The *COF* adds these words about good works: **Good works encompass not only those deeds of service and mercy exemplified by Christ, but also those ethical and moral choices that reflect Christian values and principles in all of life's relationships** (6.09). Here the *COF*, as does the scripture upon which it is based, extends the concept of good works beyond particular and concrete acts of neighbor and stranger love. The Gospel announcement is that "Jesus is Lord" of all of life. Therefore all human existence is covered by this lordship.

The church is that community which, by grace, has come to recognize this lordship. This means that "all ethical and moral choices" made by Christians and congregations are to reflect and serve this lordship.

About this, the *COF* says: **The covenant community, governed by the Lord Christ, opposes, resists, and seeks to change all circumstances of oppression—political, economic, cultural, racial—by which persons are denied the essential dignity God intends for them in the work of creation.** For purposes of illustration, imagine a Christian, or a congregation, discovering that certain stock earnings have been realized by investment in companies which exploits children as laborers. What ethical and moral choices are to be made by the Christian, or congregation, which makes this discovery? I have read that in the 1950s, in most popular publications, the most commonly used word used to designate the average American was "citizen." However, by the 1970s, the most commonly used word was "consumer." What ethical and moral choices are to be made by Christians who live in a highly materialistic and consumption oriented world? These examples could, of course, be multiplied almost without limit. We live in a fallen, sinful world and the covenant community will never be done with asking what it means that all of life is to be lived under the lordship of Jesus Christ? There can be no compartmentalization of life into areas which are not under both the judgment and grace of the Lord. But this, of course, is hardly bad news. It is good news in that in our ethical and moral choices we may progressively experience more of what it means to live in the freedom of Jesus Christ. We can be progressively freed to bear more authentic witness to the world, for the sake of the world, that it, too, may be freed from its various idolatries. This form of Christian witness is also good works.

Chapter Twenty-Nine

CHRISTIAN STEWARDSHIP

Christian stewardship acknowledges that all of life and creation is a trust from God, to be used for God's glory and service. It includes the conservation and responsible use of natural resources as well as the creative use of human skills and energies. These gifts of God are to be shared with all, especially with the poor (6.10). Through stewardship, Cumberland Presbyterians bear witness to the world that, "The earth is the Lord's, and all that is in it" (Ps. 24:1; see also Ps. 50:10-12; 1 Cor. 4:7; James 1:17). The world, either because of ignorance or the outright rebellion of sin, refuses to acknowledge, accept, and honor this truth. So the church freely, and with thanksgiving, does on behalf of the world what the world does not know how to do, or that it should do, or that it refuses to do. It is not that the world is incapable of acts of benevolence. It most certainly is, and for this the church rejoices and gives thanks. The difference has to do with acknowledging God and that "all of life and creation is a trust from God, to be used for God's glory and service." Stewardship is what the church is called to do for the sake of the world (and not simply for the purpose of "supporting" the church). Stewardship is a form of evangelistic witness.

A biblical study will reveal that there are twenty-six direct references to "stewards" and "stewardship" in scripture. "The biblical term 'steward' (Greek=*oiknomos*) describes the office of one who is entrusted with the property of another. The Old Testament usage confines itself to the technical meaning of the term but in doing so establishes the two dialectically related ideas that inform the symbolic use of stewardship—accountability and responsibility. On the one hand, the steward is a servant (often a slave!) and strictly accountable to his master; on the other, the servant is given an exceptional range of freedom as one bearing great responsibility. Being accountable, he may be judged severely for the misuse of trust placed in him (Isa. 22:15-16); yet that presupposes the honor of the office (e.g. Gen. 43, 44)."[1]

The term steward is carried forward in the New Testament and employed by Jesus, Paul, and other witnesses along the lines set forth in the Old Testament. Paul can say, for example, that "We are stewards of the mysteries of God" (1 Cor.4:1). The twin emphases of accountability and responsibility are everywhere present in the texts of the New Testament. Stewardship, most broadly understood, is accountability and responsibility with respect to the whole of life and creation as it has been entrusted to us by God. The *COF* says: **The motive for Christian stewardship is gratitude for God's abundant love and mercy accompanied by the desire to share all of God's good gifts with others** (6.11; see Lu. 21:1-4; Acts 4:34-37; 2

Cor. 8:1-15).

Stewardship, of course, includes being accountable and responsible with respect to the place of money in the Christian life. It has been noted often that the Gospels reveal Jesus spoke as more about money than any other single topic. So our understanding of discipleship in relationship to money will begin with carefully studying the teachings of Jesus. But consideration also needs to be given to the fact there is a special history relative to North American Christianity which has influenced the way in which Cumberland Presbyterians, and other American Christian traditions, have been trained to think about money.

In the fourth century, with the conversion of the Roman emperor Constantine, the Christian church was established as the religion of the empire. This meant, among other things, that the churches would now receive financial support from the government. This practice continued as the Roman church moved into Europe and continued even through the divisions brought about by the 16th century Reformation. The various European churches, during and after the Reformation, were financially supported by their given kings, princes, or magistrates. This was true for the Lutherans in Germany, the Presbyterians in Geneva, and, later, the Anglicans in England. Each in turn became the "official religion" of the state. It should be noted that certain Christian groups, belonging to what is called the radical left wing of the Reformation—Anabaptists, Hutterites, Mennonites, etc., rejected state support based on the fact that the Christians of the New Testament "enjoyed" no such support by or relationship to the government.

As a result of the church-state establishment, stewardship, with respect to money, was an underdeveloped theme in the theologies and practices of most of the churches in Europe. State support had compromised the need for attention to the theme. However, when these churches moved to "the new world" and after the American Revolution, they now faced an altogether new situation. In light of the separation of church and state, churches now had to depend on the voluntary sharing of members. As one writer has observed, "with the loss of legal establishment in the new world Protestant churches found in stewardship a significant biblical basis for responsible financial support of the church's mission. But at the same time, this practical necessity reduced the profundity of the biblical understanding of stewardship by applying it almost exclusively to church giving."[2] So there we have it. Stewardship understood almost exclusively as giving money to support the church has a deep, if somewhat limiting, root in our American church history.

What is the teaching of Jesus concerning money and discipleship? As already mentioned, leaders, or perhaps especially appointed groups in congregations, would do well to make a careful study of all the sayings of Jesus, and other biblical teachings, related to money in order to offer instruction and guidance to their congregations. The most that can be done here is to offer some informed summaries by those who have actually engaged in such carefully done studies.

Reginald White, a very accomplished New Testament scholar, writes, "Jesus did not condemn wealth, but he considered it quite dangerous. Positively, the power of wealth to provide hospitality, feed the hungry, clothe the naked, do good and lend, finds frequent expression in his parables; it is always possible to consecrate the 'unrighteous mammon' by the way you use it. Employment for wages, buying and selling, banking and interest are all mentioned without comment. Jesus' main concern is with one's attitude toward wealth and its right use. Here, unquestionably, he introduced new perspectives of compassion, service, and the golden rule equality of need. But, Jesus also emphasized the perils of wealth. Great riches made entry into God's kingdom infinitely harder. It even might be the case that someone seeking entry into the kingdom might need to completely divest to make it possible (Mk. 10:21, 23). If right use could consecrate money, wrong use could betray its owner into exploitation, dishonesty, selfishness, and merciless use of power. Worship of mammon excludes the worship of God. Jesus would reject the view that human behavior is determined by economic forces, but agree that persons can allow themselves to become so determined, so corrupted and decayed, by the love of money. Neglecting all other security, the soul may—Jesus said—come to *trust* in riches, and that spells ultimate disaster; for if the heart's treasure be vulnerable to the moth and rust of corruption and the thieves of time and death, the soul must be bankrupt at the last (Lu. 12:13-21)."[3]

Donald Kraybill offers a similar perspective on Jesus' teachings concerning money: "Jesus makes it clear that he expects forgiven and converted people to live an upside down economic life. . .People on the way with him respond financially to God's great love for them by sharing with those in need around them. One cannot conclude that Jesus was condemning private property or that he was calling for a new Christian commune. But his message did strike at the heart of the economic structures of his day. His gospel was a harsh judgment on the financial practices in Galilee and Judea. We must remember that wealth doesn't simply drop out of the sky. It is a commodity in a system of social norms and rules which control its acquisition and use. In speaking out against wealth, Jesus questioned the accepted economic rules which allowed for a great disparity to emerge between the affluent and the poor. He never says that material things are evil or sinful in and of themselves. But he does warn that they are dangerous. They can quickly assume a demonic character that unseats the rule of God in our life."[4]

One important, perhaps the most important, stewardship witness the church can make to the world concerns our market system of economics. Christians cannot "deify" the market for this would be (is?) a form of idolatry. It is quite beyond dispute that the market system dominates our lives. It is likely that it is the system which provides the greatest good to the greatest number in a given society. But Christians also must bear witness against its dangers, limitations, and false claims. For one thing, if the market place is allowed to determine morality (what is good is what sells), then there is no bottom to it. Morality is lost in an abyss of buying and selling. For another, if the meaning and conduct of life is determined entirely by the standards of the market, what place is there for the claims of Jesus upon us?

As Leslie Newbigin writes, "The chance workings of the free market become the "invisible hand" of Adam Smith which mysteriously coverts private selfishness into public good. This particular example of an invisible power ruling over human affairs is particularly relevant to the present, since it is one of the key arguments of the religious right against the religious left that one cannot speak of justice or injustice when describing the huge differences between the rich and poor in our society. These, on this view, cannot be called unjust because they are not the work of conscious human agency but the result of chance. *Thus in our economic life we are no longer responsible to Christ; we are not responsible at all, for economic life has been handed over to the goddess Fortuna.* It is not difficult to recognize that as one of the principalities and powers of which Paul speaks."[5]

With respect to stewardship as giving money, the *COF* says: **Proportionate and regular giving of all that God entrusts to the human family is an act of devotion and a means of grace. Giving to and through the church is the privilege of every believer. Tithing, as a scriptural guide for giving, is an adventure of faith and a rich and rewarding practice. The tither not only experiences the grace of God but even the grace of sharing** (6.13; see Gn. 28:22; Dt. 14:22; Mal. 3:8-12; Mt. 23:23; 1 Cor. 16:1-2). And, perhaps in light of the twin themes of accountability and responsibility, the *COF* says: **All believers are responsible to God and to the covenant community for their stewardship** (6.14; see Mt. 12:36-37; Lu. 12:47-48; Ro. 14:10-12; 1 Cor. 4:1-2; 2 Cor. 5:9-10).

Chapter Thirty

MARRIAGE AND THE FAMILY

The church has responsibility to help persons prepare for marriage, for parental responsibilities, and for family life under the lordship of Jesus Christ (6.21). It is significant that the *COF* discusses family and marriage at this particular point. It comes after the treatments of God, Christ, Holy Spirit, the nature of the church. This is because, contrary to a commonly held view, the church (meaning the church as God declares it to be) is prior to the family. That the church comes before the family in priority is clearly evident in the teachings of Jesus about the kingdom of God. The important point is that the nuclear family cannot know who it is, what it is, or what its possibilities are without seeing itself, and understanding itself, in the light of the Gospel of Jesus Christ. It is also important to note that the *COF*'s treatment of the family comes after the chapter on the abuse of human freedom (sin). The family, then, as is true of all earthly institutions, stands in need of God's redemption.

The *COF*, then, is not talking about family in general. That is, it is not talking about the family as it is organized and exists (in many different patterns) in the United States or in other places around the world. Rather, it is talking about the family that lives and exists under the lordship of Jesus Christ. It is talking about the family, and the marriage, that has come to define itself and conduct its life, however inadequately, in the light of the Gospel—in the light of God's revelation in Jesus Christ. Hopefully in this chapter we can explore at least something of what this means for us in light of the scriptures and the statements of the *COF*. And, of course, what the statements about family and marriage mean for the world around us. Because family and marriage are distinct means by which, and through which, Christians bear witness to the world about the love of God in Jesus Christ. In what follows below, I am strongly indebted to the work of biblical scholar Rodney Clapp and the material in his informative book, *Families at the Crossroads: Beyond Traditional and Modern Models.*

The Family

The Christian understanding of family begins with Jesus Christ. And Jesus, of course, drew upon his Hebrew background, the Jewish scriptures, and the traditions of Israel for his understanding and teaching. We will note, shortly, that he especially depended upon a strain of thought in the history of Israel that led him to radically re-interpret the meaning and significance of family. But, first, some attention needs to be given to this background. The first thing to note is that we can hardly go to the Hebrew Scriptures and find the modern picture of the family as consisting of a husband, a wife, and 2.63

children (this “model” of family became “traditional” only in the 18th century and largely as a result of the economic forces of modern industrialization). In the Hebrew Scriptures, family was husband and wife (often multiple wives among the wealthy) and numbers of children forming large clans. “The average Hebrew household numbered close to 50 or even 100 people (Jacob’s, we are told, consisted of 66 {Gen. 46:26}). The Israelites had no real conception of a nuclear family. What we call the nuclear family they saw seamlessly woven into the multigenerational extended family. Every family centered on a patriarch. Each son, with his wife, children, and (in some cases) servants, lived in a separate shelter. So a Hebrew “household” or family would actually be a small village consisting of several adjacent buildings. What’s more, these households would sometimes induct and include as members of the family alien or sojourners who had permanently taken shelter with them. So Judges 17:12 speaks of a sojourning Levite being “installed” in the house of Micah.”[1]

Many things about family had changed by the time of Jesus. Among them, the Book of Genesis had been committed to paper in its final form by the time of the Babylonian exile (586-538 BCE). The creation accounts in Genesis established that marriage was now understood to be between one man and one woman. Jesus confirmed and extolled this understanding (Mk. 10:1-16; Mt. 19:1-15; Lu. 18:15-17). Thus polygamy had been abandoned in Israel. Also, in the developing history of Israel and by the time of Jesus, "marriage and family were at the marrow of Israel's identity and purpose. They were the greatest signs of Israel's election by God. The prophets could use marriage as a metaphor of the ups and downs of the relationship between God and Israel (Is. 50:1, 54:6; Jer. 3:1, 7-8, 20; Ezek. 16:23; Hos. 2:19-20). And, of course, the God whom Israel came to know through God's free, grace-full promise making and promise keeping (the covenant) is the Creator God. This God is the one who calls humankind into families to 'be fruitful and multiply, and fill the earth and subdue it'" (Gen. 1:28).[2] Their election by God could, and sometimes did, lead the people of Israel into thinking that the all important matter was blood purity and blood kinship.

However, and this is a very critical point for understanding Jesus' teaching about family, there is a strain of thought in the Hebrew Scriptures that does not associate God's covenant with blood relationships or kin. Rather, the true Israelite was one who was obedient to God. Such obedience trumped blood or ethnicity. Consider the following: "Biblical scholarship widely affirms that those who followed Moses out of Egypt were a ragtag collection of slaves—even of different races and places of origin. As Exodus 12:38 notes, a 'mixed multitude' left Egypt. In a real sense, the exodus created the people Israel. It was not bloodstream, racial stock, or language that set early Israel apart from its neighbors. It was a particular tradition, the living and developing tradition of a people that responded to a promise-making God who acted decisively in Egypt—and who was then seen, through that lens, to have acted earlier in parts of what had become the people the people Israel (the most significant parts being the lines of Abraham, Isaac, and Jacob). As Old Testament scholar John Bright writes, 'Speaking theologically, one might with justice call Israel a family; but from a historical point of view neither her first appearance nor her continued existence can be accounted for in terms of blood kinship,'"[3]

It was these facts that appear to have been the background for Jesus' teaching about family. The teaching can be summarized with the following points:

- Jesus' primary family is not comprised of those who share his genetic make-up, but of those who share his obedient spirit (Mk. 3:31-35). Jesus creates a new family. It is. . .a family of his followers that now demands primary allegiance. In fact, it demands allegiance even over the old first family, the biological family. Those who do the will of the Father (who, in other words, live under the reign of God) are now brothers and sisters of Jesus and one another.

- Allegiance to the kingdom precedes the family. It does not destroy the family. Jesus affirmed the existence of the family in a number of ways: 1) He spoke strenuously against divorce (Mt. 19:3-12)—"What God has joined together, let no one separate." 2) He welcomed children and recognized the importance of their nurture, desiring to bless them (Mk. 10:13-16; Luke 18:15-17). 3) He affirmed the family when he condemned those who defrauded their parents of wealth and due honor through the abuse of the Corban (Mk. 7:9-13).

- Jesus did not expect biological family to be denied or eliminated. He did, however, de-center and relativize it. He did not see it as the vehicle of salvation. He expected first family, the family of the kingdom, to grow evangelistically rather than biologically (Mt. 28:19-20). Entrance to the kingdom was not through biology but by water and Spirit (Jn. 3:5-6). Now, for those who follow Jesus, the critical blood, the blood that most significantly determines their character and identity, is not the blood of the biological family. It is the blood of the Lamb.[4]

All of this is forms the background of the *COF*'s statement: **The church has responsibility to help persons prepare for marriage, for parental responsibilities, and for family life under the lordship of Jesus Christ** (6.21). "There is nothing about family, simply as a collection of spouses and offspring, which makes its members Christian. Instead, families and individuals gain a distinctive Christian identity through their participation in the church and its story. In the church, we are 'born again' and re-socialized as a peculiar people whose lives would make no sense if the God of Israel and Jesus Christ were not living and true."[5] It should be noted that there are many other possible identities of family other than the Christian one. In the free-market economy and culture, the family may be viewed as a collection of consumers who, when functioning properly, serve a set of economic interests and concerns. The family may be viewed only as a medium of socializing persons for good citizenship. The family may be viewed only a as a form of "social contract" that works to provide a certain stability to societal life. And, of course, family may be lived out simply as the aggregation of two autonomous human beings who may or may not have children. So what is family? Who says what family is? CP's believe, of course, that we are told the meaning and purpose of family through the story that scripture and church tells. This is why church comes before family. Family cannot possibly know who or what it is, in Christian terms, apart from its being told by the church.

The *COF* of 1984 seems, at least partly, to address the question of family through the lens of the "traditional" family model: **God created the family as the primary community in which persons experience love, companionship, support, protection, discipline, encouragement, and other blessings. It is the normal relationship into which children are born** (6.15). But it does affirm that **the church recognizes and ministers to people living in a variety of family patterns, including those persons who by choice or circumstance are single. It seeks to embrace each person and all groups of persons within the**

family life of the covenant community (6.16). More will be said about this at the end of the chapter, but here it should be said that **"the family life of the covenant community"** should not be understood to imply that the modern traditional model of family (a husband, a wife, and 2.63 children) is the "correct," and especially not "a superior," one to other possible forms or patterns of family. We do well at this point to be especially cognizant of Jesus' teaching about family. It is striking that both Jesus and Paul seem to have thought of "singleness" as perhaps a better option than marriage for those who were awaiting the full arrival of the kingdom of God (Mt. 19; 1 Cor. 7).

Marriage

As with family, who can tell us the meaning and purpose of marriage? Will society tell us? Will government tell us? Will economics tell us? Will we make it up as we go along and by and for ourselves? Once again, it is the Jesus story and the church faithful to this story which can and does tell us the meaning and purpose of Christian marriage. **Marriage is between a man and a woman for the mutual benefit of each, their children, and society. While marriage is subject to the appropriate civil law, it is primarily a covenant relationship under God. As such, it symbolizes the relationship of Jesus Christ and the church and is that human relationship in which love and trust are best known** (6.17).

A young couple comes to a pastor for pre-marriage

counseling. The pastor asks them to reflect on the questions, "What is the meaning of a Christian marriage? And, "How is a Christian marriage different from other possible understandings of marriage?" They stumble a bit with how to answer but then say things such as, "It's letting God be important for the marriage. It's coming to church regularly. It's trusting that God is there so you can go to God when times are rough." The pastor replies, "Good answers all. " But then she adds, "As Cumberland Presbyterians, we believe that Christian marriage is a form of *ministry*; a special form of service to God." And, "Marriage is a special form for learning how to love another person for a lifetime the way Christ loves the church, and all persons all the time." The pastor adds, "Married persons, of course, must grow in this love and there will be times when such growth is challenged. But we are to remember that Christ is patient, compassionate, and forgiving."

The pastor continues, "In our culture, the prevailing conception of marriage is that two people somehow meet, date and discover they are in love. They marry, proceed with careers, may have children, and, above all, they *seek to live, as much as possible, the American dream*. But, of course, marriage will be much more than this for you. Your marriage covenant (and, for us, marriage is not just a legal, civil, and social contract) before and with God will be a Christian sign to the world, a testimony, a ministry. A Christian marriage doesn't have to do with realizing the "American dream," but with bearing faithful witness to the Triune God. It is bearing witness, in a fallen world, to the truth that God's love *(agape)* is truly possible; that it really works. Again, will you always love one another perfectly, as Christ loves us? Hardly! So you will need the help of Christ, the Spirit, and the church as you seek to be to one another as Christ is to all of us. Your marriage, then, will also be a form of witnessing to the Christian faith. It will be an act of evangelism. It will bear witness to the good news that God's love in Christ is powerful to establish a union of persons in love. And that God will nurture, deepen, enlarge, and extend this love. As such, it will bear witness that this union is analogous to and symbolic of Christ's union in love with the church. And, the first thing that your children, if there are children, will know about God's love is the love they experience from and through you."

And, the pastor continues, "I would like to remind you that human sexuality is the good gift of God. It is not God, but it is a gift of God. The church believes the God of the incarnation blesses not only 'spiritual love' but also 'physical, fleshly love.' The relationship of "two becoming one" is so intense and meaningful that God placed a boundary of fidelity around it. This boundary should never be compromised or violated. Finally, I would like to tell you that 'making promises,' to God, to one another, and to the covenant community, stands at the very center of the Christian marriage service. Therefore it is at the center of marriage itself. Many mature married persons report that often it has been 'the promise' that has carried their marriages through times of storm and strain. Fidelity to the covenantal promise has enabled them to remain faithful to one another in a way that passing moods, feelings, and grievances never could have. The power of the promise is especially made known to us in and through God's faithfulness to the one covenant of grace."

The *COF* also says: **The church has responsibility to minister to the needs of persons in every crisis, including physical and emotional illness, economic distress, natural disasters, accidents due to carelessness, and death** (6.22). Perhaps this statement, utterly worthwhile in its own right, is included in this section because there is hardly a greater crisis than divorce in the lives of persons, families, children and societies. It is for this reason that the *COF* says: **If a marriage is dissolved by divorce, the covenant community is responsible to minister to victims, including any children of the marriage, and to counsel divorced persons who are considering remarriage** (6.20). Morrow writes, "As the family of God, the church is responsible to reach out in caring love and helpfulness to persons whose lives have been shattered by the destruction of their primary community. In effect, the church may become a surrogate family for those whose primary families have been disrupted if not destroyed. This is an important part of the witness of Christians through family life."[6]

The church recognizes and ministers to people living in a variety of family patterns, including those persons who by choice or circumstances are single (6.16). Again, the meaning of singleness changed dramatically in the revelation of God that is Jesus Christ. Theologian Stanley Hauerwas can write, "One of the most distinguishing aspects of the early church was the discovery of singleness as a necessary way of life among Christians. Christians do not 'need' to marry, since their true family is the church. It is only against the background of such presumptions that marriage becomes a calling to be tested by the community. That two people may be in love is therefore not a sufficient condition for their marriage to be witnessed by the church, since the church must be convinced their marriage will 'build up' Christ's body."[7]

What a profound change! "The Old Testament provides no real place for single people. Even ascetics such as the priests and the Nazirites were not single (Lev. 21:1-15; Num. 6:1-21). In fact, for a Hebrew not to get married was catastrophic. So Isaiah has seven women pursuing one man, pleading, 'We will eat our own bread and wear our own clothes; just let us be called by your name; take away our disgrace' (4:1). Blessing, in the Old Testament, means bountiful crops, thriving community—and many children. A man's or a woman's life was simply incomplete if he or she did not marry and procreate. Needless to say, there were no 'bachelor jokes' in ancient Israel. In fact, marriage was so taken for granted that biblical Hebrew has no word for 'bachelor.'"[8] It is unnecessary here to go into all of the known reasons contributing to this situation. In short, marriage did provide for procreation. Marriage did assist with economic life. Marriage, before a fully developed view concerning the after-life, meant to the Hebrews some sort of future hope through their children. And, in Israel, marriage and the producing of children was understood as God's way of insuring that one day Messiah would come and all the nations of the earth ultimately would be blessed.

In an earlier chapter, we discussed the fact that Jesus means freedom. One of the freedoms he brought was that lack of marriage and children no longer meant that one was meaningless and useless, or cursed (It is worth remembering that neither Jesus or Paul were married or produced children). Single persons could come into, serve, rejoice in, and be totally valued in the kingdom of God proclaimed by Jesus. Even more, singleness could be chosen in its own right as a vocation from God. Thus, the church cannot, and remain faithful to Jesus, regard singleness as a lesser status, an inferior status, to marriage. Not realizing this can lead to some misguided ideas and practices relative to single persons. "Frankly, most churches treat their singles ministries as little more than a substitute for singles bars. They see singles as peripheral to the core or central members, who belong to families. They assume that

that the 'normal' single will sooner or later marry and start a family. True to this assumption, a church in my area once called its adult social group 'Pairs and Spares.'"[9] It should not be so in Cumberland Presbyterian congregations. Singleness, like marriage, can be, and is, a form of service to Jesus Christ who is lord of the church and the world. Our *COF* strongly affirms this.

An Excursus: Same-Sex Marriage?

My original intention for this book was to comment only on what the *COF* actually says, and refrain from commenting on what it does not say. However, as of the moment I am writing, same-sex marriage has been legalized in thirty-seven states. And the United States Supreme Court is currently considering a case that may result in same-sex marriage becoming legal in the entire country. These facts, in and of themselves, are not the reason I am choosing here to offer a few reflections on this issue, and in doing so going beyond the statements in the *COF*. The reason comes out of my last pastorate. Several people sought from me an opinion, scriptural guidance, and discussion about these culture-changing civil, legal, and human developments. And they wondered, as they learned of changing positions on the issue by some other denominations, what was "happening" in our own church? As perhaps to be expected, some people had come to definite convictions on the subject, both "for" and "against," and some others were simply confused and uncertain. I suspect that people in many Cumberland Presbyterian (and CPCA) congregations were dealing with, struggling with, or not dealing and struggling with, the same questions, feelings, and convictions one way or the other.

As background to a consideration of the subject, I think it is good to recall the *COF* says, under its treatment of Civil Government: **The covenant community affirms the lordship of Christ who sought out the poor, the oppressed, the sick, and the helpless. In her corporate life and through her individual members, the church is an advocate for all victims of violence and all those whom the law or society treats as less than persons for whom Christ died. Such advocacy involves not only opposition to all unjust laws and forms of injustice but even more support for those attitudes and actions which embody the way of Christ, which is to overcome evil with good** (6.31). Cumberland Presbyterians, as have Christians in many traditions, have repented of their part in the way in which gay persons have been victims of violence, in attitudes and actions, and treated as less than persons for whom Christ has died. Cumberland Presbyterians have supported the elimination of unjust laws and other forms of injustice that gay persons have suffered for generations. Cumberland Presbyterians have recognized that the way of Christ compels them to become advocates for the civil rights of gay persons and, what is more, to rid themselves of all barriers, inward and outward, that have set the church over and "against" gay persons. In spite of this, it remains the case that Cumberland Presbyterians will and do differ with respect to the ways in which they read the Bible, and interpret it, with respect to homosexuality and especially homosexual sex.

It also is true that Cumberland Presbyterians will and do differ with respect to same-sex marriage. Not, hopefully, with respect to whether gays are due the same civil and individual rights that belong to all citizens of the United States. This, for some, will include the right to marry. But the major question is whether Cumberland Presbyterians will bring the practice of same-sex marriage into the orbit of its own life? Or is this a practice, more and more endorsed by the larger society, at which the church must draw a line and say, "No?" There are Cumberland Presbyterians who will take the latter position. They will do so based on their own faithfulness to their reading of scripture and what they hear God saying that bears on this subject. Concerning this point, it should be noted that such a reading and hearing of scripture is consonant with what the church has said throughout the centuries, what the historical Reformed confessions of faith have said, including the present Cumberland Presbyterian *COF*. Many will conclude that the matter is simply settled. Altering the traditional understanding of marriage as being between "a man and a woman" will be considered a bridge too far. For many, their understanding of biblical authority and faithfulness to this authority will compel them to reject same-sex marriage as an acceptable practice within the church.

There are other Cumberland Presbyterians who will and do wonder if God the Holy Spirit is at work in the world in a way that the church is being called to recognize. They will affirm the words of the English bishop who said, “The church that marries the spirit of the age will be a widow in the next.” But, at the same time, they will wonder if what they are see happening with respect to same-sex marriage is the spirit of the world or the work of the Holy Spirit? But how is it possible to read the scripture in such a way as to be open to, within the church, the recognition, blessing, and marriage of same sex persons (same-sex Christian persons)? It seems to me that the only possibility lies in what Cumberland Presbyterians have always affirmed. Namely, that scripture is to be read and understood Christologically and Pnuematologically—that is, in the light of Jesus Christ and the Holy Spirit.

Of course, Jesus himself taught that marriage is monogamous, permanent, and between a man and woman. Doesn’t that settle the question? It most certainly would except for the fact that Jesus remains alive and at work in his church and in the world through the ministry of the Holy Spirit. Christological interpretation of scripture has often been a source of controversy, even division, within the life of the church. The world it may be remembered, and not the church, put an end to slavery in America. Entire denominations were divided over this issue.

Only later, did the church, as more a less a whole, come to recognize that the Holy Spirit was at work in and through the world, in historical attitudes and events, and that a proper Christological reading of scripture would never have allowed for an argument for or endorsement of the practice of human slavery on supposedly biblical grounds. The world, and not the church, gave women suffrage in the early twentieth century. Only later did many Christian traditions recognize the work of the Spirit in this history, and that all texts previously read in support of the subordination of women should have been read in light of Christ and the Spirit. The question is whether or not marriage as being only between “a man and a woman” is so fundamentally a part of God’s design, and is attested to in scripture in such a way, that same-sex marriage simply must be rejected as a practice within the church.

It is probable, already but certainly in the years to come, that Cumberland Presbyterians will be called upon to engage in moral discernment about this issue. Congregations, presbyteries, General Assemblies, and individual Cumberland Presbyterians will wrestle with their thoughts and feelings about it. They will pray and search the scriptures for guidance. Some will seek to listen to the testimonies of gay Christians already among them, or to whom they may otherwise listen. They, above all, will desire to be faithful to the God who is revealed in Jesus Christ and the power of the Holy Spirit. Who, at the present time, can say with absolute certainty that same-sex marriage is wholly the work of the world and wholly opposed to the work of the Spirit.

I consider the following words both hopeful and helpful when thinking about the process of moral discernment under the guidance of the Holy Spirit: "*How to change*, so continuing to be relevant, while *remaining the same*, so continuing to be Christian, has been the challenge perpetually confronting Christian ethics. Man's conscience moves more slowly than his mind, but in the end Christian ethics must keep faith with maturing faith; merely residual attitudes, conventional pieties, less rational inhibitions, must be left behind. That the canon of Christian ethics was never closed, any more than the canon of Christian theology, is the consequence of another great doctrine of the gospel—as influential in ethics as the incarnation—*the doctrine of the presence of the living Spirit of Christ in the ongoing church* (italics mine for emphasis). Already within the Old Testament, but much more clearly and consistently in the New, the heart and secret of man's moral development is seen to lie in the presence within human experience of the Divine Spirit, revealing in law and the prophets the divine will, inspiring in apostles and reformers the divine protest against evil, creating and indwelling the divine community as the earnest and agency of the ideal, and constantly renewing in godly persons the hunger and the capacity for good. . .The supreme insight of the Bible concerning the Spirit is precisely that which seems him less as the bestower of gifts and the generator of power than as the source of Christian morality and the form of the contemporary Christ in the experience of believers."[10]

Chapter Thirty-One

THE LORD'S DAY

Our Confession says this about the Lord's Day: **The creator has given one day in seven for special reflection on God's nature and deeds. From the beginning of the world to the resurrection of Christ the seventh day of the week, known as the Sabbath, was the Lord's Day. Subsequent to Christ's resurrection, Christians celebrate the first day of the week as the Lord's Day** (6.23). The first thing to say about the one day in seven is that it is a gift of God to God's people. Therefore, it is not a burden to be borne, but a joy in which to delight. It is an especially theological day in that it is a day to reflect on God's "nature and deeds." For Israel, two things were intended for special reflection. First was the fact of God's act of creation (see Ex. 20:8-11). The world in which Israel works and then rests is the world that God has made and which God sustains. It was remembered that God "worked" for six days and on the seventh day God "rested." That God rested does not mean that God was tired, but that God was finished. There was nothing more to be done.

But, secondly, Sabbath was a day for reflecting on God's awesome act of salvation on behalf of his people (see Dt. 5:12-15). This meant recalling God's rescuing of his people from slavery in Egypt. When the Book of Exodus opens, the Egyptian pharaoh is quite literally working the Hebrew people, and other people, to their deaths on his various building projects. They were little more than beasts of burden. They have no value beyond production. They are merely cogs in a cruel wheel. Authoritarian rulers have always behaved in this fashion. We can recall the piece of mocking cruelty that was on the sign at the entrance to the Auschwitz concentration camp—*Arbeit Macht Frei*—"Work will set you free."

But God raised Moses and, after the lengthy contest with pharaoh (systems of oppression do not yield easily), God's people are delivered. Now things will be different. God gives the Ten Words at Sinai. God's people are given guidance for the flourishing of life. Among the words are these: "Remember the Sabbath day, and keep it holy. Six days you shall labor and do all your work. But the seventh day is a Sabbath to the Lord your God; you shall not do any work—you, your son or your daughter, your male or female slave, your livestock, or the alien resident in your towns. For in six days the Lord made heaven and earth, the sea, and all that is in them, but rested the seventh day; therefore the Lord blessed the Sabbath day and consecrated it" (Ex. 20:8-11).

The Exodus narrative indicates it is God's intention that no one will ever be worked to death again! No human being is to be seen as a beast of burden. No human being will be regarded as a means to someone else's end. No human being is to be seen merely as a means of production. The fourth commandment extends this attitude to the servants, the aliens, and even the animals! For Israel, the one day in seven was a time to give thanks for the God given dignity of human life (and the dignity of all creation) recovered in and through God's salvation as wrought in the Exodus. The Sabbath was a day to do nothing except to worship, enjoy, and delight in the goodness of God. Israelites were to imitate God according to the double emphasis of resting as God did following the creation, and by treating the aliens among them, and any slaves (servants), as God had treated them in the deliverance from Egypt.

However, as recorded in the Hebrew Scriptures, the faithful observance of Sabbath in and by Israel had a checkered history. This is the same as saying that God's people went through periods of covenant faithfulness and periods of covenant disobedience (Isa. 58:13f). It was felt that the dishonoring of the Sabbath was one of the causes of the exile to Babylon (586-543). By the time of Jesus, religious leaders, in order to prevent the repeat of exile and hasten the coming of Messiah, had imposed rigorous demands with respect to Sabbath observance. They also had elaborated detailed rules and regulations as to behavior—what was permissible and what was not—with respect to the Sabbath. The religious leaders (scribes and Pharisees) were determined that this mistake would not be repeated again. So they "fenced the

Sabbath" with careful instructions and regulations. However, Israel was still under the oppression of the Roman Empire. Perhaps, so the thinking went, careful Sabbath observance would speed a return to God's favor and the coming of God's kingdom. Until that time, faithful Sabbath keeping would be one means, a very important means, for the people to maintain their identity as God's people.

The New Testament records a series of conflicts between Jesus and the scribes and Pharisee party over Sabbath practice (see Mk. 2:23-28; 3:1-6 for examples). Jesus, a faithful Jew, was certainly not opposed to Sabbath faithfulness. It was his practice to regularly attend synagogue on Sabbath. And he most surely understood Sabbath as the day for remembering, honoring, and celebrating God as the creator of the world and redeemer of his people. However, it clearly appears to have been Jesus' attitude that the Pharasaic regulations were too fastidious. They had turned the Sabbath from being a joy and delight for God's people into being a yoke and burden. It is also to be remembered, again, that the religious leaders felt that strict Sabbath observance would speed the return of God's kingdom to Israel. Jesus, however, understood that this long-awaited kingdom was now breaking in and upon Israel. He proclaimed that the kingdom was now present in his own ministry and that of his followers. This, of course, meant an altered view of the Sabbath. It was no longer a burden to be borne in hope of the soon return of the kingdom. Now, given the presence of the kingdom in Jesus, the Sabbath was to be returned to its original meaning of being a gift to and delight for God's people. This is the probable meaning behind Jesus' statement to his critics that, "The Sabbath was made for humankind, and not humankind for the Sabbath" (Mk. 2:27).

The one day in seven was the Sabbath for Israel. Following the death and resurrection of Jesus, the one day in seven became, for Christians, the first day of the week, the day of resurrection. The original Sabbath was, for Israel, a festival of God's creation. Early Christians understood the day of resurrection as the inauguration of the beginning of God's new creation. God in Jesus Christ was not redeeming and re-creating the world. Israel understood the original Sabbath as a time for remembering God's great act of salvation on behalf of Israel (exodus). Early Christians understood the day of resurrection as representing God's great act of salvation for both Israel and the Gentiles. God was now saving the whole world in and through Christ.

Cumberland Presbyterians believe in the importance of the Lord's Day. They understand themselves as bearing witness to the world, for the sake of the world, when assembling for worship on this day. Cumberland Presbyterians also recognize that this witness is being borne in and to a world, especially in North America, in which respect for the Lord's Day has been greatly diminished and compromised. There are multiple factors that brought about this development. The industrial revolution meant that you couldn't shut down the massive factories in order for persons to recognize and honor the one day in seven. Following World War II, Americans began their love affair with the automobile and Sunday travel. The post war era also saw a movement of people from living in their small towns, and near family, to living all across the United States. The weekend, including Sunday, became an opportunity for many to visit relatives who now lived at some distance. In the last fifty years, business world invented the concept of the weekend as a time for recreation and entertainment. Factors such as these, along with many more, contributed to the Lord's Day becoming, for many, simply another day of the week. Perhaps, at bottom, attitudes toward the Lord's Day are simply as old as ancient Israel in her times of covenant faithlessness. Humankind, when it regards itself as the standard of measurement and importance, simply wishes to claim all time for its purposes. This, of course, is an act of idolatry.

Cumberland Presbyterians find joy and delight in the observance of the Lord's Day. And they understand themselves to be bearing witness to the world, for the sake of the world, to the creator and redeemer of the world. The Confession says: **Appropriate activities on the Lord's Day include worship, study, doing good works, and other acts leading to renewal. The proper observance of the Lord's Day enriches the quality of life for all other days** (6.24). Cumberland Presbyterians will continue to rise from sleep, dress, and make their way through the streets of their villages, towns, country-sides, and cities to assemble together on the Lord's Day. This is not only something they will do for themselves, but also that which they will do for the sake of the world.

Chapter Thirty-Two

LAWFUL OATHS AND VOWS

Recently the news carried a story about a homeless man in Boston. He found a backpack containing $3000 in cash and $40,000 in traveler's checks. He went into the street, flagged a police car, and turned the money over to a policewoman. It became such a "feel good" story that the news people looked the man up. During the interview with him, he said, "I may be down on my luck at the moment, but I still have my integrity." There's a man who, somewhere along the way of his life, made a *vow* to himself that he would maintain his personal character no matter what. The *COF* has two brief statements about lawful oaths and vows: **Christians should bind themselves by oath or pledge only to those good and just promises they are reasonable able to perform. A vow is similar to an oath and should be made with care, performed with faithfulness, and honored with integrity. Persons should vow to do only that which is consistent with the scriptures** (6.25, 6.26).

During the decade of the 1980s, I served as director of our presbytery's junior/junior high camp which met at Crystal Springs in Kelso, Tennessee. For nearly all of those years, Miss Ruth Brandon also served in the camps. She began this ministry when she was in her mid 70s. During camp week, she would be up first for breakfast every day and she would stay up until the lights went out at ten at night. On some of those days the temperature reached triple digits! Anyone who has worked in camp knows that the days can be long and tiring. One evening, when the staff was relaxing after the kids had gone to bed, I said to Miss Ruth, "You are a blessing and inspiration to all of us and all of the children." She said in return, "Well, one day, a few years back, I promised God that I would do this as long as I am able." It is simply amazing what people do because they have promised God they will do it.

The practice of oath-taking came out of ancient Israel's judicial and civil world. It usually involved criminality of some kind. Oaths were extremely important to defendants. If you were charged with theft, for example, and there were no witnesses to help exonerate you, you could call upon God as your witness. The defendant could "swear by God" that he or she was innocent. When you called upon God, involved God in this way, your testimony was absolutely binding. If it was discovered that you were lying, the penalty was severe. Very often it was death.

Overtime, lesser oaths were developed. These were oaths that did not implicate God. A person could, for instance, swear by heaven, or earth, or his head, or Jerusalem. If he or she were found guilty of lying the penalty would be less severe. In the Sermon on the Mount, Jesus said clearly that such oaths should be unnecessary and for two reasons: 1) God is involved whether one swears or not. There is no part of life that is not under the province of God, and 2) a person's integrity should be such that no oath is required (see Mt. 5:33-37). It is for this reason that some Christians historically have refused to take oaths or makes pledges—for example, Quakers, Amish, and Mennonites. The latter will not take the oath in courts or make pledges such as to the flag, or even say the pledge of allegiance.

Vows come primarily from ancient Israel's religious life. Vows were promises made to God, and to one another, as members of God's covenant community. A vow was a binding promise to keep your word to God or to your neighbors. The foundation of this practice was the conviction that God is a God who keeps covenant with his people. God's promises are irrevocable and absolutely sure. Thus members of God's people would themselves reflect the image of God, God's character, by keeping promises, or vows. Such vows were a matter of utter seriousness.

The writer of Ecclesiastes says the following, "1) Guard your steps when you go to the house of God; to draw near to listen is better than the sacrifice offered by fools for they do not know how to keep from doing evil. 2) Never be rash with your mouth, nor let your heart be quick to utter a word before God, for God is in heaven, and you upon earth; therefore let your words be few. 3) For dreams come with many cares, and a fool's voice with many words. 4) When you make a vow to God, do not delay fulfilling it; for he has no pleasure in fools. Fulfill what you vow. 5) It is better that you should not vow than that you should vow and not fulfill it. 6) Do not let your mouth lead you into sin, and do not say before the messenger that it was a mistake; why should God be angry at your words, and destroy the work of your hands" (Eccl. 5:1-6).

Cumberland Presbyterians, by having words about the ancient tradition of oaths and vows included in the *COF*, seek to bear witness to the world that promising to God is one of the most important things, if not the most important, that human beings will ever do. For one thing, it is a way of saying that life is not just about our individual choices and wants and desires. It is not about the person as a glorified, autonomous self. To vow to God is to acknowledge that human beings are called to be a part of something larger than them-selves. A vow to God is integrative. It integrates life with a Greater Reality than is otherwise possible. A vow to God is a confession that we are made in the image of God. We can reflect the image of God, the character of God, through promise keeping. Ultimately, vows make Christian community, and authentic love within this community, possible. Keeping our word to one another is a matter of expressing and experiencing covenant love.

Recently I performed a wedding. In the pre-wedding counseling sessions, I told the couple that, in the view of the Christian faith, sometimes it will not be love that holds them together. It will not be sex. It will not be money. It will not even be children. Sometimes the only thing that will hold them together, until all conflicts have been resolved and love can truly flower to its fullness, is the promise that they have made to God and to one another. Life is utterly diminished, even destroyed, when people lose their integrity, when their word is no longer good, and when their promises are made in vain.

Chapter Thirty-Three

CIVIL GOVERNMENT

Cumberland Presbyterians bear witness to the world, for the sake of the world, through their relationship to civil government. The *COF* has six statements about this relationship. The first three are: **The purpose of civil government is to enable God's creation to live under the principles of justice and order. As it faithfully upholds the welfare of God's creation, civil government lies within the purpose of God and functions as a useful instrument to enable people to live in harmony and peace. It is the duty of people to participate in civil government in such ways that are open to them, especially in exercising the right to vote. It is the duty of Christians to enter civil offices for which they are qualified and for the purpose of working for justice, peace, and the common welfare. Civil government and persons elected to civil office may not assume control over the administration of the church in matters of faith and practice. Yet their duty is to protect the religious freedom of all persons and to guard the right of religious bodies to assemble without interference** (6.27—6.29).

These statements reveal that the CP Confession stands in continuity with the attitudes and practices toward civil government that were characteristic of the magisterial reformers of the 16th century. By "magisterial" is meant those reformers who were supported, even sponsored, by the political magistrates (princes, kings, governors) who reigned over the governments in which the reformers lived and led their particular movements. These states (e.g. Germany for Luther and Switzerland for Calvin) were almost exclusively "Christian." Therefore, the issue for the reformers was defining the church's proper relationship to the governing powers.

It should be noted that there also were non-magisterial reformers (e.g., Anabaptists) who rejected sponsorship by the state. They especially rejected such sponsorship because potentially it would include participation in state sponsored violence such as war. Roland Bainton describes the three basic reformation responses to the church-state relationship based on how each interpreted Paul's words in Romans 13:1-7, especially relative to the government's right to use the sword: 1) "The first was that the coercive power of the state was ordained by God because of sin and should be administered by sinners. The saints should submit to all commands not contrary to conscience but should not collaborate. This was the Anabaptist position in the age of the Reformation. 2) The second position was that the state was indeed ordained because of sin; but Christians, though they would not need the state for themselves, should nevertheless assume political responsibilities, because in a nominally Christian society the state would collapse without their help. This was the position of Martin Luther. 3) The third view was that the state was ordained not only because of sin but also to foster righteousness and faith. Such, it was claimed, had been the view of the Old Testament theocracy. This view was espoused by John Calvin."[1]

Before saying more below about the attitude of the magisterial reformers (Cumberland Presbyterians stand in the lineage that began with John Calvin), I would like to briefly discuss what can be learned from the Bible relative to the relationship between Christians and the state:

The Bible and Government

- The Bible is not a purely religious book. The writers of the Bible clearly are interested in and concerned about human, political, social and historical existence.
- The Bible does not present any systematic view of government. It covers many centuries and its writers lived under widely divergent forms of government, from early Israelite tribal society to the rule of the Roman Empire.
- Many of its remarks about government are hints rather than clearly stated principles.
- It is doubtful that a clear and unitary political view can be deduced from the Bible.[2]

- In the New Testament, the state seems to be regarded as an expression of God's common grace extended to all humankind. It is God who ordains the institution of government (Ro. 13:1-7).

- The function of the state, in the New Testament, is two-fold: 1) the administration of justice (Ro. 13:4), and 2) the promotion of the general welfare (2 Sam. 23:3-4; 2 Chr. 19:5-7; Ps. 72:1-4; 82:1-4; Ro. 13:1-7; 1 Ti. 2:1-2; 1 Pt. 2:13-17).

- Peter and Paul called for Christians to submit to the powers that be (Ro.13:1; 1 Pt. 2:13).

- Both Jesus (Mt. 17:24-27) and Paul (Ro. 13:6ff) called for the paying of taxes. The view of the New Testament seems to have been that those who enjoy the benefits of the state should share in the cost of the state.

- Christians were to obey the law, pray for civil authorities, and to give honor to whom it was due (Ro. 13:1-7; 1 Tim. 2:1-3; Tit. 3:1; 1 Pt. 2:13-17).

- Some suggest that the New Testament did not forbid Christian to work in government service. This view is based on the observation that people such as the Ethiopian eunuch, Cornelius, Sergius Paulus, and the Philippian jailor were not, after becoming Christians, called upon to abandon their stations in life.

- The New Testament clearly suggests that government is not unlimited in its power. The clearest expression of this is found in Acts 5:29 in which Peter says to the authorities, "We must obey God rather than men." Neither could Christians be coerced into saying, "Caesar is Lord." And, by the time of the writing of the Revelation, the Roman Empire is presented as having turned from promoting justice and the general welfare to having become usurpers of the place of God.[3]

The Reformation and Government

- It is to be kept in mind that the 16th century reformers lived in predominantly "Christian states," ruled by "Christian magistrates" so the main concern of the reformers was to define, on the basis of scripture, the sense in which the church and the government were to be related. All of the magisterial reformers considered civil government to be an institution that was ordained by God. Martin Luther summed up the magisterial point of view in these words, "God operates in history with a left hand that is the coercive state and a right hand that is the persuasive church."[4]

- The magisterial reformers were not democratic, nor were they particularly concerned about individual rights.

- Governments, as already said, were ordained by God to

establish just order and to restrain the archaic drives of human sin.

- Among the magisterial reformers, there was no general right of resistance to tyrannous authority. God will judge and destroy tyrants in God's own way. Christians living under tyrannous government should speak prophetically to leaders who are misusing their authority. But Christians living under tyrannous authority are to crown their witness by suffering under, rather than seeking to overthrow, these leaders.5

- The general perspective of the magisterial reformers is summarized in the Scots Confession of 1560. "Governments are appointed by and ordained of God and are to serve for the good and well-being of all. Those who rebel against duly established civil power are both enemies to humanity and rebels against God's will. Those in authority are God's lieutenants who use the sword for the defense of the good and the punishment of evil-doers. Such magistrates, whether kings or city magistrates, are appointed also to maintain true religion and suppress all religion that is idolatrous. David, Josiah, and other kings may be appealed to as examples. There is only a brief hint in the Confession that rulers might be resisted in the oblique statement that no rebellion is allowable 'so long as princes and rulers vigilantly fulfill their office.'"[6] It is to be remembered that the assumption seemed to be that the rulers would, themselves, always be Christians.

Post Reformation Developments

- As is to be expected, Reformed teaching on the relationship between the church and civil government has undergone considerable development since the 16th century Reformation. Historical developments also have been considerable. For one thing, the Western world, for the most part, witnessed the collapse of belief in "the divine right of kings." This belief was still operative at the time of the Reformation. Secondly, subsequent centuries have witnessed the emergence of constitutional democracies. It is an interesting point that many scholars see the seeds of modern constitutionalism in the form of church government espoused and enacted by John Calvin in Geneva. This government was representative, from bottom up. Some scholars believe that the founders of the United States were strongly influenced by Presbyterianism and found in it a model for constitutional democracy.

- The prevailing view of government (politics) in the Reformed tradition can be summarized, at present, by the following sentence: "Politics is a relative, sinful, yet promising area for the achievement of provisional, reformable justice which bears external witness to the realization of human community and love in Jesus Christ."[7]

- The statements in the Confession appear fairly consistent with the ideas of the 16th century reformers, with modifications due to post Reformation developments. The Confession stresses that 1) the purpose of government is to "**uphold justice and order**"; 2) "**civil government lies within the purposes of God;**" 3) "**it is an instrument of harmony and peace;**" 4) Christians may seek civil service, it is even the duty of those so qualified, "**for the purpose of working for justice, peace, and the common welfare:"** and 5) **"civil government should not assume control of church affairs and should protect religious freedom;"** 6) the *COF* says "**civil government should protect the religious liberty of all persons."**

The Church's Prophetic Responsibility

The *COF* continues by saying: **The covenant community affirms the lordship of Christ who sought out the poor, the oppressed, the sick, and the helpless. In her corporate life and through her individual members, the church is an advocate of all victims of violence and all those whom the law or society treats as less than persons for whom Christ has died. Such advocacy involves not only opposition to all unjust laws and forms of injustice but even more support for those attitudes and actions which embody the way of Christ, which is to**

overcome evil with good (6.31). In this statement, we can hear the echo of the Reformation teaching that Christians have a responsibility for speaking prophetically to civil government (and to society). The voice of the state and the voice of the church are not the same.

We can also hear an echo, particularly from the Scots Confession, that Christians may engage in civil disobedience when laws and government are unjust or treat persons as "**less than persons for whom Christ has died**." Here is a direct challenge to the often expressed idea that, "Christianity (often called religion) and politics do not mix." The history of Jesus Christ, the history of the early church, and the history of the Reformation deny this claim. Rather than a biblically shaped view, it is more likely a conviction based on the "privatization of the Christian life and ethic" (a contemporary form of the first century Gnostic dualistic heresy). Such privatization of the faith has come to prevail in much of the Christianity of the western world. It forgets that the church in the New Testament did not reject the political world, but offered that world an alternate political reality (based on the ethic of Jesus). It forgets the strong witness against political injustice made by Israel's great prophets. It forgets that Jesus died on the hard wood of the cross as a political criminal. The church exists in the world, for the sake of the world, to speak prophetically to the powers that be when those powers are unjust. In my lifetime, Martin Luther King is one of those "prophets" who combined both of these

Reformation principles. He led a movement that spoke prophetically to the powers of the world and he accepted that his witness, both his and other's civil disobedience, would be met by legal and civil hostility. For him, the voice of God was more compelling than the voice of the state.

The *COF* concludes its section on civil government by saying: **God gives the message and ministry of reconciliation to the church. The church, corporately and through her individual members, seeks to promote reconciliation, love, and justice among all persons, classes, races, and nations** (6.32). At first glance, this statement might seem to be a bit out of place. But nothing could be further from the case. This statement goes beyond the affirmation that civil government is ordained by God to uphold justice and order and to promote the common welfare of all. It is included here to say that the church has a similar but different, and profoundly theological, mission. The church bears witness to the world, governments, and societies that God in Jesus Christ has given the church a message and ministry of reconciliation that is for the world. It is the message that the purpose of God in Christ is peace in the shared experience of being human beings

The reconciliation that the church proclaims to the world is something more than a matter of legal rights, more than "the pursuit of life, liberty, and happiness," and more than that various groups of people may learn to live in some degree of harmony. While all of these are important, even to be treasured, the message and ministry of the church is that persons also may experience a reconciliation and unity that is based on the gracious work of a loving God in the self-donation of Jesus Christ (Gal. 3:28). This message and ministry is not for the sake of the church but for the sake of the world. In scripture, when Christians said "Jesus is Lord" they meant that he is Lord over every realm of human existence.

In an unrelated but fascinating article about the effects of modern technology on the mission of the church, Richard Hong says, "The business and technological changes of the last 35 years have catered to or even taken advantage of our innate desire to fragment into homogeneous subcultures. This is a fundamental issue that the church is called to address. The church is called to the task of challenging us to go against our instincts and fight the hard, upstream battle for truly inclusive human community. . .The safe response is to pursue peaceful, separate, co-existence, but this isn't reconciliation. True reconciliation is hard and uncomfortable. Are we willing to fight for it?"[8] Perhaps we can say here that Jesus called this work of reconciliation, among other things, "taking up your cross." God has a mission for Cumberland Presbyterians directed to the 21st century world. It is to proclaim and to be, for governments, society, community, and persons, the message and ministry of God's reconciliation in Jesus Christ.

God Consummates All Life and History

(7.01—7.08 in the Confession of Faith)

Chapter Thirty-Four

DEATH AND RESURRECTION

The final section of the *COF* brings us to the doctrine of the Christian hope for the future. Even without appealing to this doctrine, we know as a matter of course that there will be a future. We know this because there has been a past and a present, therefore there must be a future. We, of course, can only speculate about what the future will be or bring. People have always had many attitudes toward and ideas about the future. Probably, most of the time, we are primarily concerned about our personal and immediate future. Despite the knowledge of our human finiteness (the fact that we die), we make plans for this future: for tomorrow, for next week, next month, next year or years. We hope that the future will be at least as good as, or sometimes better than, the past and the present. Sometimes, of course, we may find ourselves thinking about the "ultimate" future. We may wonder about what life means, where we are going, and whether there has been any purpose to all of it, any ultimate meaning.

Some beliefs about the future are quite ominous. Human beings now possess the power and knowledge (and freedom) to commit nuclear suicide. Some observers warn that climate change may have catastrophic consequences for our survival. Physicists tell us that our solar star—the sun—will burn out in approximately five billion years. They also debate whether the larger universe will go on expanding or come to an end in a violently destructive "crunch." Bertrand Russell, the 20th century English philosopher, expressed the thoughts of many who have lost faith in God and therefore ultimate meaning and purpose and life. He once said, on the basis of his reading of modern science, that the earth will one day explode in a ball of fire, the debris of earth will float off into the universe, and it will be as if human beings never existed! Sometimes contemporary philosophers and scientists can sound something like old-fashioned religious "dooms-day prophets."

The point is that thinking about the future is not a peculiar thing done only by Christians. All people inevitably get in on the act. But there is something Christians have in common with anyone, and everyone, who considers the future. Namely, the most reliable tools for imagining the future are *the past* and *the present*. For instance, the history of unrestrained human violence, which continues unabated in the present, leads some to wonder if the nuclear genie really can be kept in the bottle. Or, the history of human disregard for the environment that continues in the present leads some to wonder if we can avoid complicity in destroying the habitat that is our planet. The only way any individual person can negotiate the ever approaching future is by drawing upon what has been learned from the past and the present.

This human fact is precisely true of and for our Christian faith. Cumberland Presbyterians do not regard their view of the future as being a matter for wild and uninformed speculation. Rather, they envision the future in light of the known (to faith) past and present. Cumberland Presbyterians believe God has given to faith a key that fits the lockbox of the future. This key does not "open" the future to an extent that it is possible to know all of the details we might like to know. And we should be extremely careful to avoid supplying the details ourselves, as if they were, in fact, knowable. But, still, our past and present experiences do open up upon that which lies ahead. The key is the past actions of God in creation, providence, the history of Israel and *especially* God's mighty act in the resurrection of Jesus the Christ, and the continuing presence of the Holy Spirit in the church's life.

As for the decisiveness of the resurrection, I have sometimes sought to communicate something of what it means for faith by using a personal story from my childhood. My father worked hard as a welder in an industrial plant that produced railroad box-cars. After a long week in the plant, he looked forward to Saturday mornings. It was when he would gather with his friends at a small country store for weekly checker tournaments. The games were friendly but taken seriously. When I was seven or eight, he began taking me along. I took toys to play with and sometimes other Dads brought their children. We played together and looked forward to being treated to a Moon Pie and milk at some point before lunch. Daddy was an excellent player. Sometimes he would make a move on the board and quietly say, "That's it." At first, I thought this meant the game had ended. But often he and his opponent would continue to play. I finally understood that when Daddy said, "That's it," he meant he had made a move on the board that had turned the game decisively in his favor. His opponent might continue to put up a good fight, but Daddy was almost always right. The move he made had sealed the outcome of the game no matter how long it continued.

CP's believe a "That's it" event, a movement by God, occurred in historical time (in the past) that has sealed the outcome of the entire process of human history. That moment, of course, was God's mighty act in the life, death and resurrection of Jesus Christ. The Apostle Paul insisted that the Christian faith rises or falls with the historical factualness of this event (1 Cor. 15:12-20). Apart from it, the Christian faith has no purchase on the future. It is this past event that shines a light forward into the present and onward into the future. There are, to say the least, significant consequences of God's action in Christ for how Christians regard the ultimate future. Most significantly, Christians believe they have been given insight into where history is going and why it is going there. As one theologian puts it, "History itself is nothing else than creation in the process of becoming the kingdom of God. . .the meaning and purpose of all history is the full realization of God's reign over all creation. "[1] God, the one who brought forth creation, began to redeem and reclaim creation (make new through transformation) in the resurrection of Jesus. In one sense, then, Christians do not believe in "the end of the world." Scripture teaches that God is at work to bring about a "new heavens and earth" (Isa. 65: 17, 25; Rev. 21:5). This is why the *COF* speaks of the "consummation of all life and history" rather than the end of all life and history. Consummation suggests not an ending, but a completion of something already begun, and not its annihilation or destruction.

A second consequence of the event of the resurrection of Jesus is that the consummation of history will bring about a new form of personal community (a kind the church or earth was created to sign and signal!). About this, it is important to remember, as noted in the very first chapter of this book, that God, ultimate Reality, is profoundly personal. This, then, is where history is going—it is moving toward the full realization of reconciled, restored community between God and God's people. God is at work to bring about a setting for truly personal community to exist. This setting must and will include the transformation of the entire cosmos. The new community of persons is not imagined as existing in an ethereal something or other. Rather, it will be a fully restored creation (including the animal kingdom—Isa. 11: 6-9; 65: 17, 25). The most direct and beautiful symbolic expression of the coming of the new community is found in the vision of John on the Isle of Patmos: "Then I saw a new heaven and a new earth; for the first heaven and the first earth had passed away, and the sea was no more. And I saw the holy city, the new Jerusalem, coming down out of heaven from God, prepared as a bride adorned for her husband; and I heard a great voice from the throne saying, 'Behold, the dwelling of God is with men. He will dwell with them, and they shall be his people, and God himself will be with them; he will wipe away every tear from their eyes, and death shall be no more, neither shall there be mourning not crying nor pain any more, for the former things have passed away.' And he who sat upon the throne said, 'Behold, I make all things new'" (Rev. 21:1-5).

The nature of this transformed and personal community –the kingdom of God—will be fully consistent with what was revealed about the kingdom in and through the life and ministry of Jesus Christ. It will be the kingdom as he lived and demonstrated it in his very own person and life. The Christian hope for the future is not based on special or secret knowledge (gnosis) that has to be mined from the scriptures by supposed experts—as in much of the millennial theology present in the church and world today. The kingdom Jesus proclaimed and enacted publicly and visibly before the world will come to its full realization. "Nothing accursed will be found there anymore. But the throne of God and of the Lamb will be in it, and his servants will worship him; they will see his face, and his name will be on their foreheads. And there will be no more night; they need no light of lamp or sun, for the Lord God will be their light, and they will reign forever and ever" (Rev. 22: 3-5).

Death and Resurrection

Everything the *COF* says about God's consummation of all life and history is grounded in God's past actions in the history of Israel, the history of Jesus Christ, and the present and continuing actions of the Holy Spirit. The *COF* employs four words to speak about this consummation. Since, as has been said, the goal of history is profoundly personal, these words help us think about the personal aspects for human beings of the consummation of all life and history. The first two words are: *death* and *resurrection.* **Death is both a spiritual and physical reality. Therefore the church has the privilege and duty to proclaim that in Jesus Christ, God acts to redeem persons from bondage to death both in spirit and body** (7.01). It does not require special divine revelation in order for persons to know that biological death is a fact of human existence. It is simply so, as all human beings know. Human life is finite, limited, has a definite boundary set against it, and finally ends. We all die. In the view of modern science, physical death is biologically natural. It may even be seen as positive and contributory in terms of making space and resources for living things to come, including other human beings.

Scripture, however, speaks of a second form of death: "spiritual death." It speaks of rebellion against our being created in the image and likeness of God. The Bible's primal story tells us that Adam and Eve fell for the promise they could be "like gods" in and of themselves (Gn. 3:5). This delusional hope introduced "spiritual death" into the world. Understanding this form of death, of course, does require a revelation from God. Unlike the fact of biological death, the fact of spiritual death is not something persons can know in and of themselves. It is a theological truth. According to the biblical revelation, the fact that we are pride-fully rebellious against our finitude, that we harbor the desire to be our own gods, and that we futilely and foolishly behave in ways that deny the boundary set against us by physical death, constitute the roots of our separation and estrangement from God and reveals that our situation is one of spiritual death.

The fact of spiritual death is portrayed in any number of passages in both the Old and New Testaments. As we might expect, one of the most illuminating occurs in a parable told by Jesus. In this parable, spiritual death is graphically pictured as life lived without the revelation that frees persons from their prideful self-centeredness. Listen to the use of the personal pronouns (I have taken the liberty to italicize them for emphasis): "The land of a rich man produced abundantly. And he thought to *himself*, 'What should *I* do, for *I* have no place to store *my* crops?' Then he said, '*I* will do this; *I* will pull down *my* barns and build larger ones, and there *I* will store all *my* grain and *my* goods. And *I* will say to *my* soul, Soul, *you* have ample goods laid up for many years; relax, eat, drink, and be merry.' But God said to him, 'You fool! This very night your life is being demanded of you. And the things you have prepared, whose will they be?' So it is with those who store up treasures for themselves but are not rich toward God" (Lu. 12:16-21). Spiritual death is life that begins and ends with misguided self-reference, self-regard, and self-concern. It is hard to imagine a passage that better describes the belief in, and glorification of, personal self-autonomy and blind rebellion against finiteness (and God). But, of course, scripture tells this story in first one way and then another all throughout its pages.

The good news that Cumberland Presbyterians have to share with the world is that God has not chosen to leave persons in bondage to either physical or spiritual death. As to what this means concerning hope for the future, the *COF* says Christians can live with the joyful expectation that **after death their redemption will be complete in the resurrection of the body** (7.02). N.T Wright, commenting in particular on Paul's affirmation of this truth, lifts up an important point. "In Colossians 3:1-4, Paul does not say that 'one day you will go to be with him' (Jesus). No, you already possess life in him. The new life, which the Christian possesses secretly, invisible to the world, will burst forth into full bodily reality and visibility."[2]

"The resurrection of the body" is a theologically important truth. Especially so given the fact that the Greek idea of the "immortality of the soul" has exercised such a profound impact on Christian thinking. According to Greek thought, human beings have a body *and* a soul and the two, while obviously related, are quite distinct from one another. The body was regarded as material, inferior, evil. It, therefore, was considered to be a "prison house" of the pure soul. But at death the pure soul escapes from its earthly, bodily, fleshly prison and continues existence in some other form. There was, in the Greek view, something inherently divine in human beings, "a person's innermost essence was divine, and therefore an undying principle."[3] This, however, was not a concept entertained by the Hebrews. For them, body and soul were a unity (it is interesting how this view corresponds to that of modern science). A person does not *have* a soul. A person *is* a soul. The person is a whole –body and soul. The two are quite indivisible. The Hebrews also believed that human beings are absolutely mortal and do not have a divine essence within them. Therefore, if survival after death is a possibility, it is so only as a result of an act of God. Otherwise death is final. But if God decides to act (and God has acted in Jesus Christ), it is not a spiritual soul that is resurrected to new life but the totality of a person—body and soul. The ancient Hebrew, and then Christian, hope for the future was not based upon anything inherent in human beings themselves—anything they were or could do. Rather, it was based on who God is and what only God can do.

It is to be remembered that when Jesus was resurrected it was not as a soul. He was bodily resurrected. Scripture reveals that it was a glorified body to be sure. But also that it was somehow continuous with his earthly body. After the resurrection, Jesus carried the wounds of the cross in his glorified body (Jn. 20:24-27). Some of the ancient Hebrews (Pharisees in contrast to Sadducees) believed in a final resurrection of the body for righteous persons at the end of the age. It was believed that this general resurrection would occur at some point in the future. The astounding claim of the New Testament is that one righteous Hebrew, *the* righteous one, was resurrected to life not at the end but in the very middle of history!

It is to be recalled that the early followers of Jesus (almost all were Hebrews) were astounded not by the idea of resurrection itself, but to whom it had happened and when it had happened! In light of the resurrection of Jesus, Paul (in 1 Cor. 15) spoke of the future resurrection body for those who were "in Christ." He employed the image of the planting of a seed and then the coming forth of its fruit. The two, seed and fruit, are very different, yet continuous. This was the only time Paul speculated on this subject and in this fashion. Perhaps, for him, once was enough. It is a reminder that such speculation is unnecessary. The Christian hope for the future is grounded in what God has done in Jesus and, therefore, Christians do best to keep their eyes, and thoughts, upon this. But that the Christian faith should remain biblically rooted and properly Hebraic is the point of the *COF* when it says: **As in regeneration the whole person is resurrected to new life in Christ, so in the resurrection of the dead the whole person is raised to live in and enjoy the presence of God forever** (7.03).

The words "**whole person**" are intended to communicate that we, as Cumberland Presbyterians, do not view the body as a prison from which the soul will one day escape. We believe, on the contrary, that the body is the good creation of God and will be redeemed along with all the rest of God's creation. Many Cumberland Presbyterians recite the Apostles' Creed every Sunday. It includes the words, "I believe in the resurrection of the body." In the end, however, and to repeat, we do best by looking to Jesus for our belief in the resurrection of the body, and not by engaging in (fruitless) speculation as to the exact nature of the glorified body promised to believers. Nor can we profit or benefit from speculation about how these mortal bodies can be resurrected, or what their state will be between physical death and when the resurrection of the body of believers is to happen. We do well to keep our eyes upon

Jesus. He is the one whom we already know in the power of the Holy Spirit. Again, he is the key to the Christian future hope for the future.

The *COF* adds a final important point about death and resurrection. It is the teaching of the New Testament that believers have already passed from the death of sin (spiritual death) into life with God. Therefore, they can **confidently await full redemption without fear of judgment** (7.04). It is to be remembered that in the Bible, and this especially may be seen in the Psalms, the people of God ordinarily regarded the judgment of God as a good thing. God's coming judgment was something that the people of God "celebrated, longed for, and yearned over."[2] Judgment will mean that one day God's justice, righteousness, and *shalom* (peace) will permeate the entire creation. Sin and wickedness will no longer hold sway. In fact, they will be banished from God's renewed creation. Judgment is a positive element of the Christian hope because the God present to people in the historical Jesus will be the same God present to them at the end. For Christians, "It (judgment) is good news because the one through whom God's justice will finally sweep the world is not a hard-hearted, arrogant, or vengeful tyrant but rather the Man of Sorrows, who was acquainted with grief; the Jesus who loved sinners and died for them; the Messiah who took the world's judgment upon himself on the cross."[4] Christians are those who already know of this judgment that happened in the cross of Christ. They know that the judge is Christ. They know they have received his grace and forgiveness. Therefore, they await "full redemption without fear of judgment." **Thanks be to God who gives this victory through the Lord Jesus Christ** (7.04).

Chapter Thirty-Five

JUDGMENT AND CONSUMMATION

In its final paragraphs, the *COF* employs two additional words about the Christian hope for the future: *judgment* and *consummation*. The first two statements in this section emphasize God's judgment as it is experienced in this present life. **The judgment of God is both present and future. Persons experience God's judgment in many forms, including broken relationships with God and others, the guilt and consequences of their own actions, and the sense of anxiety that comes from lack of confidence in God's faithfulness and the purpose of life. God's judgment is experienced in history in the freedom of persons to choose to engage in such evils as war, civil strife, slavery, oppression, destruction of natural resources, and political and economic exploitation. God abhors all such acts which cause needless suffering and death (7.05 -7.06).**

These statements point to what is readily observable in human life and history. This is simply what happens again and again. A biblical revelation is not required in order to acknowledge that this is the human situation. The art, literature, history, and poetry produced by human beings, and their experience of life in the world, bear witness to the sinful and often tragic nature of life. Cumberland Presbyterians, however, have been given a revelation. The fact of present judgment constitutes the sub-story that the Bible tells—the story of a world in rebellion against God. The *COF*'s statements describe some of the kinds of things that happen to human beings as a result of sin—of being separated from God. They are the sad, painful, tragic, and often evil consequences and circumstances of life lived in and from spiritual death. As a result of God's revelation in Christ and through scripture, we can speak of these things as the judgment of God.

It is the passive judgment of God. Because God respects human freedom, and therefore is not a God of coercion, God gives us up to our own pursuits. Note the thrice-used phrase, "God gave them up," in Romans 1: 24, 26, and 28. That God does not force human beings to be reconciled to him brings about such human devastation as stated in the *COF*. In John's language, God's judgment is the result of the fact that human beings "love darkness rather than light" (Jn. 3:18-19). Paul says that when we human beings sow the seeds of sin, we inevitably reap the whirlwind (Gal. 6:7-8). God cannot be mocked. But it was to, and into, this world that God sent Jesus the Son. God's judgment is first of all the judgment of God's free and gracious love in the Christ. God's response to our being under the judgment of God is to open up a way to return to fellowship and communion with God and one another.

The *COF*, however, also says: **God's judgment transcends this life, ever standing against all human attempts to deny dependence on God and to live without repentance, faith, and love. Those who reject God's salvation in Jesus Christ remain alienated from God and in hopeless bondage to sin and death, which is hell** (7.07). Here we come upon the biblical idea of a final judgment (Jn. 5:25-29; Acts 17:29-31; Rom. 14:7-12; 2 Cor. 5:9-10; Heb. 9:27-28; 2 Pt. 3:5-10; Rev. 20:11-15). Donald McKim summarizes the Reformed view of last things: "We believe that the end of the world will initiate certain events that belong to God's ultimate reign, or kingdom. The scriptures describe a last judgment (Mt. 25:31-46), a resurrection of the body (1 Cor. 15), and eternal life lived in the presence of God, when God is 'all in all" (Eph. 1:23). God's judgment on evil and wickedness will be real, and the images of a 'lake of fire' into which the 'devil,' 'Death,' 'Hades,' are cast (Rev. 19:20; 20:10; 14, 15) are dramatic ways of establishing that God's purposes and reign will be total and complete, overcoming all sin (Rev. 21:17), and that all things will ultimately be reconciled to God (Col. 1:20). The end of this world is the prelude to God's establishing 'a new heaven and earth' (Rev. 21:1) marked by God's eternal presence and peace. This is why Christians pray, 'Come, Lord Jesus'" (Rev. 22:20).[1]

It might be asked, "What is the relationship of the final judgment to the judgment Christians have already experienced in Christ, and to the fact that they await this final judgment "**without fear**?" (7.04). As previously mentioned, the anticipation of a final judgment by God was an ancient hope of the Hebrew people. It is expressed throughout the scriptures of the Old Testament. As discussed in chapter thirty-four, the people hoped for, looked forward to, and longed for this judgment. It would be that time when God would banish all evil and bring about justice and peace to God's kingdom and God's people. Therefore, final judgment was a positive rather than a negative concept. What, it could be asked, is the meaning of life and history if there is no final justice?

The Hebrew belief in and hope for a final judgment was continued in Jesus and in the New Testament church. This is clear from the scriptures. But the New Testament reports two kinds of judgment. "On the one hand is the judgment of God upon sin and human guilt, for instance in Romans and Galatians, with reference to condemnation. In this context, we are judged not by our works, but by our faith. Those who believe undergo judgment not on the basis of what they did, but on the basis of the work of Christ on their behalf, whereby they are freed from condemnation (Rom. 8). But the eschatological (from the Greek word *eschaton* meaning "goal or end") passages in the New Testament continue to refer to a judgment on the basis of works, even in Paul. This judgment is before 'the great white throne'" (Rev. 20:12).[2] How are we to harmonize these passages in light of the fact that the final judgment is said to be not only for the wicked and sinful, but for all people, therefore including Christians? What can it mean that in the New Testament Christians are said to be finally judged on the basis of their works? How can this be harmonized with salvation by grace alone?

A possible, and probable, harmonization lies in the fact that the Christians of the New Testament clearly continued to think in Hebraic terms. Christians understood themselves to be promised the hope of final judgment for the same reason as the Hebrews. God's justice must one day be established in all the earth. Works, however, were never for salvation, either for the Jews of the Old Testament or the Christians of the New Testament. Rather, works gratefully flowed from God's salvation. That Christians will be judged, along with all others, on the basis of works continues the Hebraic thought that the point of salvation "isn't that God suddenly ceases to care about good behavior or morality."[3] And it stresses the point that after salvation, "There is a place in God's plan for our effort, our work, service, and generosity."[4] Christians will participate in the final judgment based on works not for the purpose of securing their salvation, but on the basis of demonstrating that human effort and human purposefulness were and are always a part of God's intention for humanity.

A second thing to be kept in mind at this point is that in Christian theology it is the person of Jesus who defines what judgment is. This is not meant to exclude God but to say that "the relation between God and ourselves is governed, even in the future, by the same principles that were laid down by Christ. . .(in Jesus Christ) I have been granted the freedom to lay bare the roots of my life and stand before God as I really am, the guilty one who has been given the chance through faith to freely confess my guilt. The judgment is the opportunity in the future to stand before God in freedom and without illusion and to confess my guilt. In this sense, the expectation of the judgment is transformed into freedom in the world: freedom from the illusion of hiding my guilt from myself, freedom to stand for the truth in a hopeless situation, freedom to serve others without profit and even danger to myself. The expectation of the judgment makes me free for death. In Paul's Epistle to the Romans (8:31-39), we find the unsurpassable explanation of the interplay of salvation and judgment."[5]

What about Hell?

The *COF* affirms the Cumberland Presbyterian belief in the reality of hell. But it does so without employing the dramatic symbolic imagery of the New Testament (that has often been taken in a literalistic way) or the lurid medieval and Roman Catholic pictorial images of persons undergoing perpetual torture. The *COF* simply says: **Those who reject God's salvation in Jesus Christ remain alienated from God and in hopeless bondage to sin and death, which is hell** (7.07).

Let it be said that Cumberland Presbyterians believe in

the reality of hell. It is a hell that, like judgment, is both present and future. But let it also be said that Cumberland Presbyterians believe in the reality of hell because they also, and foremost, believe in the love of God. The love of God, who grants freedom to the ones who are made in his image and likeness, is the foundation of the biblical teaching concerning hell. Hell, either in the present or future, is not the punishment of God but the choice of human beings. Hell is a symbol for expressing God's respect for the freedom of God's beloved. "The only reason for hell is that people persist in a rebellion for which there is no good reason. It is not our business to argue it, to use it as an evangelistic tool or attempt to prove it to people. It is just the seriousness of being human beings that the choices you make are final choices, permanent choices, and God will respect that. God loves creatures that much. Part of God's triumph includes the promise not to bulldoze or steamroller people who have chosen to resist."[6] Hell? Yes. That God sends people to hell? No!

Consummation

The final words of the *COF* are: **In the consummation of history, at the coming of Jesus Christ, the kingdoms of the world shall become the kingdom of the Lord and of the Christ, and he shall reign forever and ever**" (7.08 see Rev. 11:15). I would like to close this portion of the study by including the following words by William Placher:

"Beneath all its gold and jewels, the crowns of French monarchs supposedly contained a fragment of the crown of thorns placed on Jesus' head. No doubt the crown of thorns was buried deep beneath layers of gold, and most French kings lived lives with little in common to that of Jesus. Yet from its hiding place, might a fragment of thorn-wood, authentic or not, call rulers to an ideal at odds with the world's general pattern of things? Sometimes it happens, on a small scale even fairly often. We see the town mayor or the charity president who really does hold an office for the good of others, and at personal sacrifice. Even on a national scale—Ghandi liberated India, Mandela held South Africa together, and no one could doubt that a different sort of life would have been easier for them. In different ways they gave their lives for the good of their peoples. But the temptations are great—wealth and attention can come so easily to those who have power, and the excuses come just as easily. For the sake of public order, after all, surely one must have proper respect for the nation's ruler, and a little pomp encourages respect. But once one starts down that road, it is hard to stop. *Jesus offers us a different model of one who reigns*"[7] (italics mine for emphasis).

At his temptation in the Judean wilderness, Jesus was offered kingship over the empires of this world (Matt. 4:1-11). He, of course, refused this offer. Jesus came, rather, to bring us the kingdom of God. He indeed came to offer a different model to the world of what it means to reign. Jesus reigns as a servant. But the world rejected Jesus and his talk about and enactment of the kingdom of God. However, he finally *was* given a crown—of thorns; he *was* given a robe—in cruel jesting by Roman soldiers; he *was* given a throne—the hard wood of the cross; and he *was* proclaimed a king—in the total mockery of Pontius Pilate. After his death, most of the world simply continued, and continues, on its way and doing what it does. But Cumberland Presbyterians have been stopped. We have been stopped by the witness that has been made to us in and through scripture. We have been stopped by a voice calling to us. We have been stopped by the Holy Spirit illuminating us. We have been stopped by having heard the Gospel. We have come to know the servant king who reigns and will reign. Nothing more need be said about the future than that which is said in the final statement in our *COF*. These words point out the fundamental faith of a people called Cumberland Presbyterians. When we think about the future, we say, along with the earliest Christians, "Jesus is Lord."

Excursus: Modern Millenialism

The Revelation of John and the Book of Daniel (the last half) are literary works of extraordinary interest and importance to many Christians. The exotic imagery, symbolism, and poetic strangeness found in these works have resulted in their becoming a kind of Rorschach test for many of their readers. People throughout the centuries have read many quite unusual things into and out of them, and quite often what they have been predisposed to find and proclaim. The only thing seemingly more odd and bizarre than some of the apocalyptic imagery contained in the material in question has been the explanations given as to what this imagery means.

The last one hundred and twenty years have given us an interpretation of the apocalyptic texts of the Bible than millions of Christians swear by. This interpretation is called Millenialism, or Dispensationalism. Millenialism came from England to America in the 1890s, largely by way of the work of an Englishman named J.N. Darby. The millennial views of Darby were then popularized in America through the efforts of a man named Charles S*COF*ield. He edited a Bible (The S*COF*ield Bible, 1917) with an extensive system of footnotes that introduced millenialist ideas to countless Americans in the early part of the 20th century.

What is millennialism? For beginners, it is a view that takes literally the "1000 year reign of Christ" on earth mentioned in the twentieth chapter of the Revelation. In fact, it tends to interpret all of the poetry and symbolism of the Revelation and Daniel in a literalistic way. Basic to the millenialist view is that the events described in the Revelation (after chapter 4) have not yet happened, but will happen sometime in the near future, usually considered to be in the very near future. If you can de-code the many symbols, which millennialism claims it has done, you have a leg-up on being ready for the end of time that is soon approaching. Millenialism is responsible for certain biblical words being popularized in the American religious vocabulary, and even in the vocabulary of the wider public. Words like: the Rapture, the anti-Christ, the War of Armageddon, the Tribulation, the Millenium, the Great White Throne Judgment, etc. One fundamental idea, that will appear quite strange to many Christians, undergirds the millenialist view. It is that Jesus, when he was on earth, failed in his mission to the Jewish people. Therefore, he literally has to come back again and complete the mission of converting them. This is a truly strange idea, given the overall message of the New Testament, but millions are convinced that it is true.

The millenialist interpretation "exploded" on the American religious scene in the early 1970s with the publication of *The Late Great Planet Earth* by Hal Lindsey. This book enjoyed a spectacular success among religious readers, and also readers in the general public. Lindsey advanced millenialist views by arguing that the "signs of the time," especially the reconstitution of the state of Israel in 1948, indicated that the end of time was fast approaching. More recently, in the 1990s, Lindsey's success was rivaled, even exceeded, by the publication of several novels set against the background of millenialist views. These novels, in the *Left Behind* series, have also enjoyed enormous public success. They have been further popularized through a couple of *Left Behind* movies. "Left behind" is a reference to the belief that when "the Rapture" occurs millions of "truly authentic Christians" will be whisked away and off the earth while the more unfortunate ones will be, well, left behind. They will be left behind to endure the horrors of "the Great Tribulation." On the other hand, the raptured Christians will be in the grandstands of heaven watching (enjoying?) the mayhem on earth.

There has been another vehicle for the wide-spread propagation of millentialist end-time views. Nearly all the important television evangelists of the last two generations have been committed to this theology. Thus millions of people in America and around the world who watch these programs regularly hear that the millenialist interpretation of the Bible is the only true and correct one for understanding the enigmatic Christian writing known as apocalyptic.

Pardon me, but I am not convinced. For one thing, the idea that Jesus failed in his mission on earth is difficult to accept given what I regard as orthodox Christian theology and faith. Secondly, there is a much older and, I think, more credible interpretation of these writings than the almost entirely modern one that I have been describing. I have tried my best, through the years, to give the various millenialist views a fair hearing; partly as a pastoral concern given the religious culture in which I have lived has been dominated by these views. But, in the end, this theology (or lack of it) has wound up leaving me far behind, quite literally. I remain convinced that the more historical readings of the apocalyptic literature are the best and most fruitful (for the life of faith) for understanding this literature. These readings have been bequeathed to us by a much earlier generation of Christian interpreters stretching back into the earliest centuries of the church.

The older interpretations maintain that the Revelation, all of it, was written to and for the generation of Christians to whom it was first addressed. And that its message applied to the times in which they lived. But it also maintained that the book's message of comfort and hope in the 'Lamb that was slain" is timeless in its application. As such, the Revelation is indeed a book about our time. But not in a way that is different from its significance for Christians who lived in the first century, the fourth, the tenth, the twentieth, and so on. As I write, many Christians in the Middle East are undergoing immense suffering given the turmoil, warfare and terrorism that now marks that region. When the Revelation speaks of the "Four Horsemen of the Apocalypse,"- famine, plague, warfare, and death—there is no need for an esoteric understanding of what is meant. These Christians are living the meaning of the texts. That the Revelation and other apocalyptic texts contain a general, universal, and timeless message from God is not a view readily entertained by millennialism. And it is a perspective that is not nearly as titillating, exotic, or financially rewarding.

I have included this brief excursus because millennialism has impacted the people in the congregations I have served as pastor over the past forty years. It has been in the religious and cultural air which we have breathed. Many people have wondered, as perhaps people in many CP congregations have wondered, if millennialism is espoused in and by the Cumberland Presbyterian Churches? I am grateful, for very many reasons, that the Cumberland Presbyterian Churches *have not* espoused this relatively modern interpretation of certain scriptures. We have not succumbed to placing an artificially constructed grid over the Bible's apocalyptic texts. I am deeply grateful that what the *COF* has to say about "the end-times" is expressed with four words: death, resurrection, judgment, and consummation. This economy of words keeps us biblically faithful and hopeful, but without being encumbered (or worse) by the fanciful, exotic, and largely unfounded claims of modern millennialism.[8]

CONCLUSION

A LOOK BACKWARD—A LOOK FORWARD

In 1813, at the meeting of Cumberland Synod, a committee of four persons was appointed to prepare a *COF* for the Cumberland Presbyterian Church. The four, all ordained ministers, were William McGee, Finis Ewing, Robert Donnell, and Thomas Calhoun. This committee did its work in a timely fashion and the Cumberland Synod of 1814 adopted their work as the first uniquely Cumberland Presbyterian confession of faith. The church had operated, from 1810-1813, under the Westminster Confession of 1647. The new confession for Cumberland Presbyterians made extensive use of the Westminster Confession, even adopting some chapters in whole. In his book *Studies in Cumberland Presbyterian History,* Dr. Thomas H. Campbell discusses the first truly Cumberland Presbyterian confession and some of the important changes made by the committee of four and then adopted by the Synod of 1814:

"The principal changes made were in Chapters III, VIII, X, and XI. The Westminster Confession states that God from all eternity ordained 'whatever comes to pass.' The Cumberlands stated that God 'determined to bring to pass what should be for his own glory.' Where Chapter VIII of the Westminster Confession implies that Christ has purchased salvation for only a part of mankind, it was written into the Cumberland Confession that 'Jesus Christ, by the grace of God, has tasted death for every man.' The Presbyterian doctrine of the Effectual Calling of 'All those whom God hath predestinated unto life, and only those,' gave place to the statement that, 'All those whom God calls and *who obey the call*, and those only, he is pleased by his Word and Spirit to bring out of the state of sin and death in which they are by nature, to grace and salvation by Jesus Christ.' The Cumberlands based their doctrine of the Perseverance of the Saints upon 'the unchangeable love and power of God; the merits, advocacy, and intercession of Jesus Christ; the abiding of the Spirit and seed of God within them; and the nature of the covenant of grace' instead of the 'immutable decree of election' as stated in the Westminster Confession. Chapter III, sections 3, 4, 6, and 7, and Chapter X, section 4 of the Westminster Confession were omitted entirely. Two new deliverances were also made regarding sanctification and the gift of the Holy Spirit. Our church fathers believed the Westminster Confession tended too much to view as inevitable the likelihood of the believer's yielding to his fleshly nature. 'While they retained as true the phrases about the remains of depravity continuing to affect the believer as long as he remains in the body, yet they feared these expressions might be abused so as to 'make provisions for the flesh', and they sought to guard against this abuse by two very strong declarations. These declarations were to the effect that while the remains of a depraved nature *may* continue to affect the believer as long as he is in the flesh, it is his duty and privilege, by availing himself of God's grace, 'to maintain a conscience void of offense toward God and toward men,' and that in this enlightened gospel age it is not to be expected that a true Christian will fall into gross sins."[1]

The point of this glance backward is to note that from the very beginning of the church Cumberland Presbyterians were convinced that theology was important. They decided that they could no longer accept the pernicious doctrine of election as it was set forth in the Westminster Confession. Their concern, however, was not for theology in and of itself. Rather, it was for the faithful preaching and teaching of the Gospel of Jesus Christ. They believed that this Gospel was offered to every person and not just to a pre-determined elect. Early Cumberland Presbyterian preachers went everywhere possible proclaiming this new understanding of the Gospel with fervor and freedom. They understood that theology was always for the purpose of supporting the church's proclamation. It also served the other great concern of the original Cumberland Presbyterians. It was that every person might have the opportunity to truly *experience* the saving grace of God that comes through faith in Jesus Christ and the power of the Holy Spirit. Theology's purpose was that an experience of Christ might happen in human hearts and that this experience might be rightly (biblically) interpreted and understood.

Theology and experience, then, were both important to early Cumberland Presbyterians. C.S. Lewis once illustrated the relationship between the two in a way that perhaps most Cumberland Presbyterians can and will endorse.[2] He said that the personal experience of Christ is like a person going to the beach. At the beach, the person feels the wind in his or her hair, the sand beneath his or her feet, the sound of waves crashing onto the shore, and enjoys the absolute beauty of it all. There is, Lewis said, no substitute for such an experience. A person might read about the beach, see pictures of the beach, be told about the beach, but nothing can compare with or substitute for actually going and standing on the beach.

Theology, Lewis said, is like a map of the beach. It is actually like a map of all the beaches in the world. The map may not be inspiring. It certainly cannot compare to actually experiencing the beach. But the map is also very important. It represents what millions of others have seen of the beach. It is because of the experience of millions of people, overtime, that the contours of all the beaches can properly be known to any single person. It is, in fact, impossible to imagine that a single person could ever stand on all the beaches of the world. While there is no substitute for experiencing the beach in person, it is the map that enables any single person to get a sense of the whole. According to Lewis, it is just so with theology. Theology represents the combined experiences of millions of Christians throughout the centuries. We cannot help but be, in our personal and congregational lives, supplemented, enriched, inspired, informed, guided, and corrected by the map of Christian experience that is called Cumberland Presbyterian theology.

Cumberland Presbyterians, now two hundred years later, still believe in the importance of both personal experience and common theology. We believe they belong together and are complementary. I would like to add that theology itself can be quite an *experience* in its own right. Like worship, theology can be a means by which we experience, praise, and serve the Triune God. In the history of the Western church, there was a time when all theological work was understood precisely in this way. Theology was prayer. Theology was devotion. Theology involved not only the head but also the heart. There was no wedge driven between thinking about God and praising God. My sense of the early Cumberland Presbyterians is that they sought to recover and celebrate this way of understanding and doing theology.

In the introduction, I stated that Cumberland Presbyterians have a good theology. I also stated the hope that this theology will come to have more of us. The scripture verse that guides the whole of our Confession of Faith is John 3:16, "For God so loved the world that he gave his only begotten Son, that whoever believes in him should not perish but have eternal life." It is my belief that the world desperately needs for us to take our theology to head and heart. The world needs for our theology to have us. Because the world cannot possibly know that it is the world and that God loves it, and has given the Son to and for it, unless we bear witness to these facts.

The pursuit of theology is a way of taking our witness to the world with utmost seriousness. The world that God loves is in darkness. It does not know about God the creator, or about the purpose of creation, or the real nature of human rebellion, or the calling of Israel, or the incarnation of the Son, or his message, his ministry, his cross, his resurrection, his exaltation, his giving of the Spirit, his reconciliation, his coming in judgment, or about the calling of the Holy Spirit, or the Spirit's works of repentance and confession, saving faith, justification, regeneration and adoption, sanctification and growth in grace, preservation of believers, and Christian assurance, or that God has created the church for mission, or the meaning of the sacraments, or Christian freedom, or Christian stewardship, or the meaning of marriage or singleness, or the Lord's Day, or civil government, or death and resurrection, or judgment and consummation.

The world deserves to know these things. They must not be kept from the world. The world deserves to come into the light. Someone must know these things so that the world that God loves may be told. Cumberland Presbyterians can tell these things to the world. We must tell them to the world. As the church, or even as individual Christians, we are not here for the salvation of ourselves bur for the salvation of the world. To be here for the salvation of ourselves is to misunderstand the Gospel and to short-change the world (as well as short-changing ourselves). We have been given deep things to say to the world. They must be in us so deeply that we cannot help but tell them to the world, in both word and deed. They must be in us so profoundly that they truly constitute who we are and what we do. We Cumberland Presbyterians have a good theology in our *Confession of Faith*. But we are not only to have this theology but *become* this theology. It is in and through becoming this theology that we may be more faithful both to God and to the world that God loves.

With most of the twenty-first century still ahead of us, what is the future of the Cumberland Presbyterian Church? The short, but complete, answer is that the Triune God is the future of the church or there is no future for it at all. There can be no doubt that the God who was at work bringing this movement into being is the God who is also at work in the world now and who will be at work in the future. Therefore, it is being joined to God's work that is the future of the church. For the church, or any of its congregations, to seek a future in some other way, or on some other basis, is for the church to become like "salt that has lost its saltiness," or a "lamp that has been hidden under a bushel basket" (Matthew 5:13-14). The only program that will work is one grounded in who God is and what God is doing. Understanding who God is and what God is doing is the work and the blessing of theology.

I close with a prayer by an early Christian who knew his Lord, his theology, and who loved both the church and the world. May this prayer animate and inspire all of us who are a people called Cumberland Presbyterians: "For this reason I bow my knees before the Father, from whom every family in heaven and on earth takes its name. I pray that, according to the riches of his glory, he may grant that you may be strengthened in your inner being with power through his Spirit, and that Christ may dwell in your hearts through faith, as you are being rooted and grounded in love. I pray that you may have the power to comprehend, with all the saints, what is the breadth and length and height and depth, and to know the love of Christ that surpasses knowledge, so that you may be filled with all the fullness of God. Now to him who by the power at work within us is able to accomplish abundantly far more than all we can ask or imagine, to him be glory in the church and in Christ Jesus to all generations, forever and ever. Amen." (Eph. 3:14-21).

Notes

INTRODUCTION

[1]Clark M. Williamson and Ronald J. Allen, *The Teaching Minister* (Louisville: Westminster/John Knox Press, 1991), p. 47.

CHAPTER ONE "THE LIVING GOD"

[1]Gordon Kaufman, *Systematic Theology: A Historicist Perspective* (New York: Charles Scribner's Sons, 1968), p. 514.

[2]Richard A. Norris, *Understanding the Faith of the Church* (San Francisco: Harper and Row, 1979), xv. Also see Harvey Cox, *The Future of Faith* (New York: HarperOne, 2009) for his illuminating discussion of the interplay of faith and belief in the history of the church in the Western world.

[3]Joseph Sittler, *The Care of the Earth* (Minneapolis: Fortress Press, 2004), p. 113.

[4]Norris, *Understanding the Faith of the Church,* p. 55.

[5]Langdon Gilkey, *Message and Existence: An Introduction to Christian Theology* (New York: The Seabury Press, 1981), p. 46.

[6]Christoph Blumhardt, *Action in Waiting* (Rifton, New York: Plough Publishing Company, 2012), pp. 29-30.

[7]Gilkey, *Message and Existence*, p. 73.

[8]*Ibid.*, p. 76.

[9]Norris, *Understanding the Faith of the Church,* p. 90.

[10]*Ibid.*, p. 89.

[11]John Howard Yoder, *Preface to Theology* (Grand Rapids: Brazos Press, 2002), p. 204.

[12]Shirley C. Guthrie, *Christian Doctrine* (Louisville: Westminster/John Knox Press, 1994), 78.

[13]*Ibid.* Also, "If we Christians understand the doctrine of the Trinity aright,

we will realize it implies that God is not about power and self-sufficiency and the assertion of authority but about mutuality and equality and love. . .'The doctrine of the Trinity,' as Robert Wilkens has written, 'reaches to the deepest recesses of the soul and helps us to know the majesty of God's presence and the mystery of his love. Love is the most authentic mark of the Christian life, and love among humans, or within God, requires community with others and a sharing of the deepest kind.' The doctrine of the Trinity is the account of that community and its sharing in the life of God." William C. Placher, *Narratives of a Vulnerable God* (Louisville: Westminster John Knox Press, 1994), p. 55.

CHAPTER TWO "THE HOLY SCRIPTURES"

[1]N.T. Wright, *Simply Jesus* (New York: HarperOne, 2011), pp. 182-184.

[2]Kaufman, *Systematic Theology,* p. 488. Also, "Like Peter and the rest of the Twelve,who walked alongside Jesus during his earthly ministry and yet so often misunderstood his mission, we, too, must return again and again to the story of Jesus seeking to make sense of his call to "Follow me." Through the discipline of learning to read the Scriptures well, we hope that our vision will not be clouded by that cataract which would make us falsely believe 'the end justifies the means,' or that we should 'spiritualize' Jesus' teachings because of fear of what would happen if 'everybody took Jesus seriously.' Through submitting ourselves again to the authority of Scripture, we hope to find an alternative reading to that of Eusebius that it is not through the power brokers of human history that God will effect God's purposes, but through the little minority band of peoples committed to walking in the way of Jesus of Nazareth, bearing witness to the new reality, the new creation, the kingdom of God. And all this requires besides great trust is that: it is not our task to make things turn out right but instead to be faithful witnesses. We will have to trust that God will be God, and do what God has promised.". Lee C. Camp, *Mere Discipleship* (Grand Rapids: Brazos Press, 2003), p. 54.

[3]Joe Ben Irby, *This They Believed* (Chelsea, Michigan: Joe Ben Irby, 1997),

p. 52.

[4]Hubert Morrow, *The Covenant of Grace* (Memphis: Board of Christian Education, 1996), 29.

[5]Eugene Peterson, *Eat This Book:* (Grand Rapids: Eerdmans Publishing, 2006). An analogy for how to read Scripture: "Years ago I owned a dog who had a fondness for large bones. Fortunately for him we lived in the forested foothills of Montana. In his forest rambles he often came across the carcass of a white-tailed deer that had been brought down by coyotes. Later he would show up on our stone, lakeside patio carrying or dragging his trophy, usually a shank or a rib; he was a small dog and the bone was often nearly as big as he was. Anyone who has owned a dog knows the routine: he would prance and gambol playfully before us with his prize, wagging his tail, proud of his find, courting our approval. And, of course, we approved: lavishing praise, telling him what a good dog he was. But after awhile, sated with our applause, he would drag the bone off twenty yards or so to a more private place, usually the shade of a large moss covered boulder, and go to work on the bone. The social aspects of the bone were behind him: now the pleasure became solitary. He gnawed the bone, turned it over and around, licked it, worried it. Sometimes we could hear a low rumble or growl, what in a cat would be a purr. He was obviously enjoying himself and in no hurry. After a leisurely couple of hours, he would bury it and return the next day to take it up again. The average bone lasted about a week." Peterson, *Eat This Book,* p. 1.

[6]Williamson and Allen, *The Teaching Minister*, p. 57.

[7]Yoder, *Preface to Theology*, p. 347.

[8]John C. Vander Stelt, "Witness to the Holy Spirit," *Encyclopedia of the Reformed Faith*, edited by Donald K. McKim (Louisville: Westminster/John Knox Press, 1992), p. 397.

[9]Jack Rogers, *Presbyterian Creeds* (Philadelphia: Westminster Press, 1985), p. 163.

[10]Norris, *Understanding the Faith of the Church,* pp. 11-12.

CHAPTER THREE "GOD'S WILL"

[1]Bruce K. Waltke, *Finding the Will of God* (Grand Rapids: Eerdman's Publishing Company, 1995), pp. 11-12.

[2]*Ibid.*, p. 12.

[3]*Ibid.*, pp. 10-11.

[4]William Sloan Coffin, from the website *"William Sloan Coffin Quotes," @AZ Quotes.*

[5]Kaufman, *Systematic Theology*, p. 194.

CHAPTER FOUR "CREATION"

[1]Kaufman, *Systematic Theology.*
[2]*Ibid.*

[3]Norris, *Understanding the Faith of the Church,* pp. 61-62.

[4]Gilkey, *Message and Existence,* p. 91.

[5]*Ibid.*

[6]John Lennox, *Has Science Buried God?* (Oxford: Lion Books, 2007), p. 41

[7]Gilkey, *Message and Existence*, pp. 43-44.

[8]*Ibid.*, p. 49.

[9]See the footnote on Genesis 1:26 in *The Oxford Annotated Bible* (Oxford: Oxford University Press, 2007), p. 12.

[10]Morrow, *The Covenant of Grace,* p. 36.

[11]Kenneth Carder, *Living Our Beliefs* (Nashville: Discipleship Resources, 1996), p. 43.

[12]Ibid., p. 40.

[13]Jurgen Moltmann, *The Spirit of Life* (Minneapolis: Fortress Press, 1992), p. 121.

[14]See many helpful articles on eco-theology at the online *Encyclopedia of Science and Religion.*

[15]Gilkey, *Message and Existence*, pp. 200-201.

CHAPTER FIVE "PROVIDENCE"

[1]Guthrie, *Christian Doctrine, p. 166.*

[2]Kaufman, *Systematic Theology,* pp. 262-263.

[3]Morrow, *The Covenant of Grace,* pp. 10-11.

[4]William Sloan Coffin, *Credo* (Louisville: Westminster/John Knox Press, 2004), p. 137.

[5]Wendell Berry, *Jayber Crow* (Berkeley, California: Counterpoint, 2000), p. 133.

CHAPTER SIX "THE LAW OF GOD"

[1]John Barton, *Ethics and the Old Testament* (Harrisburg, Pa.: Trinity Press International, 1998), p. 11.

[2]Walter Harrelson, *The Ten Commandments and Human Rights* (Philadelphia: Fortress Press, 1980), p. 168.

CHAPTER SEVEN "HUMAN FREEDOM"

[1]Guthrie, *Christian Doctrine,* p. 119.

[2]Ibid., p. 133.

[3]Kaufman, *Systematic Theology,* pp. 440-441. Also, "For the main contention here is that God, who finally through this long and painful historical process succeeded in making himself known to man, desires to reveal himself to all men, rescuing and saving them from the self-destruction into which they, in their sin, are hurling themselves. The slowness of the process of salvation is not an indication of God's injustice or ineptitude; it is rather a measure of his inexhaustible patience; he deals with man in such a way that the frail and sickly plant of human freedom is healed, not destroyed." Kaufman, *Systematic Theology*, p. 16.

[4]Rodney Clapp, *Families at the Crossroads* (Downer's Grove; InterVarsity Press, 1993), pp. 101-102.

[5]Morrow, *The Covenant of Grace,* p. 36.

CHAPTER EIGHT "THE ABUSE OF FREEDOM"

[1]Gilkey, *Message and Existence,* pp. 104-105.

[2]*Ibid.*, p. 144.

[3]Gordon J. Spykman, "Original Sin," *Encyclopedia of the Reformed Faith,* p. 264.

[4]Serene Jones, "What's Wrong With Us?," *Essentials of Christian Theology* edited by William C. Placher (Louisville: Westminster/John Knox Press, 2003), p. 149.

[5]Yoder, *Preface to Theology,* p. 310.

[6]Jones, "What's Wrong with Us?," p. 149.

[7]Guthrie, *Christian Doctrine,* p. 221.

[8]David L. Mueller, *Karl Barth* (Waco: Word Books, 1972), p. 134.

[9]Norris, *Understanding the Faith of the Church,* p. 77.

[10]Quoted by Mark Thiessen Nation, *John Howard Yoder* (Grand Rapids: Eerdman's Publishing Company, 2006), pp. 185-186.

[11]Eugene Kennedy, *A Sense of Life: A Sense of Sin* (Garden City, New York: Image Books, 1955), p. 130.

[12]R.E.O White, *Biblical Ethics* (Atlanta: John Knox Press, 1979), p. 86.

[13]Clark Williamson, "The Human Question," *Essentials of Christian Theology,* pp. 177-178.

[14]Noel Leo Erskine, "How Do We Know What to Believe?," *Essentials of Christian Theology,* 36.

[15]Samuel A. Meir, "Evil," *The Oxford Companion to the Bible* edited by Bruce Metzger and Michael D. Coogan (Oxford: Oxford University Press, 1993), p. 208.

[16]Mark W. Thomsen, *Christ Crucified: A 21st Century Missiology of the Cross* (Minneapolis:

Lutheran University Press, 2004), p. 25.

[17]Morrow, *The Covenant of Grace,* p. 40.

[18]Merwyn Johnson, "Sin," *Encyclopedia of the Reformed Faith,* p. 351.

[19]Gerard S. Sloyan, *John* (Atlanta: Westminster/John Knox Press, 1988), p. 189.

[20]Gilkey, *Message and Existence,* p. 149.

[21]Morrow, *The Covenant of Grace,* p. 39.

[22]Blumhardt, *Action in Waiting,* p. 17.

CHAPTER NINE "GOD'S COVENANT"

[1]William C. Placher, *Jesus the Savior* (Louisville: Westminster/John Knox Press, 2001), p. 139

[2]Yoder, *Preface to Theology,* p. 318.

[3]*Ibid.*

CHAPTER TEN "CHRIST THE SAVIOR"

[1]Edward Humphrey, *Emil Brunner,* (Waco: Word Books, 1976), p. 103.

[2]Colin J.D. Greene, *Christology in Cultural Perspective* (Grand Rapids: Eerdman's Publishing Company, 2003), p. 4.

[3]Guthrie, *Christian Doctrine,* pp. 94-95.

[4]John Howard Yoder, *He Came Preaching Peace* (Scottsdale, Pa.: Herald Press, 2004), pp. 48-49.

[5]Wright, *Simply Jesus,* p. 69.

[6]Gilkey, *Message and Existence*, p. 194.

[7]Luke Timothy Johnson, *The Writings of the New Testament,* (Minneapolis: Fortress Press, 1999), p. 413.

[8]Kaufman, *Systematic Theology,* p. 383.

[9]*Ibid.*, pp. 193-194.

[10]Guthrie, *Christian Doctrine*, pp. 255-256.

[11]"Jesus *saves*. He saves us for life, for giving ourselves over to its sorrows and joys, to its predictable and unpredictable occurrences, its routines and its surprises. He saves us from the awful habit we have of saving ourselves, of sparing our energies, of protecting our minds and souls and bodies from the life struggles they are in fact well-equipped to undertake. He saves us from the spend-thriftness of love, of work, of play. He saves us from the Promethean but also Sisyphean fatalism and for the 'freedom of the Christian person.' He points us back into the earthly city, its disappointments and tragedies not withstanding, whose tribulations are (apart from grace, recognized or unrecognized) impossible to bear, yet the scene of the unfolding city of God. Jesus the Christ, Savior, trains our souls for creaturehood, weaning us from our needs to be gods and to be less than-human too." Douglas John Hall, *Professing the Faith: Theology in a North American Context* (Minneapolis: Fortress Press, 1996), pp. 552-553.

[12]Anna Case-Winters, "Salvation," *The Encyclopedia of the Reformed Faith*, pp. 334-335.

[13]Morrow, *The Covenant of Grace,* p. 58.

[14]Norris, *Understanding the Faith of the Church,* p. 187.

[15]Kaufman, *Systematic Theology,* p. 510.

[16]James Alison, *Knowing Jesus* (London: SPCK, 1998), p. 7.

[17]Thomsen, *Christ Crucified*, p. 24.

[18]D.E. Holwerda, "Ascension," *The International Standard Bible Encyclopedia* edited by Geoffrey W. Bromiley (Grand Rapids: Eerdman's Publishing Company, 1979), p. 312.

[19]Alison, *Knowing Jesus,* pp. 26-27.

[20]See, Luc Ferry, *A Brief History of Thought* (New York: Harper, 2011), pp. 56-91.

CHAPTER ELEVEN "THE CALL AND WORK OF THE HOLY SPIRIT"

[1]Morrow, *Covenant of Grace,* p. 71.

[2]Ibid., p. 72.

[3]Norris, *Understanding the Faith of the Church,* pp. 183-184.

[4]Sinclair Ferguson, *The Christian Life* (Edinburgh: Banner of Truth, 1981), p. 33.

[5]Morrow, *Covenant of Grace,* p. 72.

[6]Gilkey, *Message and Existence*, pp. 50-51. Also, "Spirit is the pressure upon us towards Christ's relation with the Father, towards the self secure enough in its rootedness and acceptance in the 'Father,' in the source and ground of all, to be 'child,' to live vulnerably, as a sign of grace and forgiveness, to decide for the cross of powerlessness. The sign of Spirit is the existence of Christlikeness (being God's child) in the world. And the connection of Spirit with ecclesiology (church) belongs here. We are so used to the rhetoric of the Church as the 'Spirit-filled community' that we have frequnetly lost a sense of the Church as sign of the Spirit rather than its domicile. The Church signifies (means, points to) the humanity that could be, that could exist in this tension between security and powerlessness, so that it is indeed in one sense *the* place where Spirit is seen." Rowan Williams, *On Christian Theology* (Oxford: Blackwell Publishers, 2000), p. 164.

[7]Morrow, *Covenant of Grace,* p. 71.

[8]Louis Berkhof quoted by Derek Thomas in "Salvation and the Mission of God," in *Christianity Today Online,* January 7, 2015.

[9]Irby, *This They Believed,* p. 408

[10]Guthrie, *Christian Doctrine*, p. 293.

[11]Moltmann, *The Spirit of Life*, p. 230.

[12]Guthrie, *Christian Doctrine,* p. 294.

CHAPTER TWELVE "REPENTANCE AND CONFESSION"

[1]Carder, *Living Our Beliefs*, p. 14.

[2]Paula Fredriksen, "Repentance," *Oxford Companion to the Bible*, p. 646.

[3]Norris, *Understanding the Faith of the Church*, p. 123.

[4]M. Eugene Boring and Fred B. Craddock, *The People's New Testament Commentary* (Louisville: Westminster John Knox Press, 2004), p. 186.

[5]Morrow, *The Covenant of Grace,* pp. 76-78.

[6]Ibid., p. 77.

[7]Ibid., p. 78.

[8]Marcus Borg, *The Heart of Christianity* (San Francisco: Harper, 2003), p. 180.

CHAPTER THIRTEEN "SAVING FAITH"

[1]G.W. Bromiley "Faith," *The International Standard Bible Encyclopedia, Volume Two E-J* , general editor G.W. Bromiley(Grand Rapids: Eerdman's, 1982), p. 271.

[2]Daniel Migliore, "Faith," *Encyclopedia of the Reformed Faith,* p. 133. Also, "There is nothing anti-intellectual in the leap of faith, for faith is not believing without proof but trusting without reservation. Faith is no substitute for thinking. On the contrary, it is what makes good thinking possible. It has what we might call a limbering effect on the mind; by taking us beyond familiar ground, faith ends up giving us that much more to think about. Certainly Peter and Andrew and James and John, in deciding to follow Jesus, received more to think about than had they stayed at home. And so it is with all of us: if we give our lives to Christ, if we leave familiar territory and take the leap of faith, what we receive

in return fills our minds altogether as much as it fills our hearts . . . Christ came to take away our sins, not our minds." William Sloane Coffin, *Credo* (Louisville: Westminster John Knox Press, 2004), p. 8.

[3]Bromiley, "Faith," p. 271.

[4]Ferguson, *The Christian Life*, pp. 44-45.

[5]Bromiley, "Faith," p. 272.

[6]Borg, *The Heart of Christianity,* pp. 32-33.

[7]Migliore, "Faith," p. 134.

[8]Guthrie, *Christian Doctrine*, p. 325.

[9]Daniel N. Schowalter, "Faith," *The Oxford Companion to the Bible,* p. 222.

[10]Irby, *This They Believed*, p. 482.

CHAPTER FOURTEEN "JUSTIFICATION"

[1]Guthrie, *Christian Doctrine*, p. 320.

CHAPTER FIFTEEN "REGENERATION AND ADOPTION"

[1]Ferguson, *The Christian Life*, pp. 48-49.

[2]Sandra Hack Polaski, *A Feminist Introduction to Saint Paul* (St. Louis: Chalice Press, 2005), p. 84.

[3]*Ibid.*

[4]Ferguson, *The Christian Life,* p. 51; Morrow, *The Covenant of Grace,* pp. 82-83.?

CHAPTER SIXTEEN "SANCTIFICATION"

[1]This quote from Barth is copied from my preaching notebook. Unfortunately, I am unable to locate the original source in Barth's writing.

[2]Waldo Beach, *The Christian Life* (Louisville: Westminster/John Knox, 1966), pp. 46-47.

CHAPTER SEVENTEEN "PRESERVATION OF BELIEVERS"

[1]Irby, *This They Believed,* p. 465.

[2]Thomas H. Campbell, *Studies in Cumberland Presbyterian History* (Nashville: Cumberland Presbyterian Publishing House, 1944), pp. 135-136.

CHAPTER EIGHTEEN "CHRISTIAN ASSURANCE"

[1]Philip Hughes, "Assurance of Salvation," *Encyclopedia of the Reformed Faith,* pp. 12-13.

[2]*Ibid.*

[3]*The Worshiping Church: A Hymnal* (Carol Stream, Illinois: Hope Publishing Company, 1990), p. 531.

CHAPTER NINETEEN "THE CHURCH (1)"

[1]Karl Barth, *God Here and Now* (New York: Routledge Classics, 2004), p. 80.

[2]*Ibid.*

[3]G.W. Bromiley, "Church," *The International Standard Bible Encyclopedia,* p. 694.

[4]*Ibid.* Also, "The church knows that she must be a reconciling rather than a dividing community, because she was established in and by a historical event in which God was reconciling the world (2 Cor. 5:19-20): she knows she must bind up men's wounds and forgive rather than hurt and destroy, since her master was a healer and one who forgave; she knows she should be willing to suffer and give up all claims on others, rather than strive for power and glory, 'because Christ also suffered for (her), leaving (her) and example' (1 Pet. 2:21); she knows she ought even to love and serve her enemies (Mt. 5:44) rather than seek their punishment or destruction, for she is founded on an event in which God himself manifested forgiveness to his enemies (Rom. 5:10) through Jesus' forgiveness of those who were destroying him (Lu. 23:34). It is the particular history from which she comes, and especially the Christ-event culminating in the cross, that provides the church with the concrete knowledge of who God is and what he requires." Gordon Kaufman, *Systematic Theology,* p. 486.

CHAPTER TWENTY "THE CHURCH (2)"

[1]See, Morrow, *The Covenant of Grace,* pp. 96-97, for his excellent remarks on this subject.

[2]Nation, *John Howard Yoder,* p. 65.

[3]Barth, *God Here and Now,* pp. 85-87.

[4]Rowan Williams, *On Christian Theology* (Oxford: Blackwell Publishers, 2000), p. 31.

[5]N.T. Wright, *Simply Christian* (New York: HarperCollins, 2006), pp. 203-204. Also, "In the 21st century the laity will not be passionately involved in the institutional mission of the church until the institutional church is passionately concerned about the calling or vocation in daily life of homemakers, students, teachers, farmers, truck drivers, police officers, factory workers, corporate execu-

tives, soldiers, lawyers, bankers, builders and nurses . . . the future will focus upon the role of the layperson in the world, or the church will wither in a death spiral of institutional maintenance." Mark W. Thomsen, *Christ Crucified*, pp. 14-15. And, "Of course the church is conservative for it has much to conserve. But let it conserve a vision of the world's destiny and not the structures of the world's past. Let the church in remembering Christ remember that it is conserving the most uprooting, revolutionary force in all human history. For it was Christ who crossed every boundary, broke down every barrier. He crossed the boundaries of class by eating with the outcasts. He crossed the boundary of nations by pointing to a Samaritan as the agent of God's will. He transgressed religious boundaries by claiming the Sabbath was made for man and not man for the Sabbath. Everywhere he manifested his freedom and called others to theirs, calling them forth from family, national, and religious loyalties to loyalty to the world at large. If ever there was a man who trusted his origins and had the courage to emerge from them, it was Christ." William Sloane Coffin, *Credo*, p. 138.

CHAPTER TWENTY-ONE "CHRISTIAN COMMUNION"

[1]Clapp, *Families at the Crossroads*, p. 76.

[2]Wright, *Simply Christian*, p. 211.

[3]Williams, *On Christian Theology*, p. 212.

CHAPTER TWENTY-TWO "CHRISTIAN WORSHIP"

[1]Morrow, *The Covenant of Grace*, p. 112.

[2]Larry W. Hurtado, "Worship, NT Christian," *The New Interpreter's Dictionary of the Bible, S-Z, Volume 5,* edited by Katherine Doob

Sakenfeld (Nashville: Abingdon Press, 2009), pp. 915-916.

[3]Hughes Oliphant Old, "Worship," *Encyclopedia of the Reformed Faith*, p. 410.

[4]Hurtado, "Worship, NT Christian," p. 912.

[5]Geoffrey Wainwright, "Worship," *The Oxford Companion to the Bible,* p. 820.

[6]*The Directory of Worship* in the *Confession of Faith* (Cordova, Tn: The Office of the General Assembly, 2010 Printing), p. 80.

CHAPTER TWENTY-THREE "BAPTISM'

[1]Williams, *On Christian Theology,* p. 209.

[2]*The Directory of Worship*, p. 99.

[3]*Ibid.*

CHAPTER TWENTY-FOUR "THE LORD'S SUPPER"

[1]Morrow, *The Covenant of Grace,* p. 113.

[2]*Ibid.*

[3]*The Directory of Worship*, 102.

[4]*Ibid.*

CHAPTER TWENTY-FIVE "THE CHURCH IN MISSION"

[1]Donald K. McKim, *Presbyterian Questions: Presbyterian Answers* (Louisville: Geneva Press, 2003), p. 69.

[2]This story comes from *Christianity Today Online* on February 23, 2015.

[3]Guthrie, *Christian Doctrine,* p. 370.

[4]See, D. Mark Brown, *The Cumberland Presbyterian Handbook* (Cordova, Tennessee: The Ministry Council of the General Assembly of the Cumberland Presbyterian Church, 2012), p. 84.

[5]William C. Placher ,"What About Them?" *Essentials of Christian Theology,* p. 298.

[6]Nation, *John Howard Yoder,* p. 106.

[7]Irby, *This They Believed,* p. 420.

[8]Williams, *On Christian Theology,* p. 170.

CHAPTER TWENTY-SEVEN "CHRISTIAN FREEDOM"

[1]Nation, *John Howard Yoder,* p. 25.

[2]Karl Barth, *The Call to Discipleship* (Minneapolis: Fortress Press, 2003), p. 17.

[3]Karl Barth, *God in Action* (Manhasset, New York: Round Table Press, 1963), p. 28.

[4]John Howard Yoder, *Body Politics* (Scottsdale, Pennsylvania: Herald Press, 2007), p. ix.

CHAPTER TWENTY-EIGHT "GOOD WORKS"

[1]Beach, *The Christian Life,* pp. 55-56.

[2]*Ibid.*

[3]White, *Biblical Ethics*, p. 83.

CHAPTER TWENTY-NINE "CHRISTIAN STEWARDSHIP"

[1]Douglas John Hall, "Stewardship," *Encyclopedia of the Reformed Faith,* pp. 358-359.

[2]*Ibid.*

[3]White, *Biblical Ethics,* pp. 93-95.

[4]Donald Kraybill, *The Upside Down Kingdom* (Scottsdale, Pennsylvania: Herald Press, 1978), pp. 113-114.

CHAPTER THIRTY "MARRIAGE AND THE FAMILY"

[1]Clapp, *Families at the Crossroads*, pp. 35-36.

[2]*Ibid.*, p. 70.

[3]*Ibid.*, p. 71.

[4]*Ibid.*, pp. 77-78.

[5]*Ibid.*, p. 84.

[6]Morrow, *The Covenant of Grace,* p. 142.

[7]Stanley Hauerwas, *In Good Company: The Church as Polis* (Notre Dame: Notre Dame Press, 1995), p. 161,

[8]Clapp, *Families at the Crossroads*, pp. 95-96.

[9]*Ibid.*, p. 89.

[10]White, *Biblical Ethics,* pp. 232-233.

CHAPTER THIRTY-THREE "CIVIL GOVERNMENT"

[1]Roland Bainton, *Christian Attitudes Toward War and Peace* (Nashville: Abingdon Press, 1990), p. 59.

[2]James Barr, "Politics and the Bible," *The Oxford Companion to the Bible,* pp. 599-601.

[3]P.R. Gilchrist, "Government," *The International Standard Bible Encyclopedia,* pp. 545-546.

[4]Bainton, *Christian Attitudes Toward War and Peace,* p. 138.

[5]Charles C. West, "Social Ethics," *Encyclopedia of the Reformed Faith,* pp. 124-126.

[6]W. Fred Graham, "Civil Government," *Encyclopedia of the Reformed Faith,* p. 159.

[7]West, "Social Ethics," p. 126.

[8]Richard S. Hong, "Business, Technology, and the Task of Reconciliation," *Church and Society,* edited by Bobbie Hargleroad (Louisville: Presbyterian Church USA, May-June, 2002), p. 163.

CHAPTER THIRTY-FOUR "DEATH AND RESURRECTION"

[1]Kaufman, *Systematic Theology,* p. 319.

[2]N.T. Wright, *Surprised by Hope* (New York: HarperOne, 2008), p. 149.

[3]Kaufman, *Systematic Theology*, p. 466.

[4]Wright, *Surprised by Hope,* p. 137..

CHAPTER THIRTY-FIVE "JUDGMENT AND CONSUMMATION"

[1]McKim, *Presbyterian Questions: Presbyterian Answers,* pp. 96-97.

[2]Yoder, *Preface to Theology,* p. 253.

[3]Wright, *Surprised by Hope,* p. 139.

[4]Yoder, *Preface to Theology,* p. 255.

[5]Hans Conzelmann, *A New Look at the Apostle's Creed* (Minneapolis: Augsburg Publishing House, 1969), pp. 59-61.

[6]Yoder,*Preface to Theology,* p. 280.

[7]Placher, *Jesus the Savior,* p. 190.

[8]For an illuminating study of the classic interpretation of *Revelation* see Barbara R. Rossing,*The Rapture Exposed: The Message of Hope in the Book of Revelation* (New York: Basic Books, 2004).

CONCLUSION "LOOKING BACKWARD–LOOKING FORWARD"

[1]Campbell, *Studies in Cumberland Presbyterian History,* pp. 123-124.

[2]I have used this illustration by C.S. Lewis for over thirty years. However, I am unable to cite the source in which it occurs.